GREAT-GRANDMAMA'S WEEKLY

This magazine will aim at being to the girls a Counsellor, Playmate, Guardian, Instructor, Companion and Friend. It will help to train them in moral and domestic virtues, preparing them for the responsibilities of womanhood and for a heavenly home.

from the Editor's Prospectus, *1880*

D1500606

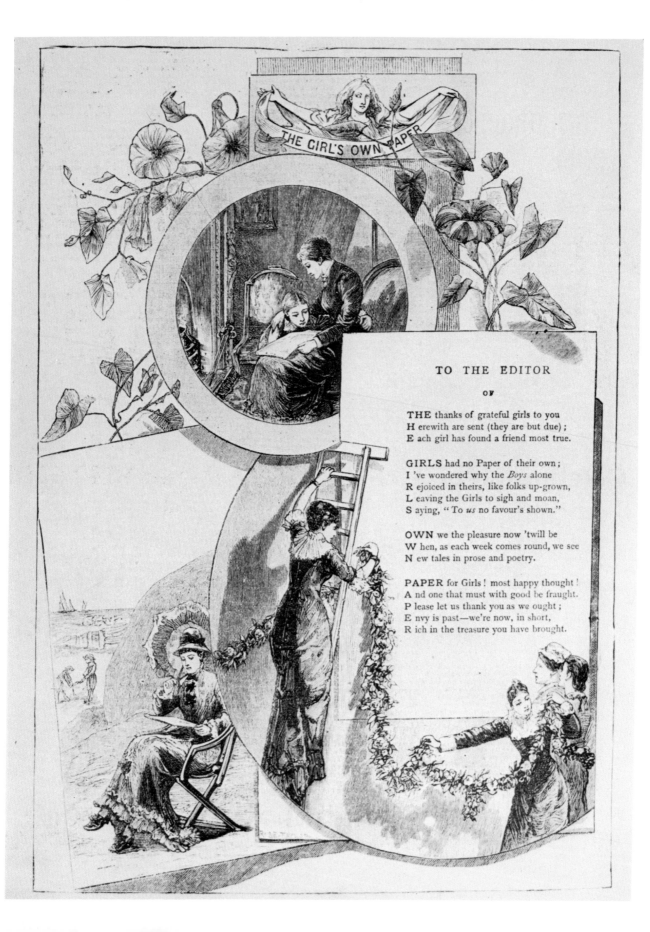

THE GIRL'S OWN PAPER

TO THE EDITOR

OF

THE thanks of grateful girls to you
H erewith are sent (they are but due) ;
E ach girl has found a friend most true.

GIRLS had no Paper of their own ;
I 've wondered why the *Boys* alone
R ejoiced in theirs, like folks up-grown,
L eaving the Girls to sigh and moan,
S aying, "To *us* no favour's shown."

OWN we the pleasure now 'twill be
W hen, as each week comes round, we see
N ew tales in prose and poetry.

PAPER for Girls ! most happy thought !
A nd one that must with good be fraught.
P lease let us thank you as we ought ;
E nvy is past—we're now, in short,
R ich in the treasure you have brought.

GREAT-GRANDMAMA'S WEEKLY

A Celebration of The Girl's Own Paper 1880-1901

Wendy Forrester

LUTTERWORTH PRESS
Guildford and London

First published in Great Britain 1980

ISBN 0 7188 2450 4

Filmset in Bembo 270, 11 on 12½ pt, quotations 10 on 11 pt, captions 10 on 11 pt italics and index 9 on 10 pt.
Printed offset litho in Great Britain by
Butler & Tanner Ltd, Frome and London

To
my Grandmothers
FLORENCE WILLIAMS
and
MARY FORRESTER

The author would like to thank Ann Hugh-Jones for a considerable amount of help and advice in writing this book.

CONTENTS

"ALL SOLD, MISS. WOULD YOU LIKE TO ORDER THE
JANUARY PART IN GOOD TIME?"

Editorial Note

Although the full and correct title of the magazine was *The Girl's Own Paper*, it was frequently and affectionately referred to without the definite article, or merely by its initials, and both usages have been adopted for this book.

G.O.P. stands for *Girl's Own Paper*, and *B.O.P.* for its brother publication, the *Boy's Own Paper*.

Material in square brackets has been added by the author.

All quotations are from the *Girl's Own Paper* unless otherwise stated.

Illustrations

The illustrations used in this book were photographed from original issues of the magazine and are reproduced by courtesy of Lutterworth Press and the United Society for Christian Literature, descendants of the Religious Tract Society.

The title page illustration is an acrostic taken from the issue of February 21, 1880.

VOL. I.—No. 1.]   JANUARY 3, 1880.   [PRICE ONE PENNY.

Amiable ever, but weak-minded never,
Brave in your duty be rather than clever.
Choice in your friendships, then true to your friend,
Doing nothing to vex her, much less offend.
Elastic in spirit, soar high as the kite,
Finding strength in the guidance that limits your flight.
Gentle in manner and gracious in speech,
Honey distilling the youngest to reach.
Idle young fingers make old slattern hands,
Just pinning, where method good sewing commands.
Kill crossness with kindness and make it relent,
Led captive by kisses and taught to repent.
Make merry at home for mirth is a treasure
Not meant to be wasted in frivolous pleasure.
Obedient and truthful, twin sisters of love,
Priceless as pearls from God's casket above.
Quarrels! Oh, let not such evil be wrought,
Religion forbids it, yea, even in thought!
Seek (earnest in prayer) for grace to restrain
Tempers unholy which give others pain.
Useful abroad, be more useful at home,
Virtue for service need never far roam.
Woman is formed from girlhood's first plan—
Xanthippe or Claudia, Queen Mary or Anne.
Young friends to be happy, now learn to be wise,
Zeal without knowledge is a head without eyes!

The Girls' Own Alphabet
from the first issue
January 3, 1880

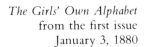

THE PRINCESS VICTORIA.

FOREWORD

When I was a child, my father brought me, as a surprise present, a giant volume, the 1890–1891 *Girl's Own Annual*. During the years which followed, this gave me a good deal of pleasure, and I appreciated it even more when I was older.

In spite of my affection for this book, it did not occur to me until long after I was grown up that Annuals for other years probably existed; but when I did realise this I started to hunt, and before long acquired my second *Girl's Own Annual*, dated some years earlier than the first. I found the second equally delightful, looked for and discovered a third, and was well on the way to a collection.

A stack of stout books grew, some in plain dark bindings, some elegantly embossed with gold designs, all with dates in the eighteen-eighties and 'nineties. Later ones I rejected—though I might not be so strong-minded now—partly because I found the twentieth-century *G.O.P.* slightly less appealing than the Victorian one, partly for the simple reason that the volumes take up a lot of space and one has to stop somewhere.

I continued to spend many a peaceful hour reading the improving serial stories, the budgets for girls of slender means, the fashion notes, the answers to correspondents, and the other enjoyable contents of my growing collection, and one day it occurred to me that I had the material for a short feature comparing this Victorian magazine with one for present-day teenagers. I started the feature, but could not get beyond the first few hundred words, and eventually came to the conclusion that what I really wanted to write was a book about the *G.O.P.*, during its Victorian years.

I believe that there may be people interested in reading a little about this popular and successful magazine for girls in the last century, and in that belief I have provided, not a history of the *Girl's Own Paper* in its Victorian years, but a dip into its pages which I hope may amuse, or inform, or perhaps both.

Although the chapters which follow review the magazine only up to the end of Queen Victoria's reign, it survived into that of her great-great-granddaughter. In its seventy-six years it underwent several changes of

Far left: this portrait of Queen Victoria as a girl appeared as frontispiece to the first issue of The Girl's Own Paper *(January 3, 1880), which included a description of her early life. "If Victoria has been a good queen, as well as a good wife, a good mother, and a good woman, this is due, under God, to the training she had in childhood and girlhood."*

GREYFRIARS.

A STORY FOR GIRLS.

By EVELYN EVERETT GREEN.

"TRIX CAME RUNNING IN."

CHAPTER XVI.

JESSIE'S FIRST APPEARANCE.

WHEN Esther's footstep had died away along the corridor, and Jessie had locked her door upon the intruder, a different look came into her face; all the would-be indifference and weariness vanished in an instant, to be replaced by a vivid excitement and triumph, which gave a wonderful brilliance to her beauty, whilst robbing it of something of its youthfulness and childlike quality.

"You can come back, Thérèse," she said, softly, "I think we are safe now. At any rate the door is locked."

At these words there appeared from an inner dressing-closet, the door of which had been carefully closed, the French maid, who bore in her hands a pile of rich white drapery, and several cases which evidently contained jewels. Upon her sharp dark face was a look of cunning which was not pleasant to see there, and in her voluble fashion, half French, half English, she began discoursing on Jessie's beauty, on the ravishing appearance mademoiselle was about to make, on the delight and astonishment of the Vicomte at the sight of his princess thus attired, and the blissful conclusion which must come as a *finale* to such a charming little romance.

And whilst she thus talked, in a fashion that would have disgusted Esther, and which no mother, even an indulgent and not overwise one, would have tolerated for a moment, Jessie sat

Above: an episode from the serial *Greyfriars*, by Evelyn Everett Green, from *The Girl's Own Annual, 1890–1891*. *Abetted by a sly French maid, Jessie decks herself for a forbidden ball, to her tomboy sister's admiration. "Oh, Jessie, you are a stunner!"*

name and format, finally disappearing under the title of *Heiress*, in 1956. The Editor's farewell letter expressed the hope that it would reappear in easier times. However, the nineteen-sixties, waiting in the wings, was not a decade in which a magazine like the *Girl's Own Paper* would have been likely to flourish, retitled or not. A 1949 copy saved from my schooldays seems nearer in spirit to the *G.O.P.* of the eighteen-nineties than to one of the teenage magazines of fifteen years ago. It would have been even less likely to survive in the nineteen-sixties than in the comparatively congenial atmosphere of the years just after the Second World War. However, it may be welcomed back by another generation. I hope it will.

INTRODUCTION

The first issue of *The Girl's Own Paper* appeared on January 3, 1880, published by the Religious Tract Society in Paternoster Row, London, price one penny.

Just a year earlier, with the express purpose of counteracting—"nay, of destroying and throwing out of the field"—the spate of "pernicious" publications arising in the wake of the 1870 Education Act, the Society had launched the *Boy's Own Paper*. The lively and progressive style of this magazine was an experiment, a departure from the Society's established religious periodicals (*Sunday At Home, Leisure Hour,* the *Child's Paper*), and considerable misgivings were voiced among the more conservative dignitaries of the Committee, dedicated as they were to the moral and spiritual welfare of the nation's youth. But—"I think every reader ... will find that however exciting or interesting it may be, it is pervaded by a Christian tone," the Earl of Aberdeen, a former chairman of the Society, assured them. The immediate success of the venture came as a revelation, as did the fact that the paper's readers numbered girls as well as boys— eighteen-year-old Georgina Hamilton, for instance, winning a prize for a competition in an early issue. Very soon it was clear that there was wide scope for a feminine equivalent of the *Boy's Own Paper.*

However, although the *Girl's Own Paper* closely resembled its brother in appearance, it was by no means a B.O.P. with the sexes changed. The adventure stories so much associated with the boys' paper are rare in the Victorian years of the girls'—the greatest adventures for them being those of love and marriage, or of earning one's own living. Nor are there many school stories of the kind so popular with a later generation, where the heroine has ten to make and the match to win, and where chums converse in elaborate slang. The tone of the paper is less "schoolgirlish" than "girlish", and possibly the Editor might have preferred it to be described as "womanly".

Fiction was the mainstay of the magazine, with two serial stories running at any one time, and occasional short stories. There were articles on health and beauty, dress, needlework, housekeeping, cookery, hobbies, music (actual scores were printed from time to time, and Queen Victoria's youngest daughter, Princess Beatrice, was a contributor), foreign countries, doing good, poems, jokes and anecdotes (termed *Varieties*), competitions and a weekly collection of answers to correspondents. Appropriately enough, the first issue was graced by a girlhood portrait of the Queen, thus setting the tone.

"There was a real want of a paper which girls could truly call *their own*," recalled the Editor years later in the thousandth number (February, 1899), going on to say:

A paper which would be to the whole sisterhood a sensible, interesting and good-humoured companion, counsellor and friend, advocating their best interests, taking part in everything affecting them, giving them the best advice, conveying to them the best information, supplying them with the most readable fiction, and trying to exercise over them a refining and elevating influence ... Success shone upon us from the very first, and *The Girl's Own Paper* at once and by general consent took a foremost place amongst the magazines of the day.

Professional critics in the press were generous, and said many a friendly word in our praise. The late George Augustus Sala [a popular journalist] elevated *The Girl's Own Paper* to the position of "first favourite", and in an encouraging notice expressed a hope that "all the girls" of Great Britain would subscribe, for he thought it would be greatly to their advantage. Much-valued approval and friendly letters of advice and help also came to us in these early days from Mr John Ruskin, who, writing to a girl friend, said that he had ordered the paper to be sent to him regularly, and added, "Surely you young ladies—girls, I ought to say—will think you have a fair sixpennyworth." [Monthly numbers containing the four weekly issues bound together in blue covers were priced sixpence.]

Evidently the girls agreed with Mr Ruskin. The magazine proved extremely popular, its circulation quickly rising to over 250,000 and eventually outstripping even that of the boys'[*]; and the timely revenue from both publications enabled the Religious Tract Society to increase its support of its many mission stations in Africa, China and Catholic Europe. At the end of the magazine's first year, the Society's annual report noted that "some of the Society's friends have complained of the [B.O.P. and G.O.P.] as being too secular in tone", but added that "the attempt to give them an exclusively religious character would be to defeat the very purpose for which they were intended". Fortunately this purpose was not defeated and by the fifth month the gratified Committee had recorded their sentiments:

There was an urgent need for such a publication. ... We earnestly and with thankfulness believe that the hopes expressed in our preliminary prospectus ... are being fulfilled—that *The Girl's Own Paper* is to its readers a guardian, instructor, companion, and friend, and that it is preparing them for the responsibilities of womanhood and for a heavenly home.[**]

The review attempted in this book of the magazine's first twenty-one years will, it is hoped, enable today's readers to judge whether at least the earthly hopes of the publishers were fulfilled.

Far right: on October 5, 1895, the G.O.P. published a setting by Princess Beatrice of a song by Queen Victoria's dear Disraeli, which recalled with "smiles and sighs" the long-lost days of youth.

[*] Patrick Dunae, *Boy's Own Paper: Origins and Editorial Policies*, The Private Library (journal of the Private Libraries Association), Second Series, Vol. 9, No. 4, Winter 1976.

[**] Rev. S. G. Green, *The Story of the Religious Tract Society*, R.T.S., 1899.

H.R.H. THE COMPOSER

THE GREEN CAVALIER'S SONG.

Words by The Earl of Beaconsfield.   *Music by* H.R.H. Princess Henry of Battenberg.

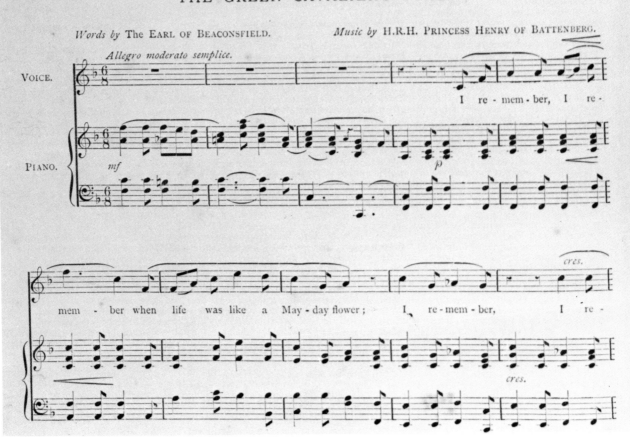

I re - mem - ber, I re - mem - ber when life was like a May - day flower; I re - mem - ber, I re -

THE EDITOR

Throughout its Victorian existence, and for some years later, the *G.O.P.* had only one Editor, Charles Peters, who came to the R.T.S. from Cassells.

In the thousandth number, in 1899, he wrote: "To the Editor-in-Chief of the Society's magazines, Dr Macaulay, the hearty thanks of the Editor are due for liberty of action and a great deal of kindly encouragement." A deleted entry in the Minutes of July 20, 1882, however, suggests that he had earlier been criticised for over-secularisation: "A hope was expressed by the Committee that Mr Peters would act more in harmony with the principles of the Society."

Clearly there is the mark of a very strong editorial personality on the magazine. His successor, Flora Klickmann, called him "an editor of strong individuality" in the appreciation which opened the 1908–1909 Annual, at the end of his tenure:

The death of Charles Peters, who had been the editor of this magazine for twenty-eight years, came as a personal loss to tens of thousands of readers who never saw him. There are piles of letters in my office at the present moment from people who never met him, nor ever exchanged a letter with him, all regretting his death as though he had been an intimate friend. And the reason for this is clear to all those who have followed, month by month, year by year, the pages of this paper. From the very first, Mr Peters had but one aim in editing this magazine, viz. to foster and develop that which was highest and noblest in the girlhood and womanhood of England, helping his readers to cherish their finest ideals, and teaching them to see the things of life in their proper perspective, putting the best things first, and banishing the worthless from his pages.

It was inevitable that before long he became something far more than an ordinary editor to his huge constituency. Not only the girls for whom the magazine was originally started, but their mothers also, made him their final court of appeal when in any doubt or difficulty, and in this way he became the personal friend and counsellor of multitudes who would not have known him had they met him face to face.

And no man took his work more seriously, striving to the last to give the magazine his very best. It was no wonder that when he passed away he left a blank that no one can really fill and hosts of friends to mourn his loss.

THE MAGAZINE

By the time these words appeared, the *Girl's Own Paper* had become very clearly an Edwardian publication. The new editor chose to re-title it *The Girl's Own Paper and Woman's Magazine*. The weekly numbers, price one penny, were discontinued, and a more compact monthly issue replaced them, selling at sixpence, as the old monthly had done. Flora Klickmann gave her reasons for the change (1908):

In the days when *The Girl's Own Paper* was started, girls had not so much pocket-money as they have at present, but now any girl can afford sixpence a month for her magazine, and would rather scorn to take it in pennyworths ... [Moreover] when the magazine started it was intended for girls only, but very soon it became apparent that it was being read by grown-ups as well ... the girls of the past have become the grown-ups of today, and are still taking in the magazine.

Far right: the Editor's Christmas greeting to his readers, December, 1881. (The same design was thriftily used again many years later.)

Throughout the eighteen-eighties and 'nineties, however, the changes were slight. Issues looked very like each other, printed in three columns of rather small type. Illustrations were line drawings, except for the rare "presentation" colour plates. In addition to fashion drawings and fiction illustrations there were occasional full-page pictures, with such titles as *Maiden Meditation*, *Sweet Seventeen*, *Fair Daffodils* and *The Flower Girl*, tending to have something of a family resemblance.

The first page of each number was headed by the upper half of a female figure with flowing hair, an expression of extreme spirituality, and no pupils to her eyes, bearing the title of the magazine on a banner. TWO LITTLE GIRLS wrote in 1880 about this figure, apparently worried about the blankness of the eyes, and were told:

> The figure at the head of our paper is not the copy of a picture or portrait, but of a statue. It is not the custom in art to put eyes on statues of pure white marble. In the later and lower periods of Greek sculpture, statues were sometimes coloured, but no one now expects white marble to have eyes like dolls or wax figures. The statue of which our heading is a copy has been greatly admired. It was called by the sculptor "The Spirit of Truth and Love", and we think this a good motto for our paper. Our engraving was made from a photograph expressly sent for *The Girl's Own Paper*, by Mr S. C. Hall, Editor of the Art Journal. . . .

In 1893 the Editor decided that this heading had been used for long enough, and held a competition for a new one, open to all, professional and amateur, men and women. It would be pleasant to relate that a girl reader was successful, but the design chosen was by Henry Ryland of Kensington. The new heading appeared in October 1894 and depicted two young women in classical draperies, one drawing, one writing. Viewed rationally, it is more pleasing than its predecessor, but perhaps things are not quite the same without the soulful lady.

Other changes began to be noticeable about the same time. Photographs appeared, somewhat fuzzy, and instead of the delicate, detailed line illustrations there were halftone ones, still monochrome—more dashing, but rather less attractive. Early in the new century there was a major change in the appearance of the magazine, with larger print and two

Above: Henry Ryland's prize-winning design for the new masthead which showed "two maidens artistically attired in white sitting in graceful ease"

Far left: Our Novel Christmas Tree, Ruth Lamb's account of preparations for a Christmas party, complete with the text of the special charade written for the occasion by Mamma, appeared in January, 1880.

17

Far right: captioned Biding Their Time, *this illustration appeared in the issue of April 16, 1892.*

columns instead of three. The extra Summer and Christmas numbers were romantically titled—*Silver Sails, Sheets o' Daisies, Lily Leaves, Victoria's Laurel, Rosebud Garden, Mignonette*—*Christmas Roses, Snowdrops, Feathery Flakes, Household Harmony, Christmas Cherries.*

THE CONTRIBUTORS

"The Editor has been assisted in his labours by a band of very willing workers—authors, musical composers, and artists—whose names are familiar to all our readers," Charles Peters wrote in the thousandth issue. To mark the anniversary, a hundred of the contributors presented him with an autographed tea-table cloth, recognising "the ability, friendliness, and discretion which have been all along displayed in his dealings with his staff". He was ready to cast his net widely, and wrote of himself:

> Whilst surrounded by a tried staff, he has made it a rule to welcome contributors—indeed, to invite them—from every quarter. . . . Amongst our occasional contributors may be seen the names of a queen, several princesses, and leading members of the nobility, and a great many more who have distinguished themselves in various lines of activity connected with the life and work of women and girls.

Lists of the year's contributors were published at the front of each Annual. To take, at random, the volume for 1888–1889, the list of seventy writers includes one Queen (of Roumania), one Countess, one Baronne, four other titled ladies, one Baronet and five Reverends★. Also present as a young man of twenty-three is the poet W. B. Yeats. Among some fifty artists listed, three are Royal Academicians, including James Sant, "Principal Painter In Ordinary to Her Majesty".

A gallery of photographs of the regular contributors was published in the 1884 Summer issue, *Sunlight*; when this idea was revived in the thousandth issue, some fifteen years later, many of the earlier faces were still there. The Editor in Chief, James Macaulay, depicted in 1884 with flowing beard and skull-cap, looked conservative and stately in 1899; Charles Peters appeared modestly in the midst, a rather solid, round-faced man.

One of the chief regular contributors was Gordon Stables, M.D., C.M., R.N.; veiled under the pseudonym "Medicus", he was the author of the regular articles on health and beauty. This seems an unlikely profession for a Naval doctor, but he must have found it satisfactory since, like the Editor himself, he was connected with the magazine for nearly thirty years, writing in addition to his health and beauty articles other features, under his own name, on a wide variety of subjects—notably on animals. (At the same time he was contributing similar articles to the *Boy's Own Paper*, and writing adventure stories.) Reference to the Medical Register of 1880 reveals him as a graduate of the University of Aberdeen (he remarks on his "kilted knees" in an article about a Scottish holiday), with

★ Contributors included the Rev. W. J. Foxell, B.MUS., a member of the Religious Tract Society Committee. The Society is now the United Society for Christian Literature, proprietors of Lutterworth Press, who are the publishers of the present book, and whose General Manager is Mr M. E. Foxell, the contributor's grandson.

BIDING THEIR TIME.

THE HOLIDAY:
HOW TO MAKE THE BEST
OF IT.

By MEDICUS.

DIFFIDENCE isn't a virtue, and it certainly isn't a vice; it is something that we rather like to see in a young girl, and can just pity and forgive in a boy; and yet—would you believe it?—it is the feeling uppermost in my mind at the present moment. And if you will listen to me I will endeavour to explain to you how it happened to come there. I looked into our Editor's room a little while ago. It was early in the day, but he was busy, as usual; he was flanked on both sides by piles of letters and flowers, and a load of manuscript lay before him, so that I could only get a kind of bird's-eye view of him.

"How do you do?" I said. "I hope I see you in good health."

"Are there two p's in apartment?" was the Editor's reply, not deigning to lift his head, but scribbling away as if writing for his life.

"No," I said, "only one p. Good morning; I must be off."

"Wait a moment," said our Editor. "I want you."

Now the fact is, I didn't want to be wanted. I had my dust clothes on. I presume I looked quite gay. I was bound for a long drive. However, there was nothing for it but to wait, so I sat down on a pile of old papers, and hung my white hat on a file. After the lapse of five long minutes he looked up.

"What are you going to give us for this month, Medicus mine?" he said. "You must write your article now."

"This is beautiful weather," I replied, "and everybody is out."

"Duty first," said our Editor; "duty first, doctor. Now what is it going to be? The eyes of two hundred thousand young girls are on you; and there is paper and here is a pen."

"What would you say," I said, "to an article on the circulation of the blood?"

"Circulation of the blood, indeed!" said our Editor, scornfully. "Who do you think would read it? Our girls can feel their blood circulating, they don't need to be told of it.

No, tell us something practical. Be useful if you can't be lively."

I cast only one longing, lingering glance at my white hat on the file, took up my pen and commenced, merely remarking to the Editor, "I don't mind losing a holiday for the sake of our girls."

So now, my fair young readers, having sacrificed my own holiday for your sakes, I trust you will let me give you some hints which, if taken and adopted, will assuredly tend to make your holiday all the more agreeable to you.

And here is where the diffidence comes in. Your boxes are all packed, your flyman is at the gate—he has come fifteen minutes before his time, as flymen often do—and you are all bustle and excitement, and I, your Medicus, touch you gently on the shoulder. No wonder I am diffident for daring to address you at such a supreme moment. Well, then, don't read my article just yet; fold THE GIRL'S OWN PAPER carefully up, and slip it in under the rug-

his address given as the Naval Medical Service—this no doubt owing to his nomadic life; he spent much of his time touring the country in a caravan called "The Wanderer", with his dogs—a St Bernard and a Newfoundland are mentioned. His photograph in the magazine reveals him wearing very long moustaches, and looking younger than the avuncular, "no nonsense" style of his articles would lead one to imagine, though he was already forty when he started writing for the *G.O.P.* in 1880.

Although the *Girl's Own Paper* was edited by a man, the feminine touch was by no means lacking. Most of the fiction and many of the features were written by women. One of the chief fiction authors was Ruth Lamb, already an established novelist when the magazine was launched. Her first by-line in the *G.O.P.* was for *Our Novel Christmas Tree* in the second issue in 1880, a charming account of the pleasantest kind of Victorian family life. Over the years she contributed a number of serial stories (*Her Own Choice, Only a Girl-Wife, One Little Vein of Dross*), among the most interesting those with a socially reforming message (*Sackcloth and Ashes*). In 1896, by then calling herself "an old lady" and signing her letters "your affectionate mother-friend", she was contributing a regular religious or "thoughtful" feature, *In the Twilight Side by Side*, and running the Twilight Circle, to which girls could write with spiritual problems:

GORDON STABLES, M.D.

LIDDLE, C. (British Guiana).—Your letter, dear girl, has made me very glad. Every day brings new proof of the delightful bond of union which our Talks in the Twilight have established between girls of many nationalities.... [1901]

IRIS (Simla).—I have not heard from NORA lately, but if this meets her eye, I am sure she must feel deeply the interest taken in her, and the many prayers offered for her by you and members of our Circle all over the world ... Your words are sweet and cheering, dear IRIS, and of late I have joyfully acknowledged so many hopeful messages from my girls.... [1901]

The names of Dora Hope and Dora de Blaquière recur frequently over a number of years—two of the contributors who seem most thoroughly journalists, both displaying a practical versatility over the whole period. Dora de Blaquière wrote, for instance, *Winter Clothes and How to Make Them, St Valentine's Day, Books Before Travel, Grilling and Devilling, On Helping in the House, What Should We Afford for Dress?* Dora Hope's most characteristic productions were articles on domestic economy cloaked as fiction (*She Couldn't Boil a Potato, The Brothers' Benefactor*) but she turned her hand to a variety of subjects—in the first volume alone, *How to Make Poor Children's Clothing, How to Embroider in Crewels, Pressed Grasses and Ferns for Ornamental Purposes, How I Managed my Picnic, A Girls' Walking Tour* and *Sunday School Work*.

DORA DE BLAQUIÈRE.

Although the very first serial story, *Zara*, was anonymous (there was more anonymity in the earlier issues), the second, *More Than Coronets*, appeared under the name of Mrs G. Linnaeus Banks, who must have been a valued acquisition, already known for her popular novel *The Manchester Man*. First published in 1876, it had gone through four editions within as many years.

Rosa Nouchette Carey was another extremely popular and prolific novelist. Her earliest book, *Nellie's Memories*, had sold thousands and was followed by many successful stories. She wrote a number of serials for

Far left: an article by Medicus published on July 30, 1881. A delicate girl going on holiday must take proper flannel underclothes, stout shoes for evening (to avoid catching cold through the feet), sensible stockings and a shawl or plaid. She must rise early, get plenty of exercise, drink as much milk as she can, and be sure to pack a good tonic.

IN CHURCH.

By W. B. YEATS.

SHE prays for father, mother dear,
  To Him with thunder shod,
She prays for every falling tear
  In the holy church of God.

For all good men now fallen ill,
  For merry men that weep,
For holiest teachers of His will,
  And common men that sleep.

The sunlight flickering on the pews,
  The sunlight in the air,
The flies that dance in threes, in twos,
  They seem to join her prayer—

Her prayer for father, mother dear.
  To Him with thunder shod,
A prayer for every falling tear
  In the holy church of God.

Above and far right: published on June 8, 1889, companion to an article called What Shall We Do With Our Sundays?, *was this poem by the young W. B. Yeats, with its gently idealised illustration.*

the G.O.P. (*Merle's Crusade, Esther, Little Miss Muffet*), while Macmillan and Co., who published many of her books (Blue Cloth, Gilt, 3s. 6d. each), quoted *The Lady* magazine describing her novels as "immaculately pure, and very high in tone", and the *Pall Mall Gazette* as doubting "whether anything has been written of late years so fresh, so pretty, so thoroughly natural and bright". In 1899 she was living in Putney with her widowed sister and another very long-standing *G.O.P.* contributor, the poet Helen Marion Burnside, who compiled the Rosa Nouchette Carey Birthday Book, with introductory verses, in 1901.

Lily Watson contributed besides serial stories (*A Fortunate Exile, The Hill of Angels*), articles such as *Self Control* ("The young lady who in any crisis instantly becomes useless by dropping into insensibility, or both useless and actively objectionable by 'going off' into shrieking hysterics, is no longer regarded as fulfilling her vocation"). Francesca Maria Steele (*The Convents of Great Britain*) wrote novels under the pseudonym "Darley Dale", and Elizabeth Emily Charlton chose the romantic name "Eglanton Thorne". Sarah Sharp Hamer (writer of children's stories as "Olive Patch") was the cookery expert "Phillis Browne" and wrote *The Girl's Own Cookery Book*. Among other important contributors were Isabella Fyvie Mayo, Sophia F. A. Caulfeild, Emma Brewer, Sarah Doudney, Nanette and James Mason. Anne Beale wrote serial stories such as *Restitution; or, Miser and Spendthrift* and articles such as *Our Tractarian*

IN CHURCH.

HER OWN CHOICE.

By RUTH LAMB.

"'COMMON, DO YOU CALL HER?' CRIED A SHRILL VOICE, CLOSE BY."

Above: an episode from Her Own Choice, *a serial by Ruth Lamb (June 28, 1884). The heroine Hilda is deeply remorseful when her careless words are overheard by the mother of an injured child whom her tender-hearted cousin, Dorothy, has rescued.*

Movement. When she died aged eighty-four, she bequeathed her diary, in twenty-six volumes, to her friend the Editor, who published some extracts under the title *Anne Beale, Governess and Writer* in 1900. The popular *Pixie O'Shaughnessy* and *Peggy Saville* novels of Mrs de Horne Vaizey began to appear in serial form towards the end of the period, under the name "Jessie Mansergh".

THE READERS

"Anyone, with half an eye, can see that 'The G.O.P.' is intended for girls of all classes," wrote the Editor in 1880 in reply to a correspondent signing herself GREY HAIRS. He went on:

Girls of a superior position—belonging, we mean, to the "upper ten thousand"—should read everything, and be well up in *every* matter upon which we give instruction. Their money, time, and superior intelligence admit of this. For girls of a less high position there are papers on economical cookery, plain needlework, home education, and health. Servant-maids communicate to us well-written letters, and by their tone we can see that our magazine has indeed helped them to an intelligent carrying out of their humble work; that it has been a companion to them in their isolation and a counsellor in times of sore temptation. There is much in our paper we humbly believe that will train these girls in living a pure and honest life, and we rejoice to help them, for their letters convince us that there is honesty and nobility even in the kitchen. From our daily letters from the girls, written upon coronetted notepaper by those of noble birth, and by others from the kitchens of humble houses, we gather that there is help needed by all, and that our paper has given a high aim to their lives and a practical and wise assistance in their various engagements.

The Editor might have added that, as well as all classes, all ages and nationalities were also catered for. Between GREY HAIRS and six-year-old TOTTY CROOKES, who enquired about removing grease spots from silk ("We think Totty writes very well for her age"), there was something for everyone. The fashion features were written for grown-up "girls", as were the health and beauty articles; few of the serial stories had heroines younger than the late teens. Early competitions were sometimes restricted to girls under nineteen, but the interest shown by older readers resulted in later competitions having entrants in their thirties. Needlework competitions attracted industrious children as young as six or seven.

The popularity of the magazine overseas, particularly in the Colonies and Dominions, but also in America and Europe, is well in evidence in

A VERY young heroine, Miss Esther Mary Cornish-Bowden, aged eight years, has just been awarded by the Royal Humane Society its medal and a handsome testimonial explanatory of the circumstances under which she bravely entitled herself to receive that medal. She is the daughter of a gentleman living at Black Hall, Avonwick, Ivybridge, Devonshire, and she saved the life of her governess, Miss Bradshaw, who, when returning from Sunday-school on the 30th of November last, with the youthful heroine and her younger sister, turned giddy, and fell into a pond six feet deep with water. Dispatching her younger sister to the keeper's lodge, Miss Cornish-Bowden bent over the pool, trying to lay hold of her drowning governess. This she did, but in the effort, she overbalanced herself, fell into the pond, and sank. Never losing her presence of mind, she retained her grip of the governess, and when she rose to the surface she still held her by the right hand, while with the left she caught hold of some short bushes. In this position they remained for about five minutes, the child calling for help. Eventually a passing workman heard the cries, and assisted Miss Bradshaw and the child out of the water. The former was partially insensible, but her brave little rescuer appeared quite unconcerned.

Right: the G.O.P. did not usually report current events, but was never averse to praising good sense, modesty and resourcefulness. A Brave Little Girl (an account of a child's courage) was published in one of the early issues (March 20, 1880).

the correspondence columns; by the late eighteen-nineties there was a regular column devoted to International Correspondence.

Taking the whole circulation of *The Girl's Own Paper* from the issue of the first number [wrote the author of an article, *Looking Back*, in the thousandth issue] we arrive at an imposing result....

Suppose that instead of distributing the copies to subscribers, they had been hoarded up and made to form a tall pillar, one copy being laid flat on the top of another. And supposing a girl wished to read the topmost number—the present number, that is to say—without using a ladder, she would have to wait till she grew to be a hundred and seventy miles high.... If all the numbers which have been circulated since Number One were laid end to end, they would make a pathway long enough to go round the world at the Equator with a bit over.

EDUCATIONAL.

DORA.—Write to Miss Leigh, 77, Avenue Wagram, Paris, and consult her. She keeps a home for governesses. Of course, she is in a position to give a reliable opinion as to the salary a teacher of your age and experience, as well as educational attainments, might obtain, could she find a suitable situation.

CHICK.—The School of Cookery at South Kensington (Exhibition Road, S.W.) trains for the post of "cookery instructor" in all branches of cooking, at twenty-one guineas for the full course of twenty weeks; plain cookery at eight guineas for a course of fourteen weeks. You should apply for a directory. There are other schools for teaching cookery.

ELLA.—Girls studying at South Kensington can find board and lodging at Miss Wüstrey's Kindergarten School, 58, Pen-y-wern Road, Earl's Court; and likewise at Worthington House, 179, Finborough Road, South Kensington.

M. BLASSOR.—The Editor does not send out the

Above: some answers to readers' queries, published on November 5, 1887. In the same issue the Editor advised LOLLY POP *and* E.B. *who wanted to be hospital nurses; referred separate enquirers to the Association for the Oral Instruction of the Deaf and Dumb, the Oxford Local Examinations Board, the Froebel Society; suggested that girls thrown out of work by the closing of a Sherborne silk factory might be sent to a training school for servants; and warned hopeful* CLARIE *that she would probably fail to make a livelihood out of embroidery.*

Chapter One

THE
MODERN WOMAN

Too often ladies hide the fact that they have to work for their living, as if it were an everlasting disgrace and could never be forgotten. This is one of the old-fashioned ideas, which, it is to be hoped, a more enlightened age will wipe out. Only this week an elderly spinster, who has lived in highly-genteel poverty for the best part of her life, remarked to me, "My grandmother was a perfect lady—she *never did anything*." May future years be preserved from such nonentities!

How to Secure a Situation
(1892)

My friends call me an old-fashioned girl, some of them say eccentric. I know they mean commonplace, but that troubles me not; what does trouble me are the ways and doings of my up-to-date friends, those who pride themselves upon being anything but commonplace.

I will show you what I mean.

Perhaps it is because I grew up in an out-of-date place where the air blew fresh and sweet straight from the heavens, where everything around us was true and genuine, because my sweet mother and I were the closest of friends and companions, she teaching me to reverence my own sex as well as to respect the other, that I can no more revolt against her ideas and desires than I could rebel against the God who made me.

Because also in this quiet seed-time of my life I acquired what has been well-called the habit of "thinking-back," I have been able to keep myself together and avoid being carried along with the stream, since like many another country girl I have entered the busiest throng of busy bread-winning girls. It is not of the bread-winning girls that I am going to speak, however, so much as of those who belong to the leisured class, yet as one imitates another so much, the defects of the latter will often be found in an exaggerated degree among the former.

My occupation has given me a back-seat view of much in life which I could not otherwise have obtained a glimpse of; and a back seat is of all seats the most enjoyable if one can so far forget one's own existence as to be thoroughly interested in other people. From my quiet corner I have been able to watch the girls of our period, to judge them critically, to admire them immensely, and to be profoundly ashamed of them at times.

For anyone above the poverty line, a good case could be made for choosing the late Victorian period as a pleasant time to live. It was an era of comparative peace and prosperity, and among its principal advantages must be counted a sense of progress, reform, improvement. The franchise was being extended, primary education becoming universal, sanitation and medical knowledge improving, trade unions being given the protection of the law. Not every citizen can have welcomed every reform, but it is difficult not to assume a feeling in the air that life was changing for the better—particularly for women.

A girl who bought the first issue of the *Girl's Own Paper* when she was seventeen would not have been able to vote in a Parliamentary election until she was fifty-five (1918), but she was living in a world where women were gaining a place in education, business, and the professions, and where women's suffrage was at least being discussed as a possibility.

The majority of the magazine's middle-class schoolgirl readers would have attended private schools (seminaries for the "Daughters of Gentlemen"), though some would still be receiving their education at home from governess or tutor. Secondary education was left practically untouched by the State until 1902, though the Girls Public Day School Trust was setting up schools—later to be called High Schools—to prepare girls for further study at universities or other institutions of higher learning.

After school, a middle-class girl who stayed at home would probably be given a dress allowance by her father. A sum of £10 or less would

Above: the opening of an article, The Girls of Today, *by Lucy H. Yates (August 18, 1894).*

normally mean making her own clothes—"On a dress allowance even of £20 per annum I think there is little or no room for dressmakers' bills" (1883). Some girls might receive £5 a year with the responsibility of buying only their own boots and gloves.

Among the well-to-do, of course, were some girls who were given very substantial allowances, even as much as £100, but these would have been a very small minority. The usual age of "coming out" for a girl in society was eighteen, and although only those readers in the upper reaches could expect to be presented at Court, articles on the subject appeared from time to time and dealt in detail with every aspect of the ordeal, from walking backwards when wearing a four-yard train, to the number of plumes worn in the hair.

When a girl "put up her hair", it was a sign that she was growing up, and readers wrote to ask at what age this would be proper. "Girls usually put up their hair at about sixteen," the Editor replied to ESMERELDA in 1883. A few weeks later, NAPOLI was told, "Your hair should be turned at eighteen. It would look like a silly attempt to make a child of you for you to wear it down your back later than that." But many of the poorer girls, of course, wore their hair up in a bun, or tucked away under a cap, much sooner than that. They often left their Voluntary or Board schools before entering their teens (not until 1918 was it illegal to leave before the age of fourteen) to earn their own living; and for them the price of their weekly Girl's Own Paper represented no small sum. Nanette Mason, in the grim little feature How Working Girls Live in London, wrote:

The average weekly earning of girls engaged in labour of all kinds cannot be more, it has been estimated, than ten shillings. . . . No wonder that many of them look as if they never had a luxury in their lives. [1888]

But for the girl seeking to improve herself and her lot, the Girl's Own Paper must have been reckoned a good pennyworth. It is worth noticing that, in the budget for a ten-shillings-a-week girl suggested in the above-mentioned article, two pence is allocated "if she belongs, as we will hope" to a trade union. The feature, which ran through a number of issues, ended with the statement:

Were wages raised many good results would follow. . . . We are confident that a better day than was ever seen before has, in our time, dawned, though it may not yet shine brightly on our sisters, the working girls of this country.

By far the greater number of poor girls went into domestic service, and the G.O.P. encouraged this, feeling that young women were safer employed in private homes than in factories or shops. A thirteen-year-old maidservant might start her career at £5 a year, rising later to £12 or perhaps £18. The factory girl's wages averaged £21 to £34 per annum; the shopgirl's slightly more. An article entitled Bar Maids and Waitresses in Restaurants, Their Work and Temptations in an 1896 issue gave the average wage of these workers as from 5s. to 10s. a week (£13 to £26 a year), "subject to a charge of from 7d. to 9d. per week for breakages"; hours worked were often twelve to fourteen—and sometimes up to seventeen—a day. An assistant teacher in an elementary school might receive £50 a year, while a Post Office clerk or a trained book-keeper could earn between £65 and £80.

Far right: the opening of a short anonymous feature, A Contrast, from June 12, 1880. This drives home a favourite G.O.P. lesson. The heedless girls who deliberately order their ball dresses at the shortest possible notice care nothing for the overworked girls at the dressmaker's, among them poor Mary, who collapses from exhaustion, and dies in her sleep.

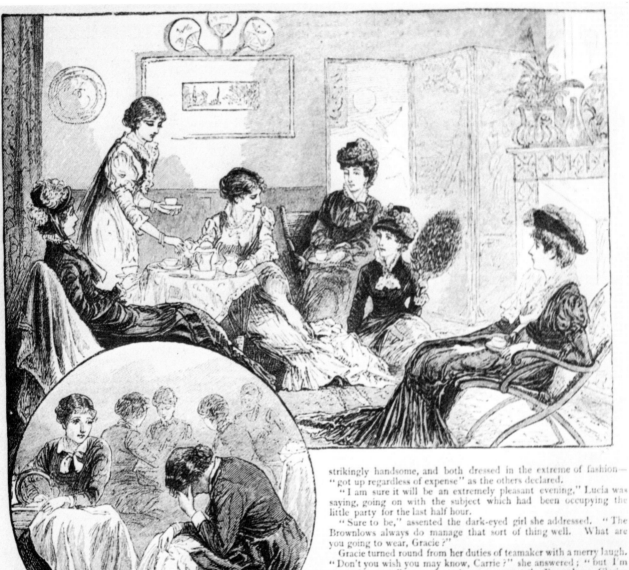

THE Misses Saunders were entertaining a select party of four of their intimate friends at afternoon tea. It was a cold bleak day in December, and without the wind was raging and howling, and fiercely driving before it the flakes of thick-falling snow.

It was the sort of day that makes you gather round the warm fire and feel thankful for the shelter of home.

The force of contrast made the cosy sitting-room where the girls were assembled all the more cheerful and inviting. It was a tastefully furnished apartment, abounding in the dead greens and black furniture so fashionable at present, and bountifully supplied with low easy chairs, which the girls had grouped round the hearth, where a glorious fire was blazing, lighting up the room, which was growing dark in the early December twilight.

Miss Saunders—familiarly called Gracie—presided at the little gipsy table, with its silver urn and tea equipage, while Lucia, her younger sister, handed cake and cups of tea to their guests.

They were all pretty stylish girls, but Gracie and Lucia were strikingly handsome, and both dressed in the extreme of fashion—"got up regardless of expense" as the others declared.

"I am sure it will be an extremely pleasant evening," Lucia was saying, going on with the subject which had been occupying the little party for the last half hour.

"Sure to be," assented the dark-eyed girl she addressed. "The Brownlows always do manage that sort of thing well. What are you going to wear, Gracie?"

Gracie turned round from her duties of teamaker with a merry laugh. "Don't you wish you may know, Carrie?" she answered; "but I'm not going to tell you. Last time we were at the Brownlows, Clarice got to know that I was going to wear pink, and then the dear good-natured creature wore red herself, and would insist on keeping close to my side all the evening, in an apparently affectionate way, but in reality because she wanted her red dress to kill my pink one. Then another time when I had ordered the dresses for Lucia and myself, what did Charlotte French do but steal the idea, and then appear at the same place in a dress exactly like ours, just for all the world as if a dozen had been made to order. I'm not going to give either of them a chance again; so Lucia and I have held a solemn conclave and have decided what we will wear, but we are not even going to give the order to Madam Robertson until two days before, by which time, I should hope, both Clarice and Charlotte will have made their own arrangements."

"That's not at all a bad idea," replied the girl who had spoken before. "It's awfully annoying to find one's ideas appropriated by some one else. But won't it be rather a hurry for you to get the things in time?"

"Oh no," answered Gracie carelessly. "Madam Robertson is very good, and always manages to let us have what we want by the time we name, and she never makes a misfit."

"But, Gracie," ventured, in a very gentle voice, a fair-haired girl, sitting on the hearthrug, holding a screen of peacock's feathers to shield her face from the fire. "Do you think it is *quite* considerate—I don't mean so much for Madam herself, as for the workgirls she employs? Mamma tells me that the poor things are sometimes almost worked to death because people give such short notices, and she always makes me give as long a one as I can conveniently."

CHRISTMAS EVE IN HAMILTON WARD.

Above: The Wards of St Margaret's, *by Sister Joan, a serial from 1894, follows the heroine, Constance, through thirty years of nursing, to end her career in spinster contentment sharing a cottage with her friend Hope.*

Requests from readers for advice on their careers were frequent, and the replies always well informed:

KATHLEEN.—Twenty-five is the earliest age to be admitted to several of the most important London hospitals, but in some institutions girls are accepted as probationers at twenty-one. Paid probationers usually receive £10 or £12 salary the first year, with board, lodging and uniform; but many girls nowadays are glad to pay £13 13s. for their training as the competition among would-be nurses is severe. [1896]

CATHERINE L.—Uniform of a hospital nurse is provided. Of underclothing, supply yourself with as much as you can afford, when of sufficient age to be eligible, which you are not till past twenty-one, even in a children's hospital. The usual age is twenty-five—very young people are liable to catch disease. [1896]

"WHAT SHALL I WRITE?"

The stage as a career was emphatically discouraged by the *G.O.P.*, which frequently warned readers against the awful dangers awaiting girls in the theatre:

Once on the stage, those wishing to leave it and live religious lives find much prejudice from prospective employers. [1884]

Too often an "educated" girl faced with the need to support herself thought no further than a post as companion or governess. A reader signing herself DESPONDENT wrote in 1896:

My father has died, and our comfortable home must be broken up. I am told that I may have £30 a year, but this is not enough to live upon. Could I become a companion?

She received the Editor's reply:

Above: The Marriage Settlement, *from the title page of the issue for September 1, 1894.*

31

Situations as companion are much harder to find than girls seem to imagine. They depend largely on private influence. Ladies take as companions girls of whose qualities they already know something. We cannot blame them for this. If there are any friends of your family who might avail themselves of your services, by all means make your wish known to them. But failing this, we earnestly recommend you to spend some portion of your money in learning a business; what this business should be we cannot suggest until we know your tastes and abilities. But think over matters, and then please give us some idea of your preferences, when we will with pleasure advise you more fully.

Governessing was a career which, although on the decline, still attracted a good many girls—though not all qualified, as a reply to one poor aspirant showed:

You seem to think that we keep a registry office. You are not sufficiently educated to take a place as nursery governess. You cannot write; and do not express yourself properly. [1894]

An article in 1884 dealt with *The Duties of a Governess*:

From the time the governess enters a house it should be her grand aim to win her pupils' love.... Continual fault-finding is too trying to a child's patience.

But the governess's patience, too, had long been sorely tried—and for such young women every year brought new options on to the horizon. In 1888 came *The Type-Writer and Type-Writing*:

Just now the type-writer is attracting considerable attention; and though its use in England is far from being so general as in the United States, we feel quite safe in prophesying that even in our comparatively conservative land, for many purposes the pen will be in a few years superseded by this ingenious machine. ... Type-writing is doing much, and will do more, towards solving the problem of finding suitable employment for ladies, it being an occupation peculiarly fitted for their nimble fingers. In the United States, lady type-writists are a large and important body, commanding good salaries, and as the instrument comes into general use in this country, ladies who have learnt to work it will have no difficulty in finding remunerative employment, especially if, in addition, they can write short-hand.

The *Girl's Own Shorthand Class* series of articles began in 1892:

The only requisites are Pitman's sixpenny "Phonographic Teacher", which can be got through any bookseller, a fine-pointed pen or pencil—not too hard to run easily over the paper, or too soft to make a delicate yet firm stroke—some ruled paper (say an old copybook), and a little patience.

Young Women as Journalists appeared in 1891:

Supposing the young woman to be mistress of all necessary accomplishments, she will still have to decide whether it would be quite seemly for an unprotected girl to travel about London or a great town in the evening until after midnight. The work also has to be done in all kinds of weather. We have seen such a girl at her work, and one who was apparently well fitted for what she was about; but we sympathised with her in regard to the hardships of her lot while we could not but admire her courage. As things are at present, the girl reporter has to assume a bold mien when, with her notebook, she takes her place at a table among perhaps a dozen men, on whose province she is encroaching. It is not an occupation which tends to the development of feminine graces; and this will be as fully realised by the girl herself as by those with whom she comes in contact....

Far right: The Tennis Players, *written by Sydney Grey and illustrated by Everard Hopkins, October 13, 1883.*

But an aspiring and talented young woman need not turn her back on journalism because she does not choose to compete with ordinary reporters.... Reporting is only one branch of the profession.... Many accomplished journalists have never been reporters.... A great deal of the most effective work on our newspapers has been done by women; and, could it be told, the public would today be surprised to learn how much of the total is still done by them.

In *A Chat With a Girl Photographer* in January, 1901, the subject of the interview was a Miss Edmonds who had started as a "receptionist and shopwoman" with a Kensington photographer, and worked her way up until she had her own studio. Still a young woman, she attributed the success of her business to her up-to-date ideas:

The monstrosities which make up the usual photographers' "accessories" are conspicuous by their absence.... Balconies and pedestals, and pictorial backgrounds, with impossible perspectives, find no place here.

Some interesting figures on women in work were given in reply to a correspondent in 1894:

A BREAD EARNER.—We can give you statistics respecting the number of self-supporting women for the year 1892. There are 288,919 in the United Kingdom who are following various professions; 26,344 engaged in commercial business; and in our various industries and manufactures 2,027,899 more. These are all unconnected with those engaged in domestic duties. In Germany half a million more women are thus earning their living than those in our own country; and in Austria, France and Italy fewer earn their living than is the case here. Altogether, the number of women thus employed exceeds that of men by four and a half millions.

If prospects of advancement for the working girl were poor, those for women aiming for professional careers were brightening. In the field of higher education, major advances had been made. In 1884 the *G.O.P.* published *Education for Women at Oxford*, dealing with the question of admitting women to the University examinations, which was one so vigorously argued that a special train was chartered to bring from London all those who would vote in favour of the ladies. The article ended:

Some twenty years hence, when it has become a commonplace event for women to enter for these examinations, we shall look back with interest and amusement on the great struggle and the triumphant victory of the champions for the Higher Education of Women.

Despite this victory, Sophia F. A. Caulfeild had need to write tartly in 1894:

The justice and magnanimity which would show "honour to whom honour is due" ... is not always found equal to the occasion when it involves the granting of a degree.... St Andrew's, and the London Universities, and those of Chicago, Pennsylvania, Brown and Tufts, and Yale, stand by themselves in their fair-dealing with women scholars, admitting them to all their privileges and honours.... Only the other day the Royal Geographical Society refused the admission of women as Fellows, when at least Isabella Bird (Mrs Bishop) and Mrs French Sheldon might certainly have been regarded as well qualified for such an honorary distinction, and both ladies very worthy successors of the wonderful Ida Pfeiffer.

(Ida Pfeiffer [1797–1858] had been the subject of an article, *A World-Wide Traveller*, in an 1885 issue.)

Far left: the title page of The Girl's Own Annual, *1886–1887, drawn by Kate Greenaway. A reproduction of her drawing* Afternoon Tea, *with its characteristic blend of freshness and formality, was one of the presentation colour plates in the same volume. When she died in 1901, the G.O.P. published an appreciation.*

"WOMAN'S RIGHTS."

By HELEN MARION BURNSIDE.

Oh, those boasted "rights of women,"—
  Rights, of which so much is said!
Yet what are they?—Can you tell me,
  Wedded wife, or learned maid?
'Tis a vexed and vexing question,
  Which I fain would understand,
Often asked, but never answered,
  Oh, my sisters in the land!

In the days lang syne, I'm thinking,
  Hearts were just as brave and true;
Woman's work was never wanting
  For a woman's hand to do.
'Twas our privilege and duty
  To shed light on Earth's dark ways,
Though we never talked, or dreamed of
  "Woman's rights" in those old days!

Ah! lang syne, lang syne, my sisters,
  There were women standing by
When the Saviour's feet went toiling
  Up the steeps of Calvary.
Women soothed the pain and anguish
  Of those hours, so dread and dim;
Theirs the right, so sweet, yet awful,
  E'en to minister to Him!

Such sweet rights are ours for ever,
  Oh, my sisters in the land!
Rights of ministry and mercy,
  To be wrought with heart and hand.
Think you that those "rights" you talk of—
  Make them whatsoe'er you please—
Can be deemed more honour-worthy,
  Or more high and dear than these?

Above: a poem by Helen Marion Burnside, whose verses frequently appeared in the magazine (January 7, 1893).

Far right: an illustration to verses by William Luff:

"Am I a lily growing?
Standing still in the light?
Drinking ever the dews of Heaven
All through the darkest night?"

(October 4, 1890)

Not all contributors, however, were so enthusiastic on the subject. In *The Vocations of Men and Women* (1890), the Reverend Dr Tremlett complained:

> There are some who wish ... to convert this gentle, yielding, believing mind into the hard, unyielding, reluctant mind of a man. And when they have done it, what then? Have they raised the nature of woman? Nay, have they not rather lowered and perverted it? Depend upon it, man cannot alter what God has designed, and surely it is both unreasonable and unchristian to attempt it.

The gentle, yielding reader was advised in *Thoughts on the Higher Education of Women* by A Man in 1891:

> The subjects to be avoided, save in an elementary manner, are mathematics, and possibly science—certainly, however, the former. The subjects most to be encouraged are classics and history. These two widen and refine, while the tendency of mathematics for women is to make them narrow, and creatures of only one idea.... Depend upon it, ladies, the judgment of the Cambridge undergraduate represents fairly the judgment of English manhood upon your sex; and if there is anything he hates and ridicules, it is a masculine, unwomanly woman.... He wants to find sympathy in his pursuits—true womanly sympathy; a helpmate, not a lady who understands differential and integral calculus, who will discourse learnedly and drearily upon one everlasting subject.

Despite objections such as these, the attitude of the magazine was in general encouraging—although early articles inclined to the traditionally "ladylike". *On Earning One's Living—Fruitful Fields for Honest Labour* in 1880 suggested sculpture in wood, engraving on wood, designing patterns, china-painting, book-binding, painting on panels, mosaic work, flower-making, frame-making and gilding, repoussé brass-work, sewing and millinery, kindergarten teaching, teaching deaf-mutes, dispensing medicine, reporting and short-hand writing, law copying, nursing, painting in water-colours, and oil painting. But in 1883 appeared a series entitled *Work for All*, in the first article of which the anonymous author wrote:

THE DISADVANTAGES OF HIGHER EDUCATION.

WE hear a great deal nowadays about the advantages of the higher education of women. During the last few years high schools have multiplied in every direction: colleges and halls have been opened at both Universities, and girl graduates are no longer *raræ aves*.

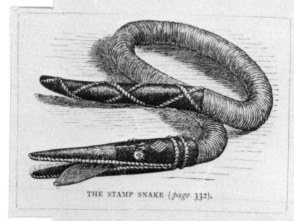

THE STAMP SNAKE (*page* 332).

Now comes a question—Is this altogether advisable? Are there not great disadvantages as well as advantages connected with this system?

It is well known that a woman's *physique* is not equal to a man's, and the brain power depends very much on the *physique* which nourishes the brain—*ergo*, the average woman will never equal the average man on his own ground. We do not deny that a clever woman can equal or surpass an average man; nor that the present system of education is infinitely superior to the old dreary round of lessons. But even to that there are two sides. While girls are learning Greek and mathematics, they have little time for the needle-work, which used to be a part of every girl's education, and which they will want to understand at some period of their lives. It is the fashion now rather to sneer at darning, mending, and other trifling household duties; but if a woman is to be a wife and mother, she will need a good deal of such knowledge. It is a great thing to know the relation of one angle to another; but it is not every mathematician who brings her knowledge to a practical issue with regard to tables and chairs, or can tell whether a room has been properly dusted or not.

Woman was created as an helpmeet for man, not as his equal or rival; and woman nowadays is very apt to forget that fact.

In our life and country the little things are the woman's work; and many of our best and noblest women are those who spend their whole lives in trifles (not trifling). Little things—soothing a fractious baby, mending a husband's shirt, doing a little for the poor, caring for servants, keeping the household machinery oiled—

"Little things
On little wings
Bear little souls to heaven."

It has yet to be proved that Cambridge examinations assist women in their household duties, and one of the Oxford nonsense rhymes has a terrible significance in its inner meaning:

"'Who will marry you, my pretty maid?'
'Advanced women don't marry, sir,' she said."

Does not that mean that while the talented women of this generation are studying to equal men on their own ground they are leaving the women's posts for the incapables? If this comes to be the rule may God help the men!

Another side of woman's influence follows naturally on this. Do we not all know dozens, if not hundreds, of cases, even among our own friends, where "the unbelieving husband is sanctified by the wife"? Where the man who has been careless and irreligious is gradually brought into the right way by his wife? Where a mother's quiet wisdom keeps her sons straight, among the innumerable temptations which beset them, at school, at college, and on their going into life? Do we not all know at least a few of the women of whom it might be said—

"She never found fault with you; never implied
Your wrong by her right; and yet men by her side
Grew nobler; girls purer, as through the whole town
The children were gladder that pulled at her gown."

We cannot help thinking that the great fault of the education of the present day is that the learning is made an end, and not a means. There is an old-fashioned notion that education is a preparation for the work of life, and that no amount of knowledge can take the place of practical usefulness. No doubt a certain amount of knowledge is necessary to fit us for this life; but, married or unmarried, a woman (if only she knows what she knows, and is taught when a child to do her work thoroughly) can find plenty of work lying ready to her hand, and she will be far more useful doing than studying.

A woman's natural quickness of perception may often be of the greatest possible use in matters which seem above her ken; but if she tries to advance too far she will certainly fail. Dwarfs on giants' shoulders see farther than giants; but we all know the fate of the dwarf who fought by the giant's side.

M. P. S.

VARIETIES.

SHORT-SIGHTED MORTALS.—When waves and trouble come over us, we say that troubles will never end; when God sendeth a fair wind, we think that the fair wind will never cease blowing.

NEW AND SECOND-HAND.
If thou wouldst tidings understand
Take them not at second-hand.

IN THE NEIGHBOURHOOD OF THE CAT.—People who have a strong antipathy to cats detect their presence by the odour, in circumstances which would be thought impossible. A lady in my study one day suddenly remarked, "There is a cat in the room." On my assuring her there was none, she replied, "Then there is one in the passage." I went out to satisfy her; there was no cat in the passage, but on the first landing-stairs, looking through the railings, sure enough, was the cat.—*G. H. Lewes.*

A GREAT INFLUENCE.
CHEMISTS tell us that a single grain of iodine will impart colour to seven thousand times its weight of water. It is so in higher things; one companion, one book, one habit may affect the whole of life and character.

Right: The Disadvantages of Higher Education, *an article by M.P.S., appeared in February, 1882. A few weeks later, in April, the Editor published an energetic reply by Bertha Mary Jenkinson, one of his teenage readers.*

The regular Varieties feature, an example of which follows M.P.S.'s article, covered a vast range of anecdotes, jokes, sayings and proverbs.

Far right: readers' verses, short stories, and essays were printed in The Girl's Own Page of Amateur Contributions. *Many compositions were sentimental, most predictable, but sometimes, as with Bertha Jenkinson's letter, they sounded a refreshingly individual note.*

AN OCCASIONAL PAGE OF AMATEUR CONTRIBUTIONS.

NOTE.

THERE are few habits so conducive to a well-regulated mind as the careful writing down of one's thoughts and sentiments in black and white, and our God-given power of influencing others for good is extended, if we are able to express ourselves clearly and correctly. These amateur compositions are inserted with a view to encouraging our girls in the practice of committing their thoughts and experiences to paper for the benefit of their sisters. Nothing thus printed is to be looked upon as perfect in composition, and the Editor wishes it to be understood that he will print only such verses or papers as shall be written in correct taste, interesting in subject to the general reader, and shall contain the age of the writer, and be certified as her *bonâ fide* work by a parent, minister, or teacher.

LIFE'S MUSIC.

Do the chords vibrate but lightly?
  Or are they full and deep?
Does the music murmur gently,
  Like a little child asleep?

Or is it harsh and broken,
  Like moanings of the wind,
While we grow weary seeking
  A tone which we cannot find?

There is a sweet note somewhere,
  If we could only see,
It would make a sweeter music
  And a fuller harmony.

Perhaps that note we're needing
  From others' life is caught;
And its melody is answered
  In our own deep train of thought.

For everyone must perfect
  His work of love and life,
Must keep it purely spotless
  In the midst of sin and strife.

And there is One to help us,
  Who knows that we alone
Can never make it holy,
  Never purify its tone.

He takes our burden from us,
  And tells us in His love
Our life-work shall be perfect
  In Our Father's home above.

    OLIVE HAWTHORNE (aged 15½).

DEAR MR. EDITOR,—The first remark I wish to make on the article entitled "The Disadvantages of Higher Education," by "M. P. S.,"* is, that it is unmistakably written by a man, and one who certainly has never had a wife who has been highly educated, or he would not have wasted his time in penning the article before mentioned. He says a woman's physique is not equal to that of a man's, and therefore the brain power of a woman can never equal a man's. That may be; but is it necessary, does it follow that a woman after she has learnt to read and write, to sew, clean a house, and cook a dinner, should allow her brains to lie dormant? I think not. A woman's education must go on all her life, exactly the same as a man's, or she will never be even a helpmeet for her husband.

If God had intended woman to be merely man's slave he would never have furnished her with reasoning powers. She need not have had even a tongue, for she could have cooked his dinner and mended his shirt quite as well without one. I think if such had been the case the emancipation of slaves would never have taken place. As for girls never learning sewing nowadays, I know that any girl educated in a Board School thoroughly understands the practical work of cutting out and putting together materials of all kinds.

Do you think, Mr. Editor, that "M. P. S." ever read Sidney Smith's "Pleasures of Knowledge"? If he did, I wonder if he skipped the following passages or read them:—"I appeal to the experience of every man who is in the habit of exercising his mind vigorously and well, whether there is not a satisfaction in it which tells him he has been acting up to one of the great objects of his existence? The end of nature has been answered: his faculties have done that which they were created to do; not languidly occupied upon trifles, not enervated by sensual gratification, but exercised in that toil which is so congenial to their nature and so worthy of their strength."

This applies equally to a woman as to one of the other sex. There is an anecdote I have read which I think is appropriate to the subject in hand. It is as follows. "When I lived among the Choctaw Indians I held a consultation with one of their chiefs respecting the successive stages of their progress in the arts of civilised life, and among other things he informed me that at their start they made a great mistake—they only sent boys to school. These boys came home intelligent men, but they married uneducated and uncivilised wives, and the uniform result was the children were all like their mothers. The father soon lost all his interest both in wife and children. 'And now,' said he, 'if we would educate but one class of our children, we would choose the girls, for when they become mothers they educate their sons.'"

In THE GIRL'S OWN a few months since I read that God did not take woman from man's head, so as to be his superior; nor from his feet, so as to be his inferior; but from his side, in order to make her his equal and companion, and unless a woman is educated she certainly cannot be either his equal or companion.

But, Mr. Editor, I fear I am taking up your valuable space, so I will be contented with merely mentioning that some women cannot be wives and mothers. They have their living to earn and must go out in the world, and if they are not educated, and highly educated too, I think the right word to apply to them would be incapables. I infer from "M. P. S." that he considers all women's reasoning faculties are not alike. He says that "While the talented women of this generation are studying to equal men on their own ground, they are leaving the women's posts for the incapables." Now, all women are not geniuses, neither are they incapables. There are some go-betweens, and these are the ones fitted to be wives and mothers. I do not mean to say that a genius would not make a good wife and mother, but possibly her genius requires her to concentrate her whole energies on one object. Then the go-betweens? They are improved, refined, and better able to train their sons to be great, good, and noble men, than if they had no sympathy with their tastes and feelings. A man enjoys talking to another, about politics for instance, and more so when he knows his opponent is "worthy of his steel." Would he not feel just the same pleasure in arguing with his wife, if she were educated, so that she could understand and talk sensibly and intelligently with him? Then, again, a talented woman is not obliged to be a heathen. Possibly, indeed most probably, she will be an earnest-minded Christian.

"M. P. S." also says if a woman advances too far she will certainly fall. I say the same of a man, but a woman cannot advance too far if she be sure of every step she takes. I could say more, Mr. Editor, but will refrain. And now, with numerous good wishes to you and "Our Girls,"—I am, yours sincerely,

    BERTHA MARY JENKINSON
    (Aged 14 years and 7 months).

* M. P. S. is *not* a man, but the daughter of an illustrious dignitary of the Church of England.—ED.

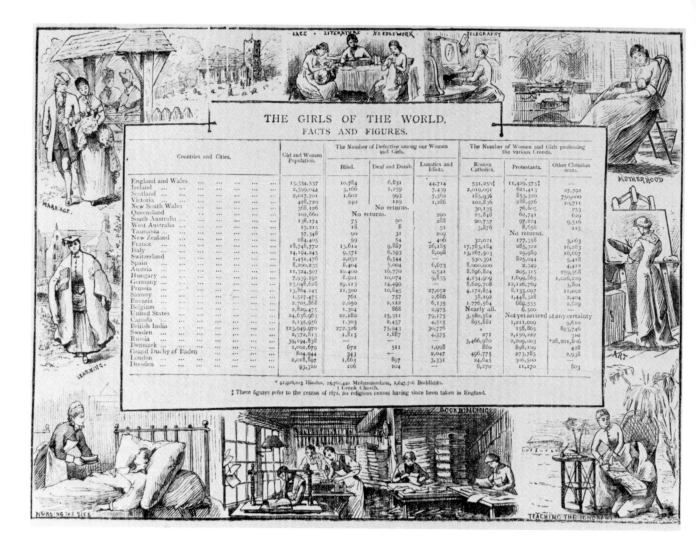

THE GIRLS OF THE WORLD.
FACTS AND FIGURES.

Countries and Cities.	Girl and Women Population.	The Number of Defective among our Women and Girls.			The Number of Women and Girls professing the various Creeds.		
		Blind.	Deaf and Dumb.	Lunatics and Idiots.	Roman Catholics.	Protestants.	Other Christian sects.
England and Wales	13,334,537	10,784	6,831	44,714	531,250‡	11,429,375‡	27,792
Ireland	2,599,044	3,166	1,259	7,439	2,016,091	621,413	
Scotland	2,617,701	1,602	993	7,562	185,936	853,320	750,000
Victoria	428,729	240	119	1,286	102,836	288,976	10,711
New South Wales	368,126	No returns.			30,135	76,605	253
Queensland	102,660	No returns.		290	25,848	62,741	629
South Australia	138,174	75	90	288	20,757	97,224	9,516
West Australia	13,215	18	8	51	3,876	8,558	115
Tasmania	57,348	90	31	209	No returns.		
New Zealand	284,495	59	54	406	32,021	177,358	3,063
France	18,748,772	13,614	9,887	26,185	17,763,184	285,322	16,283
Italy	14,194,245	9,571	6,593	8,098	13,467,503	29,969	16,667
Switzerland	1,454,476	2,032	6,544		592,391	825,044	5,418
Spain	8,200,235	8,404	3,004	6,673	8,000,000	2,349	4,412
Austria	11,324,507	10,400	16,770	9,541	8,896,824	205,315	259,568
Hungary	7,939,192	8,921	10,074	9,855	4,234,909	1,699,865	1,026,229
Germany	23,048,698	29,113	14,499		8,625,708	12,126,769	3,801
Prussia	13,804,245	11,300	10,845	27,052	4,172,854	8,135,097	17,092
Saxony	1,527,475	761	757	2,686	38,192	1,448,328	2,404
Bavaria	2,705,868	2,050	2,118	6,135	1,776,564	689,555	2,029
Belgium	2,829,475	1,304	868	2,975	Nearly all.	6,500	
United States	24,636,963	22,180	15,311	79,175	3,580,562	Not yet arrived at any certainty	
Canada	2,135,956	1,303	2,457	4,515	895,681	1,211,609	9,610
British India	123,949,970	272,326	75,943	30,776	*	158,865	893,746
Sweden	2,372,813	1,813	1,887	4,375	271	9,150,222	342
Russia	39,194,838	—	—		3,466,980	2,209,003	†28,201,896
Denmark	1,001,679	672	511	1,998	880	898,109	428
Grand Duchy of Baden	804,944	343	—	2,047	496,775	273,785	2,938
London	2,018,897	1,663	897	3,331	24,045	300,500	
Dresden	93,310	106	104		6,270	11,270	803

* 91,698,023 Hindus, 25,760,440 Mohammedans, 1,647,706 Buddhists.
† Greek Church.
‡ These figures refer to the census of 1871, no religious census having since been taken in England.

Above: in 1885–1886, Emma Brewer contributed a series of articles on The Girls of the World, *quoting facts revealed by the "wonderful science" of statistics. "It turns the bright flash of its lantern into the most secret places of a life, whether it be of an individual or of a nation, revealing at once the dark unhealthy corners ... improvement, light and health must of necessity result."*

The age of *gentility* it is to be hoped is passing away in England, and a healthy, vigorous life is coming in. No good work could, in the nature of things, be done by women who hid it away, and thought nothing did them so much honour as white hands and silk dresses. The abundant wealth of the country is no doubt largely responsible for this; men have made money so freely that there has been "no occasion" for the daughters to work, and those who have been less successful, have thought that they lost caste if their daughters did what their neighbours didn't, and, as in China, artificial restraints were resorted to, to keep the fair young things delicate and idle.... A man (using man in its widest sense of human being) who does not work, is like a chrysalis, unformed and unsightly, with the beauty in which Nature intended him to be clothed all folded up and undeveloped.

The series included comment on the medical profession, which was suggested as a possible career for the readers of the *G.O.P.* a comparatively short time after its members had grudgingly admitted women. Elizabeth Blackwell had put her name on the British Medical Register in 1859, by virtue of her American degree; Elizabeth Garrett had done so in 1869, by virtue of her Society of Apothecaries' licence; Sophia Jex-Blake, after both these means of entry had been barred, succeeded in doing so in 1877.

The objections which are urged to medicine as a profession for women [ran an article in *Work for All*] never seem to be felt when they desire to become sick nurses, although the one calling is quite as laborious as the other, and there are few of the objections which in fairness would not apply to the sick nurse.

The series ended with a plea for equal pay:

It should be remembered that the work of girls is, as it were, on its trial. If it be found to be inferior to that of men it is but just that it should be paid for at a lower rate, but if equal or superior, surely it should stand upon its intrinsic worth, and be paid for accordingly. Every woman who does what she undertakes to do in the spirit of the true workman, rejoicing in it and doing it to the very best of her ability, is a benefactor to her sex—nay, more, a true patriot.

New Employment for Girls by Sophia Caulfeild in 1891 included some original suggestions. Massage was one of these, and there were some odd comments on this:

S. F. A. Caulfeild

Too much of the operator's vital energy and magnetism may be absorbed by the feeble yet too keen recipient; or the weakly operator may, on the contrary, draw from the patient all the little vital power she possesses.

It sounds so perilous one wonders that people risked it. Medicine, surgery, chemistry, midwifery and dentistry were mentioned, and particular reference made to India as a wide field for women doctors because of the difficulties for men in "zenana practice" (the custom of segregating women in separate apartments to which no man could be admitted); *Work for All* had made the same point earlier. One very novel example appeared.

In the United States we find that a grist and planing mill is in the hands of a "Lady-Miller", i.e. Miss Addie Johnson, of West Virginia. She has studied mechanics sufficiently to "take down and put together an engine as well as any engineer in the country"; and she has worked her mill for the last three years. This is quite a new vocation, and it seems worth a notice.

MARGARET BATESON.

Another enterprising American, "Mrs Clara McAdow, the mining millionaire", was cited in 1894, and said to be "by no means 'unsexed' by the days of struggle, and fatigue, and association in her labours with working men".

A significant note was sounded in an article on employment by Margaret Bateson in 1897, dealing with the question of a fair day's pay for a fair day's work, with particular reference to the middle-class girl:

Everyone must be familiar with the usual line of attack. It takes the form of an appeal to a girl's generosity and to her fellow-feeling for other girls. The individual girl is reminded that if she remains living at home tranquilly and quietly (for movement is itself expensive), she can just manage to subsist. Then why should she insist upon doing work for pay? It is sordid of her to wish it. Moreover—and it is at this point that our tender-hearted girl succumbs—she must infallibly deprive other girls of a wage who need it more.... There is no proof that the general stock of work is growing less. It needs little imagination to foresee that manufactures may increase greatly, that trade can be indefinitely extended, and that a demand for many services is only waiting to be formulated when the services are supplied. Indeed, what we term the "Woman's Movement" means, if we regard it from one point of view, the creation of many demands. Who is it, for instance, who employs the expert

THE GIRLS OF TO-DAY.

By ONE OF THEM.

DURING the last few years it has been the fashion for people of all sorts and conditions to busy themselves about us and our position ; they have given their opinions of us very freely, they have discussed our capabilities, or rather incapabilities, together with our future prospects very much as though we were marionettes, without souls or brains or hands.

We have looked in vain among these opinions for some practical benefit to be derived from a study of them, but what we have noted is a sort of compassion for us that we should have been born into the world at all, and that our being here is a cruelty to our brothers and fathers ; for if we are stupid, they must keep us, and if we are clever, we rob them of their situations, and must keep them ; but that which hurts us most is the opinion that we are useless lumber in the dear old homes.

We beg to differ on every point : in the first place, we join heartily in the General Thanksgiving, and thank God for our creation and preservation as for great blessings, and this we do every day of our lives. And in the dear homes, however poor they be, we feel and know we have definite places, and that when we leave them, it will mean sorrow to the dear parents.

If any among us are idle, and a good many of us are credited with this disease, we are rebuked ; if, on the contrary, we are industrious and earn an independent livelihood, we are abused for taking the bread out of our brothers' mouths.

If we do not work, we are told that we cannot make good wives ; and if we do work, that we shall be unable to make our husbands happy because they want companions more or less frivolous when they have been at work all day. Alas! we should be thoroughly deserving of all the compassion showered upon us from time to time, if we were moved one iota from our steady purposes by all the conflicting advice and opinions offered us.

It is our determination not to be objects of compassion, neither will we be useless lumber in our homes, neither will we arrange our lives with the one purpose of entrapping men to marry us.

We did not ask to come into the world but were sent here by a loving Father, and whatever our position we are thankful for being here, otherwise we should have known nothing of a Heavenly Father's love and glory and majesty. We should not have known the meaning of being His children.

And as to our earthly parents, there are very few indeed who would be glad to get rid of us, be they ever so poor, and as a rule we feel so sure of their love and help that we should not believe it even if they themselves told us they wished we had never been born : but enough of this. The fact remains that we are born and that God created us male and female ; and what is more, He created us with powers for a purpose, and He surely expects us to use them, otherwise our hands, our brains, our heads, our hearts, might have been omitted.

Are we to be sorry that it is now quite rare to find, among us girls, one that sits down all day reading novels with a pet dog in her lap which she from time to time caresses, or that a girl willing to work is deterred from it by the fear of lowering her position thereby ?

We are convinced that work is good for us ; we are better for it physically, mentally and spiritually. We are altogether happier for it, and we object to being compassionated for doing that which our talents fit us for.

No girl will be the worse for a little money in the Savings Bank, but it will go doubly as far if she has placed it there out of her own earnings and not out of her father's.

We look round upon many families we know, and wherever we see a girl petted and thought too pretty or too delicate or too anything else to work, she is invariably discontented and unhappy—and why ? Because she is not fulfilling her mission in the world.

If, as people say, we are robbing our brothers of their work, it must be because we take more pains with the work and do it better than they. Therefore let them look to it.

There is work for everybody ; if not in one way, then in another. A lady whom some of us know was once very rich, and when her husband died she found herself quite poor, and would have been obliged to live upon her friends but for one gift she possessed, and peculiar as it was, she resolved to use it. It was that of mending clothes and linen, which she could do beautifully. She made her position known to several families who gladly engaged her on stated days in the month from nine in the morning till six in the evening, and needless to say, she is proving the greatest comfort possible to mothers of large families. For some years now she has kept herself not only independent, but able to put by a little for old age or sickness, and no one thinks of looking down upon her because she is doing the one thing she knew she could do well. In the same way a clergyman's daughter deprived of means had to face the world for herself and little sister, and knew that no one could clean or trim lamps better than she. So she at once made this accomplishment known, and she is getting a very tolerable income in this way without any loss of self-respect.

Working does not make us less womanly or less helpful in our homes or less affectionate to our parents, or, depend upon it, God would not have given us the capacity and the ability to work.

Who is the strength and the brightness of the home—the busy or the idle girl ? The one who uses her brains or the one who lets them rust ?

If people will interfere with us at all, let them try to build us up in vigorous, healthful work, teaching us that however humble the work we do, we give it dignity by doing it to the best of our ability.

Many of us girls belonging to the so-called upper class are extremely clever in dressmaking and millinery. Should we not prove benefactors to the small tradesmen and servant classes, if we could take rooms in various parishes where they could bring their materials and get them made up prettily and cheaply ? As it is now, their dresses and bonnets are in wretched taste and badly made, and at a sum greatly in excess of what they can afford.

We have come to the conclusion that we shall live better lives and longer lives if we work well and cheerfully at that which falls to our lot. The nation will be the better for our influence and example, and our brothers cannot and will not be content to smoke and dawdle away their time at clubs and music halls while we, their sisters, are earnestly working.

Looking at things all round, we come to the conclusion that there is plenty of work to do, not only for our fathers and brothers but for us girls also. Out of this work we will select that which we can do best, whether it be nursing, teaching, book-keeping, mending, lamp-cleaning, dressmaking, or anything else. At the same time we will endeavour to hold fast by those attributes of modesty, gentleness and patience which belong to good women, and while we enrich the home with our earnings, we will try to be its sunlight and its ornament.

Above: The Girls of Today, *a lively article published in December, 1899, when G.O.P. readers were looking forward to the new century.*

woman shorthand-writer ? It is, in many cases, the woman-lecturer, the woman of business, or the woman-doctor.... And though in London and our large towns we are slowly waking up to the fact that the capacities of women of the educated middle and upper class are not wisely allowed to atrophy, the country at large still wastes much useful labour. In how many of our rural districts is there a trained nurse, much less a cottage hospital, with a nursing staff of women ? In how many country places are educated women trying by their own practical exertions to unravel the farmers' and the labourers' problems; in how many are they idling through their days, or at best bicycling over the country to kill time—and simply because they believe paid labour to be wrong. . . .

I regard a pound a week as the average beginning salary of the middle-class girl. To the girl who in the factory or the workshop is earning less, and by very hard labour, I have no need to appeal. My only word to her is one of inducement, to try, by superior training, by combination, by whatever fair means lie in her power, to win more adequate pay. But the middle-class girl should begin with £1 a week; if possible, of course, with more; certainly not with less. And here I may say that the stories which I hear of girls who destroy each other's chances of salary, by offering to do work for board and lodging only, or for a salary less than that offered, I regard much as I should some exhibition of cannibalism.

While the *Girl's Own Paper* advocated feminine usefulness and the worth of honest labour, the unsentimental, professional note of this article, and the mention of "combination" particularly, comes as something of a surprise. Even though by the eighteen-nineties women were being allowed into men's unions (having until then usually had to form their own), the *G.O.P.* at this time is not a publication one associates with trade unionism. Obviously the writer knew that a pound a week was far out of the reach of the average working girl; many working men did not earn as much.

In general the *Girl's Own Paper* avoided matters of political controversy, although it was prepared to inform its readers on the state of the law. In 1890 A Solicitor wrote on *The Married Women's Property Acts*, discussing the greatly increased rights of married women to property of their own. And by 1898, in a series entitled *Letters from a Lawyer*, addressed to "My dear Dorothy" and signed "Bob Briefless", readers received advice on a variety of legal matters ranging from insurance and investments (2% per annum on £50 left to Dorothy by her godmother), to how to draw up a Will.

In *Some Types of Girlhood*, under the sub-title "*The Political 'Sisterhood'*, or Our Juvenile Spinsters", the indefatigable Sophia Caulfeild asserted in 1890:

Politics are by no means outside a woman's sphere of influence; and her work would grievously lack completion were she to exclude it from the list of the necessary items of a general education. But "stump oratory" may safely be regarded as quite beyond the limits of a woman's social work. What could be more revoltingly unnatural than the grim, ungainly spectacle of a woman haranguing a mob?—a woman engaged in exciting the passions of socialistic and unprincipled men; exciting them to deeds of violence and insubordination, instead of entering their homesteads in private as messengers [sic] of harmony and peace.

However, the author goes on to say:

Before concluding my description of the type so nicknamed, I must warn my readers that it has been very unjustly applied in a large proportion of cases. Those opposed to any reform as regards the work, the improvement, and general influence of the sex, seem to feel a mischievous pleasure in classing all such reformers under one and the same opprobrious designation.

Five years later, in an article entitled *Politics for Girls*, the author (Frederick Ryland) prophesied:

MELBOURNE QUAY OF TO-DAY.

Above: Melbourne Quay, from an article of July 4, 1891. The author, W. Lawrence Liston, described how men lined the quayside to welcome the families "whose futures they have pioneered in this vast country". (He was to be taken aback by the remarkable friendliness of fellow passengers on Australian trains.)

Features on colonial life appeared at intervals, and would-be emigrants sometimes wrote to the Editor for advice. "No girl should go out without a thorough knowledge of housework and housekeeping, even to washing and ironing clothes," he warned. The energy and industry of successful colonists were much praised.

It seems probable that before the girls who read this page grow into full womanhood, the Parliamentary franchise—that is, the right and duty of voting for Members of Parliament—will be given to women in the United Kingdom as it has already been given in some of the Colonies. Many of the most influential members of both our great parties—the Conservatives and the Liberals—are in favour of the change; and in all probability it will be carried into effect within ten or twelve years.

The seventeen-year-old girl who, in 1880, had envied her brother his *Boy's Own Paper* and been delighted to get her own magazine, would have been in her thirties when that article appeared, perhaps already introducing a new generation to the *G.O.P.* But not until her daughters were adults would the dream of votes for women become a fact.

Chapter Two

HEALTH AND BEAUTY

Health can make the plainest girl pleasant to behold, if her mind be pure and innocent. Health causes the rich blood to mantle in the cheeks, brings the gladsome glitter to the eye, brightens the complexion, gives music to the voice, a charm to the smile, litheness and vigour to the limbs, and sprightliness and grace to every motion. So if you have beauty and purity of mind combined with bodily health, it is indeed impossible you can be ugly.

Article by Medicus
(1884)

"What a lovely morning it is, Marion dear! How fresh the air is, and how sweetly the birds sing! I wonder if many other of the Editor's 'girls' are now taking walks in the early morning!"
"Yes, Jane, of course there are. The Editor's influence is unbounded."

Above: one of the engaging cartoons which appeared on the correspondence pages of some early issues (May 21, 1881).

Nobody will be surprised to hear that there were no articles on mascara or lipstick for the Victorian readers of the *Girl's Own Paper*. Lip salves, cooling washes, perfumed cod-liver oil, or the "little elegancy" of rose glycerine for redness or sunbrowning, were permitted. But, as MARY A. was told in 1887, "On no account use powder; nor, still worse, paint! No sensible, modest woman should resort to such measures."

However, they had regular articles on health and beauty, and although health was a long way in front, beauty was not quite forgotten. These articles appear under the name of "Medicus"—pseudonym of Dr Gordon Stables, M.D., C.M., R.N. (Introduction, page 18). His first article, in 1880, is called *How Can I Look My Best?*

Happy is the girl, I say, who can take and enjoy a bath in pure cold, soft water every day of her life.... Avoid coloured and over-scented soaps. Another mistake is the use of too rough a towel, and this rough towel, I am sorry to say, is often recommended by people who know no better. A moderate degree of friction is all very well, but, dear me, you do not need to rub your pretty skin off.... But probably the most harmless of all cosmetics, and certainly the best, is wetting the face with May-dew—I'm not joking, gentle reader—and if you have to get up quite early in the morning to go and look for it, and have to walk a mile or two before you find any, all the better.

Shortly afterwards, in *Health and Beauty for the Hair*, Medicus says:

If you want to have a good head of hair you ought to cultivate a calm and unruffled frame of mind. Nervous, fidgetty folks seldom have nice hair....

MAXIMS FOR THE NEW YEAR.

By MEDICUS.

"Look before you ere you leap,
For as you sow you're like to reap."
Old Play.

SOME people laugh at the very idea of making good resolutions; I do not. It is true we never can keep all the good resolves we may make; if we could do so we would be perfect, and that is what no merely human being ever yet was in this world. Nevertheless, it is my humble opinion that it *ought* to be our aim, and that it *is* our duty, to get as near to perfection as ever we can, both for the sake of our own happiness and that of everyone with whom we come into contact. You grant this; well, then, I'll tell you something. I mean this month not only to be your *Medicus* but your *Mentor* as well. Just for once in a way, you know, and I'm certain my fair young readers will forgive my presumption, for—it is a season of forgiveness. I would not be your accuser though, yet well I know that if you were to ask yourself this question, "Have I done all the good in my power for those around me and for myself in the year that is gone?" the answer would be expressed in a word of two letters instead of three. But, there, brighten up and read what I have to say; the year is young yet, the year is yours to do as you will with, and I would not have the hue of your resolution "Sicklied o'er with the pale cast of thought." No one, I may begin by telling you, who is not perfectly healthy can be truly happy and comfortable, and a person who is not both cannot bring joy to others, so that in resolving to do the best you can for your personal health, both mental and bodily, you are really consulting the good of others at the same time. That itself should in my opinion be inducement enough for any girl to learn and to try to abide by the common laws of health. But does obedience to these laws entail a very great deal of self-restraint and self-mortification? I do not think so, because good habits are just as easily acquired as bad ones. I pray you lay that to heart and remember, too, that—

"Ill habits gather by unseen degrees,
As brooks make rivers, rivers run to seas."

Besides, evil habits always bring wretchedness and misery in their wake, while good invariably lead to happiness and joy.

Now some of the hints and maxims regarding the care of the health, which I have embodied in my papers of last year, will bear repeating here in an epitomised form. But as I have very great objections to write anything in a dry tabulated kind of way, I will try to put before you what I have to say in the shape of a sketch.

The heroine of my little sketch I shall call Jeanie Smith, and I will try to paint you, from my imagination, just one day in her life. It is a very common, some might even say humble, name I have chosen for my heroine, and you cannot tell therefrom whether she be English, Irish, Scotch, or Welsh. But, whatever you do, don't imagine that Jeanie is a saint; she is neither more nor less a saint than any of my readers are. She has the same passions, good and bad, and the same temptations to do wrong instead of right, only, for the sake of illustration, I choose that she shall do what is right.

Jeanie's age is somewhere between ten and fifteen; she is neither rich nor poor, but she has duties to perform just the same as we all have. Jeanie lives in the country, but for all that she comes up to town sometimes in the season, and a year never passes without her having a holiday of some kind.

It is a clear frosty morning in January, with crisp crunchy snow on the ground, and the sun is shining quite brightly, although it is not much past seven o'clock. Jeanie wakes and rubs her eyes, and sits up in bed. She gives a little shiver as she does so. "Oh!" she thinks, "I do wish it were May or June once more, then early rising would not feel so hard." She would fain lie for only one little half-hour longer. It is a good thing she doesn't, for lying awake in bed of a morning is most enervating and depressing, but she remembers she has a little brother to dress, and several other household duties to perform, so she gets up within five minutes of the time she first opened her bright eyes. It is not good to spring at once out of bed; one ought to compose one's thoughts for a few minutes. This gives the heart time to prepare for the change, but do not take longer than five minutes, any more than Jeanie does. She kneels for a space of time beside her bed, and asks for guidance from Him whose guidance we all so much need.

Now the bath. The servant has brought a little hot water, to deprive the ordeal of its January chill. But it is still a cold bath. If it were not so, there would be no brace or tonicity in it. Tepid baths are only for bedtime. The glow produced by the bath—though not very great—is enough to give Jeanie heart and warmth to go on dressing. She even sings to herself as she does so, and this, by the way, is a sure sign that the bath has done her good. If young girls are healthy, they ought to want to laugh of a morning, and sing as the birds do. Jeanie's toilet adjuncts are all of the simplest, but good. Her tooth-powder is either charcoal or carbonate of soda, her tooth-brush is medium in thickness; her nail-brush strong and useful, like her little nail-scissors, which she does not forget to use. Thus Jeanie's teeth are like pearls, her hands are soft and white, and she never suffers from agnails. The soap she uses is mild transparent, the water *rain water.* Perhaps this accounts for the beauty and delicacy of her complexion, but only, mind you, to a partial extent, for Jeanie lives nearly all the day in the open air, and there is nothing in the world equal to fresh air, for not only beautifying but preserving the complexion.

Our heroine washed her hair some evenings ago, using warm soft water and yolk of egg instead of soap, so this morning it only needs well brushing to make it glitter like the wing of yonder blackbird, who is waiting for Jeanie to throw him his matutinal crumbs. A word about the bedroom itself. It is neat, and clean, and tidy, and everything is put in its place again as soon as used. Now the very fact of sleeping in such a room has an effect for good. A tidy apartment is a nerve tonic; an untidy one a nerve depressant.

But, see, Jeanie is dressed, and hurries away to perform her duties. She carries health with her, and that makes the duty seem light. Oh! what a holy thing is duty well performed. Duty! Have ever you studied the word in all its bearings?

Jeanie's is by no means a life of ease. I am sure she would not be happy if it were, nor half so healthy. Hours of leisure she has, of course, and these she devotes to exercise, to study, and to doing good. She always finds means of doing good, if only in a small way—to God's lower animals, for instance.

One of Jeanie's duties at meal times is to see that her little brother is properly served; that he doesn't eat too fast, and that he behaves himself like a young gentleman. It is good for her she has to do so, for thus her own food is not hurried down, and indigestion rendered impossible. The danger of eating too quickly is great, for the food is improperly masticated—it is not sufficiently mingled with the saliva, and too much is eaten, so the stomach is in consequence very greatly overtasked.

Jeanie has sewing to do as well as lessons to con, but neither at her needle nor at her books does she sit huddled up in an ungainly, cramped position. Indeed, she *never* sits thus; and her shoulders, in consequence, do not bend forward, nor is her spine bent, so she can walk erect; and as she never sews or reads in the dim twilight nor in strong sunshine, her eyes do not ache and her sight is as powerful as a bird's. She has learned that a great deal of work, whether sewing or reading, can be better and less laboriously performed out of doors than in; and much more pleasantly, too, because in the open air she is not only increasing her health, but learning to love life in every shape. Does she not see the flowers blooming around her, the trees gently waving their glittering leaves in the sunshine, and the bees at work, and does she not hear the birds singing? Ay, and Jeanie can sing, too, for well she knows how beneficial such exercise is, and how it keeps colds and coughs and consumption itself far away. She knows this, because "Medicus" told her; but even if he hadn't it would have been all the same, because it is as natural for a girl to sing, when healthy and happy, as it is for the lark.

Jeanie goes for a long walk, not after, but before dinner; but whether sitting or walking out of doors, she takes her mother's advice, and wears strong boots and warm stockings.

Here are a few truths or maxims about catching cold, which I throw in parenthetically. This climate being a most changeable one, it is advisable for every girl, especially if anywise delicate, to wear, winter and summer, flannel or silken underclothing, and woollen stockings or silken, with water-tight boots. Goloshes are bad. Pattens are excellent to wear about the doors in the country. In cold weather, while walking, wear a comforter; but loosen it if you feel warm. Do anything rather than sweat your neck. Don't sit in draughts, but do not be afraid of a good blow of fresh or even cold air. Avoid sudden changes from heat to cold; never go right away out of a warm room into a cold, to dress for an evening party. Thousands by doing so receive their death-blow. Avoid sitting in damp clothes; and if you get wet, don't be afraid of

FIG.1.   FIG.2.   FIG.3   FIG.4.

Exercise greatly promotes the health and beauty of the hair. So does the bath. This latter should be taken every morning and as cold as can be borne. EXERCISE AND THE BATH (Printer, put it in large type) [*sic*]. . . .

To ensure perfect cleanliness, the hair should be washed once a fortnight. Do not use soap; the yolks of two new-laid eggs must be used instead. The water should be rainwater filtered—lukewarm to wash with, cold to rinse out. Afterwards dry well and brush.

Exercise and the bath, sensible diet, and no tight-lacing are the usual lines of the advice given by Medicus. He is no advocate of "dosing" and says in one article, "To be a slave to aperient medicines is almost as bad as being a slave to opium" and in another, "If I had my will, I would clear out every bottle with a label on it from the nursery. Away with your syrups of senna and rhubarb, away with your still-waters, your slops and your oils." Girls brought up on Medicus's advice certainly ought not to have grown into mothers who gave their children a Friday-night dose of castor oil.

One of his early articles, in 1880, is headed *How To Be Healthy*:

Many girls between the ages of ten and fifteen suffer from what we medical men call anaemia, or, in plain English, poverty of blood. Such girls are often looked upon as merely delicate, and little that can be of any avail is attempted to be done for them. Here is a case in point, and it teaches a lesson that you will do well to lay to heart. Miss Julian A. is fourteen years of age; she is an only daughter and adored by her parents. But her mother says, expressively, "Julian won't make old bones." Her mother's words may come true, because this is the way in which she is treated: she is kept and coddled almost constantly within doors, she always has a little fire in her bedroom, and the window is seldom opened. If she goes out she is positively burdened with clothes, and, in addition to all kinds of good living, she is made to drink wine "to keep her up". She is pale and blanched in appearance, too weakly to work, and suffers from *back ache*. This case, and all others of the same kind, requires plenty

Above: in The Physical Education of Girls (*May, 1884*), *Mrs Wallace Arnold set out ten simple exercises with the chest expander ("procured at any surgeon's mechanist's or indiarubber warehouse"), to correct a stooping back brought about by study at desk, piano and drawing-board.*

of exercise in the open air, the companionship of other girls of the same age, good food, cod-liver oil, and tonics of iron.

And in *Why Am I So Pale?*, in 1890:

Bad meat and fish are expensive, and three times the amount of good blood can be made from pea-meal, oatmeal, good bread, lentils, and mealy potatoes, with a little butter and plenty of milk, for half the money.... In conclusion, let me remind my readers of one lamentable fact; it is this—thousands of girls suffer from paleness of countenance through tight-lacing....

Tight-lacing is regularly denounced in the *G.O.P.*:

No adult woman's waist ought to measure less in circumference than twenty-four inches at the smallest, and even this is permissible to slender figures only. [1886]

Among the answers to correspondents in 1889 is the following:

MISS MONK inquires "how she may reduce" her natural waist from the size which her Creator was pleased to make it, viz. twenty inches round, to sixteen inches. We recommend her to apply at some hospital, and see whether she can induce them to cut it open, and remove either some part of the liver or lungs (as she could not very well dispense with her heart), and then she can have her dresses reduced in the waist without stopping the action of the wonderful God-

created machinery inside. At the same time, we must frankly tell her that we could not form any idea of how long she would live with half a liver or half a lung. Apart from this question, we cannot imagine how anyone could wish to produce deformity.

It is not quite clear what a reader signing herself M. R. NORWOOD boasted of to merit the scolding she received in 1886, but it sounds rather like tight-lacing. She is told:

We pity you! To what a miserable, unwholesome state of deformity you have reduced yourself! We do not open our columns to persons who boast of having so far degraded themselves.

Although slimming is not condemned as firmly as tight-lacing, it is scarcely encouraged. DAISY is told in 1880:

[She] may be very thankful that she is blessed with such excellent indications of good health as the rosy face and a stout body. She must be very handsome indeed in face, and very unusually elegant in figure and in carriage, to look at all well if "thin". A thin little girl is a pitiable sight!

FLOSS in 1891 is told:

You will not benefit yourself by eating a lemon daily, nor trying vinegar, nor any plan of such a nature, to reduce fat. Probably you would succeed in thinning your blood, and your poor watery blood may develop dropsy, in lieu of good healthy fat. How would you like to become puffy and bloated?

Medicus does, however, admit that it is possible for a lady to become *too* stout. In *Health and the Toilet* (1890), after devoting some space to the problems of the scraggy lady, he writes:

Ladies, on the other hand, who are getting too rotund, should take time by the forelock. I can assure them that obesity, if it once commences, makes giant strides.... Avoid all oily and fatty foods, and all floury vegetables, cereals and sugar; take dumb-bell exercise daily, walk plenty; take a cold bath every morning; eat as little as possible.

The articles and the answers to correspondents in almost any present-day magazine for girls would have been inconceivable to Medicus or his Editor. The simplest gynaecological problems are absent from the pages of the *Girl's Own Paper*, and even bowels are decently referred to as "the system". One might not have expected corns to be unmentionable, but they are, or very nearly:

LADY CLARISSA has our thanks for her recipe for certain troubles connected with the wearing of tight, hard, or ill-fitting shoes; but of which (we find it requisite to tell our girls) no one ever speaks in "polite society". It is very vulgar to speak of them excepting in the privacy of a bedroom, and to a very intimate associate. However, we willingly give the recipe. "Mix some tallow and carbonate of soda very well together, and grease the painful supernumerary night and morning." We should suggest a nicer description of ointment than "tallow" as an adjunct to the soda. CLARISSA omits to name the proportions. [1887]

Beauty problems occur frequently in the answers to correspondents, but the replies tend to be brisk to a fault.

B.E.R.—We have answered both your questions over and over again. We can only now advise you to wear a veil, and keep your hands in gloves as much

Far right: an illustration from a serial by Ida Lemon (July, 1896), which makes a favourite G.O.P. point: beauty depends on the glow and sparkle of good health. Pretty as they are, sitting in their dainty dresses in a summer meadow, Kathleen and Dorothy would appeal whatever their garb and their setting, for they have the beauty of youth and health, charming manners and sweetness of expression.

as possible. Neither disfigurement is always capable of cure. Red hands and freckles are natural to many. [1883]

SCOTCH THISTLE.—We are shocked to hear that you "never wash your face with soap"! The sooner you begin to do so, the better. Use soft water, or put some bran in it. Employ a mild, unscented soap at night, and then apply a little glycerine and water before drying it, or else, after drying, a little vaseline. In the morning, you need only bathe your face with cold water, as it will then be clean. It is the nature of some skins to shine. Wear a veil. [1884]

KATHERINE.—We congratulate you on having a colour. Too many girls look sadly washed-out, described so graphically in negro parlance as "poor catsy white trash". [1894]

FATIMA (Smyrna).—As to the dangerous attempt to give additional brightness to the eyes by artificial means, we greatly object to them. Some foolish, vain women employ belladonna—a drug that extends the pupil and injures the eye. . . . [1898]

An aristocratic correspondent in 1881, signing herself DAY-DREAM, is rebuked at once for two different kinds of vanity and for faulty syntax, as though to prove that the *Girl's Own Paper* stands in no awe of Debrett:

We are sorry to hear that you, a peer's daughter, are a perfect fright to look at with your red nose and fearful complexion! Your skin is naturally tender, and you have been using a too rough towel. Until that great entertainment at which you say you are to "come out", you should bathe the face morning and night in cold rain water, to which a little toilet vinegar has been added, and use cold cream at night. Your writing is good, but no better than it should be, for, with the advantages of having a governess to yourself, you *ought* to be a superior girl in everything. That you have yet to learn English is shown by your writing, "Will you please give a pattern of how to make a *woollen man's* glove in your paper?" We are not so well acquainted with the requirements of woollen men as we are with those of careless and boasting girls.

But some straightforward beauty advice does appear unaccompanied by moralising, as in the answer to BLANCHE in 1880:

At your age you need not be alarmed at your hair getting thin; it is probable that your system is a little out of order. Attend to your health; eat and drink nothing that stimulates or heats the system; take a teaspoonful of cream of tartar now and then of a morning. Use a hard brush for five minutes every day, morn and night, and the following stimulating pomade. Go to a respectable chemist and tell him to mix you two drachms of Wilson's stimulating ointment in an ounce and a half of nicely-scented pomade. Rub a little of this well into the roots of the hair every day, and wash once a week with juniper-tar soap, or mild carbolic acid soap.

In 1884 an exasperated Editor replies to MISETOE MAGGIE:

We have already announced to our correspondents that we have ceased to answer questions respecting the hair, the complexion, cosmetics, personal defects, blushing, and nervous shyness. Read what we have said about them before.

But by 1896 the Editor has relented at least to some extent:

AMY.—The use of curling-tongs is decidedly bad for the hair. While young it is not of much consequence, as the singed, dried up, and broken hair is renewed again; but this is not so in older women. The hair naturally becomes

Far left: Twenty One, a portrait by Maria Stanley, published in the Annual of 1885–1886. The sitter, with her fresh complexion, simply dressed hair and loose white gown, adorned by just one rose, has the charm of good health and quiet manners so constantly praised by G.O.P. writers.

Number 2 is less of a nuisance than an eye-sore. She is dressed to the waist as a man; thence, as divided skirts have not yet become fashionable, she necessarily remains a woman, at least in costume; in motion she yet strives to represent a man. This figure provokes one to laughter, calling to mind as it does that hybrid, the mermaid, which was neither fish, flesh, nor fowl, nor good red herring.

Again, what is more tiring than that mincing step so many affect, and what more tiring to the walker?

One more, the 5th—the girl who carries herself too well—that is to say, who pulls her shoulders back until it appears she could fall backward at a touch; the body is perfectly rigid; all the work is done from the hips downwards, which is manifestly not right. What does a doctor tell you about walking? It is the best exercise possible *because* it brings into play *all* the muscles of the body.

The natural movement is always the more graceful, and the beauty of motion is the ripple of the whole form, the beautiful sway of a beautiful line. The wonderful construction of the human body is expressed best in walking, each muscle giving and taking its share in the work.

"WITH BODY BENT FORWARD."

Above: a cartoon from an article on deportment by An Artist (May 9, 1891) in which the author caricatures particular faults of carriage.

Far right: Our Girls A-Wheel, *an energetic group, published in October, 1896.*

thinner and is not replaced in the same way when injured, and the natural oil not so efficiently supplied when dried up. The consequence is shown in partial baldness. Curling in soft paper is more prudent, and the curl looks more natural.

The hair, the complexion, cosmetics, personal defects, blushing and nervous shyness; all very familiar subjects of queries by the present-day teenager. It is perhaps hardly surprising that the G.O.P. readers took little notice of editorial admonition. FLORENCE MABEL in 1886 still has to be told:

The use of any kind of powder to the face is foolish and injurious, and is sure to be regretted at a future time, as it makes the skin coarse.

VIOLET, in the same year, is told:

We sympathise with you, and are sorry to hear of your "wrinkles" at nine-teen; but we think you give too much attention to your face in the glass to be happy or barely contented. The wrinkles are probably caused by the sun and strong light. You must wear a veil, and bathe the face with oatmeal-water instead of soap. But do not mind your face so much; cultivate your mind and heart, and then you will be pleasant in everyone's eyes, even if plain in early youth and more deeply wrinkled still in extreme old age.

ABRUPT, writing in 1889, receives a reply which matches her pseudonym:

We cannot give you any recipe for making your hair grow dark, nor any for "getting rid of a double chin". Be thankful that you have got any hair or chin at all, and that the hair you complain of does not grow on your chin . . .

——one wonders whether ABRUPT continued a subscriber.

O.P.N. in 1891 is informed:

[She] need not feel worried at having a little down on her lip. If of a dark complexion it is very usual, and is not disfiguring, if slight, in the opinion of many; and you cannot expect *everyone* to admire you. Those who really care much for you would not wish to change any little special characteristic that marked the individuality of the face they loved.

One mysterious reply is addressed to PA'S DARLING in 1880, in which she is told to "rub the eyebrows three or four times a day with a piece of raw onion; you must not redden the skin, however". What was the raw onion intended to do, I wonder? To darken the eyebrows, to make them thicker or thinner? And did it work?

The articles by Medicus are most frequently concerned with general health matters—*When Not To Take Medicine* (1887); *Poverty of Blood: Its Cause and Cure* (1888); *Shall I Ever Get Well, I Wonder?* (1889). Once in a while, however, he becomes more frivolous; in *The Toilet Table and What Should Lie Thereon*, he gives a recipe for tooth-powder which sounds nasty:

Charcoal is unsightly but very effective, and it can be made more so by rubbing up with an ounce of it as much quinine as will lie on a sixpenny piece; a few drops of otto of roses may be added.

Recipes for cosmetics appear sometimes, as in *Lissom Hands and Pretty Feet* in 1880:

Here is a little bath for the hands, for which I am sure you will feel grate-ful. It is easily prepared, and if the hands are soaked in it for about ten

IN THE PARK.

HEALTH.

By GORDON STABLES, M.D., R.N. ("MEDICUS").

OVER-EXCITEMENT.

Would you be surprised to learn that this is very deleterious to the health of young ladies, and I don't care what the excitement may be, it has always to be paid for. Some girls are by nature finely-strung and emotional, and these have all the more need to take care of themselves. Even sentiment or what is called romance leads to emotionalism, and this in its turn to nervousness or even hysteria, and often to dire results.

I speak truly, I believe, when I say that your over-romantic, over-excitable and emotional girl is never likely to be married. Nor is the girl who is wanting in self-respect in so far as to be carried away by her feelings at any time. Therefore, I say, let girls have more solid exercise in the form of gymnastics or even athletics, and less reading of trashy suggestive novels, and less of the "moonlight on the sea" business. It may be that marriage is the goal that most young women try to reach, but they need not always be thinking about it, and the girl who looks upon every young man she happens to be introduced to as a possible suitor, generally conducts herself in such a way as to frighten that young man off, be he ever so eligible.

LOVE AND MARRIAGE.

There can be no continued happiness in married life if the marriage is not for love, and that, too, love on both sides. And if there be not compatibility of temper and tastes, love will evaporate. Of course there is true love and imaginary. I don't think that anyone tastes of the former more than once in a lifetime. Again love at first sight is a mere myth. True love can no more be built up in a day than a battleship can be built in a month, and don't you forget that, girls, please.

I heard an expression the other day which I did not quite understand, though I guessed its meaning. Two old ladies were yarning about a young lady, and said the one to the other, "She just threw herself at his head." Well, I am a fisherman, and that is not the way I should attempt to

catch a *salmo ferox*. And really there is a good deal of the *salmo ferox* about every marriageable young fellow who is worth looking at. He is possessed of splendid strength, and has a fair share of the beauty of manliness, but he has a shy kind of wildness about him also, not unmixed with suspicion, and, like the *salmo ferox*, he is easily frightened away if the bait goes in with a splash right in front of his nose. "No, thank you," he thinks to himself, and swims off to look for something less easily obtained.

GIRLS AND THE CYCLE.

I have been an ardent cyclist all my life, and am but little likely to run the wheel down.

A lady-writer says, "The bicycle is the greatest emancipator for women extant—women who long to be free from nervousness, headache and all the train of other ills. The wheel stimulates the circulation and regulates the action of the digestive canal, thus driving away headaches, and as a cure for nervousness it stands unrivalled. In every motion which the rider makes, the muscles are brought into play and gently exercised. With head and shoulders erect, those of the chest and arms are given a chance, while the pedal motion gives ample play to those of the legs."

WHAT ABOUT EMANCIPATION?

That is the only word I take objection to in the above quotation. It sounds to a man's understanding as if women had hitherto been kept in disagreeable subjection to the stronger and sterner sex. I don't think any woman, unless an old maid, hankers after emancipation of that sort, which seems to mean that, mounted on her bike, a girl can ride away anywhere and do anything all alone, without either male friend or chaperon, that she can guide and protect herself and be as free and easy as the wind. Well, I can assert, without fear of contradiction, that no man can really and truly care for a girl of this independent character, nor of one who pretends she can do everything manly quite as well as a man, only more so. Who wants a woman with a biceps, anyhow? Such a one is usually deficient in the gentler arts of her sex. Your women who scull much, or golf or hockey a deal are usually coarse in skin and in features, and far indeed from beautiful. No, girls, don't let us have too much of that emancipation business. Better to be loved and admired by a true and good man than be "emancipated."

BUT CYCLING MAY BE ABUSED.

There are times when no girl should cycle much. At any other time an hour's spin, so long as she does not race, is most delightful, provided the roads are good and the machine in order. In this case you have no occasion even to envy the swallows. But if instead of enjoying the scenery and the fresh air, you only try how far and how fast you can go, ten to one the run will do you little good and may do incalculable harm. Listen: every human being on earth has some organ or portion of the body that is weaker than the rest. It may be the lungs in some, the liver in others, or—so on and so forth, but it is on this weak organ that the strain of fatigue works its worst.

See that you have the best saddle that can be procured, and that you do not have to stoop. Ride in your very easiest corset, compatible with a figure free from actual dowdyism—I assure you I don't want you to look ungraceful, but health is the first consideration, isn't it? You will find riding from home less fatiguing than coming back, but all the same you have to return, so take care not to tire yourself out. The weakly should never ride on an empty stomach, nor after a full meal.

SLOW DIGESTION.

This is a complaint that very few girls are subject to. But it does occur sometimes, and it should not be put

minutes morning and evening in summer, it tends to keep them nice and white and free from roughness. You put a pinch or two of powdered alum and a teaspoonful of powdered sal ammoniac in about a pint and a half of warm salt water, and dissolve; then, when you have added a little toilet vinegar, this elegant hand bath is ready for use.

In 1886, in *Toilet Table Elegancies*, readers are told:

Lard 4 ounces, white wax $\frac{1}{4}$ ounce, alum in powder a teaspoonful, and a little alkanet to colour, make a beautiful and useful lip-salve. If you add to it a few drops of otto of roses, you have indeed an elegant preparation.

More recipes appear in *Rational Toilet* in 1892:

What is called virgin's milk is made by taking, say, half a pint of rose water and adding thereto three drams of Friar's balsam. This is an excellent and simple face cosmetic. Here is a wash for sunbrown or freckles; but although it is cooling as to sunbrown, I could not vouch for its efficacy in freckles. It is made with one dram—that is, one ordinary-sized teaspoonful—of California borax, 4 ounces of lime juice, and about two teaspoonfuls of candy sugar. Put all these together and mix well; then add a little eau de cologne.

It would be nice to know how many readers were tempted to experiment with these recipes; or with those given in 1898 (not under the name of Medicus) for Oriental Face Cream, Hair Restorer and Bloom of Roses —a somewhat more sophisticated note appears to be creeping in with these.

In *How To Look Well in the Morning* (1892), Medicus writes:

Perfumed cod-liver oil may be rubbed well in around the eyes before lying down. This may not seem a very fascinating way of treating coming wrinkles, but it is often an effective one, for in this way the tissues under the skin are nourished to some extent, and kept full. Face massage may also be used.

In the same article readers are told:

The peculiar diathesis that leads to the formation of these black-heads often leads also to the secretion of acid, or so-called sour perspiration; and people who suffer from either ought, in the first case, to regulate the diet. Drink warm milk instead of tea. Drink hot or warm milk with dinner and supper in preference to anything else. Take a glass of hot water some time after breakfast with a few drops of lemon juice in it. The bath daily in some form is absolutely necessary.

In *Beautiful Hands* in the same year, Medicus says:

The liquor of boiled oatmeal groats will tend to whiten the skin; but it must be made fresh every day—it won't keep. A cocoa-nut oil liniment is sometimes used to rub into the hands at night to whiten them. It is composed of half an ounce each of cocoa-nut oil, white wax, and almond oil, nicely scented.

Oatmeal is recommended again in the reply to JESS in 1888:

Many people who cannot use glycerine or vaseline for their hands in the winter, find great benefit from oatmeal and honey; mixed, and rubbed into a smooth paste. This is put on the hands when they are washed, and proves healing to many skins that grease does not help. Oatmeal alone may also be used, instead of soap, when washing the hands.

Another homely hint in 1892 is "an old-fashioned but good" remedy to clear a complexion from "muddiness":

Far left: some twenty years after his first articles on health for the G.O.P., Medicus is still writing in his incomparably personal style (August, 1901), although The New Doctor now contributes occasional, and much staider, articles to the magazine.

Above: among these Miscellaneous queries of January 22, 1887, are a number of the usual appeals, all answered in the usual uncompromising fashion.

To a pint of filtered rain-water add a wineglassful of lime juice and a few drops of attar of roses. Shake well. To use it you simply damp the face and hands with it, and let it stay on for a few minutes. This may be done three times a day.

As the *Answers to Correspondents* (Chapter 9) indicate, vanity was not encouraged in the *G.O.P.* Medicus writes in 1883:

The very first signs of a love of outré finery in a child-girl should be checked by the mother; older girls should check it in themselves, as they would the thought of a deadly sin. It often leads to the utter ruin of all correct deportment in society, and causes the girl to be looked down upon even by people of both sexes.

It is curious to turn from the beauty pages in modern magazines for girls, dealing with moisturiser, tinted foundation, blusher, powder, eye-shadow and the rest, to an article called *Beauty* by Medicus in 1888:

Health is the true basis of all female beauty. I have an observing eye, and make good use of it. Well, I declare to you that when I meet young ladies rouged, powdered and pencilled, I wonder if the world is getting worse. For deceit thus carried about openly can have no good effects on the moral character. Many girls moving in what is called good society, a sadly mixed compound nowadays, are little better than walking frauds, perambulating fibs. I will not put it any stronger, but I can let my imagination whisper to me what some of these "angelic beings" look like in the morning before they are ready to emerge from their rooms.

I would not speak so plain, I would not hit so hard, if I had not a remedy to suggest. To those girls, then, who think they are adding to their beauty by the use of cosmetics, I would say, "There would not be any occasion to use such abominations if you would attend to your health."

"My skin is not so clear as it should be," someone says, and she forthwith powders it, adding, perhaps, a tint of carmine to the lips and a little pencilling to the eyebrows; and lo! she is transformed. Yes, but very transparently so. "A thing of beauty is a joy for ever." But not in this case. This made-up girl will not be a thing of beauty after she is twenty-one, and younger girls not made-up, but happy and joyous with the true beauty of health, will laugh and call her "an old thing" when she is not within hearing.

To obtain this true beauty of health Medicus recommends restricting the diet, with more vegetables, fewer rich dishes and sauces, no stimulants, early rising, a Turkish bath once a week or a hot bath twice in ten days, a well-ventilated room with plants in it, "The Girl's Own Bath" every morning (a quick wash all over with hot water and the mildest transparent soap, followed by a cold sponge tub with a couple of handfuls of sea-salt), and as much exercise as possible.

Writing many years later, in 1898, the same author says:

There is nothing that some females will not do or suffer for the sake of being considered pretty or beautiful. There are places in London where they pretend even to excise or stretch out wrinkles and crows' feet about the eyes and give the simple semi-idiotic patient—they need to be patient—an entire new skin.

Chapter Three

FICTION

Who is wise?   She who learns from everyone.
Who is powerful?   She who governs her passions.
Who is rich?   She that is content.

Wisdom, Power, and Riches
(1890)

During the period under review, each issue of the *G.O.P.* included instalments of two serial stories; these instalments were usually quite short, but the serials frequently ran for months. They were not particularly juvenile in style or content. Heroines below marriageable age were few and most of the stories could have been read quite as happily by a granny in search of a light novel as by one of the teenagers for whom they were officially written. It would be going too far to say that all these serials were "improving", but not that the moral effect of even the lightest was taken into consideration.

On the first page of the first number in 1880 is the beginning of the first serial: *Zara: or, My Granddaughter's Money* by an anonymous author. The plot, rather more highly coloured than many which followed it, begins with an old woman spending a night in the lodging-house run by the mother and stepfather of the hero, Paul, then a child; she confides in Paul's mother that she is searching for her granddaughter, Zara Meldicott Keith, from whose mother she has been estranged and to whom she intends to bequeath her money. She leaves a bag in the care of Paul's gentle mother when she goes, and the reader is told that shortly afterwards she collapses and dies. Eventually Paul's stepfather insists on opening the bag in Paul's presence and discovers it to contain a fortune which he takes for himself, swearing the frightened child to secrecy. Before Paul's mother dies, she charges her son to make restitution to Zara Meldicott Keith if he ever discovers her. Not long afterwards the stepfather dies and leaves the money to the boy. We pass over a period of many years, at the end of which Paul is a medical student, attached, though not yet engaged, to a charming and suitable girl. Then by chance he sees a music-hall poster bearing the unforgettable name of Zara Meldicott Keith, and his mother's words return to him. At the music-hall he sees her:

THE GIRL'S OWN PAPER

VOL. I.—No. 1.]   JANUARY 3, 1880.   [PRICE ONE PENNY.

ZARA:

OR, MY GRANDDAUGHTER'S MONEY.

CHAPTER I.
AN ARRIVAL.

THE streets of a dreary London suburb were more dreary than usual on that December evening. A dense fog was fast gathering up its yellow vapour, making the shabby, tumble-down region only one degree less obscure than it would be at midnight. Jasper Meade, proprietor of the "Commercial Lodging House," stood on his own door-step, whistling a dismal refrain very much out of tune, but at the moment he was not thinking of melody — his keen, restless black eyes were striving to penetrate the mist. He watched every vehicle that rattled past, splashing through the sloppy mud, waking up the echoes for a short space, and disappearing into the obscurity beyond, and considered it another lost chance, a fresh disappointment. The secret of this was that Jasper's last venture in the world of speculation was not realising his expectations.

He had lately purchased the lodging-house before-mentioned, and found his venture was of questionable advantage. It had been described in the advertisement as "ruinously cheap," having

"WILL YOU COME TO MY LITTLE ROOM?"

spacious, well-furnished rooms, good stables, every convenience for man and beast, and doing a splendid business. Tempted by the delusive bait, he had rashly invested the whole of his capital in the purchase, awakening too late to the knowledge that much gloss and rosy tint is apt to be used in advertising, and that a bargain rarely comes up to the description given of its merits.

Rooms, many and various, there certainly were in the old house, but they looked as though generations of bygone travellers had tarried there, disported themselves without restraint, and then gone on their ways. The walls were sullied and grimy, the furniture worn out, the carpets ragged and faded, the whole place disreputable in the extreme. Jasper's wife — a pretty, bright-eyed little woman, charming with her Frenchified manner, born and bred a lady — had been driven to utter despair when Jasper took her down to that suburban establishment, and told her it was to be their future home! The meanness and vulgarity of the place were repugnant to Phillis; every instinct of her nature revolted, she

A mere child in years—little more than seventeen, who ought still to have the timid bashfulness, the sweet, delicate, blossoming freshness of early youth —shrinking from aught that was forward, obtrusive, and conspicuous. Yet there she stood, unabashed, in the full glare of the footlights, looking assured, confident, self-reliant as a woman of twenty-eight might have been. And men were clapping at her, and boys were stamping their feet at her in wild applause.

Afterwards Paul goes to see Zara, and is filled with remorse because she has grown up without the advantages of education her grandmother's money could have given her, advantages which that same money has given him. But he believes that to present a friendless girl of seventeen with a fortune would cause worse problems than leaving her in her present position, and his attempts to befriend Zara are, not surprisingly, miscon-strued. The only thing he can think of to do is to give up any thought of his former sweetheart and marry Zara as a means of restitution. This plan, going beyond quixotry into imbecility, causes trouble to everybody concerned. Mercifully, Zara resolves the problem by returning to a former suitor and emigrating with him, receiving her fortune as a wedding present from a thankful Paul.

In *The Follies of Tressida* (Anonymous, 1884), two sisters have a double wedding. Coquettish Tressida is thought fortunate in securing "the finest

Above: the concluding episode of The Follies of Tressida (*March, 1884*), *when one look at Tressy's despair convinces Susan that her sister has done wrong. "What a wicked girl I am!" cries Tressy.*

Far left: the first episode of the anonymous serial Zara, *which opened the first issue of the magazine in 1880.*

Above: an excursion for Margaret Stewart, heroine of A King's Daughter, *in the days when "the sun was still shining" for her; in the party are the worthy local minister and Margaret's protégée, May Castle.*

Right: an unusual short story, Weaving the Dusky Strand, *appeared in the G.O.P. on September 15, 1888. Set in India, it is a rare example of the dramatic adventure story, so common in the pages of the* Boy's Own Paper, *the G.O.P.'s brother publication.*

young fellow in Barstowe", while doubts are expressed over the choice, by her steady sister Susan, of a man who used to be "too fond of a drop". Once married, Susan spends her spare moments reading the cookery book and reaps a harvest of domestic happiness, while Tressy sits among the unwashed dishes reading *On the Way to a Coronet*, feeds her husband on bread and cheese, lives beyond her income, and ends by driving him to drink and herself to dishonesty. Her husband, crying, "She'll make a drunkard of me if I stay with her any longer. Curse her! I was a fool to marry her!" disappears for three years, at the end of which he returns to a repentant and reformed wife.

Some of the stories in the *G.O.P.* are of a sober nature. In *A King's Daughter* (Isabella Fyvie Mayo, 1884) there are two heroines, the queenly young Margaret Stewart, daughter of a Shetland laird and engaged to a marquis, and May Castle, a foundling, owing her name to the fact that she was discovered in the ruins of a castle in the month of May. May is

making all who are guests like yourselves wish for a similar meeting, and remember with pleasure the one that is past.

In giving invitations, if you wish your visitors, whether few or many, to be happy, bestow some thought on the elements which are to compose your party. Think whether they will be glad to meet each other; consider in what amusements they have shown an interest, what are their tastes and accomplishments, and how you may best turn these to account for the general good.

A chemist who was combining various ingredients would not put in an extra one which would set all the rest in a ferment, merely for the sake of filling up the vessel which contained them. So let me advise you, dear girls, never to spoil your party for the sake of filling up a seat or giving what may be deemed a "duty invitation," in order to pay a social debt. And let all understand beforehand just the kind of gathering in which they are to take part. In my next chapter I shall endeavour to suggest some ways of entertaining your friends when they are met together.

(*To be continued.*)

MARGARET TRENT, AND HOW SHE KEPT HOUSE.

By Dora Hope.

"How nice and soft and thick your stair carpets are, Margaret," said Dorothy Snow to her friend as they went upstairs together. It was a week or two before Christmas, and Dorothy had come to spend a long day, to take advantage of Margaret's proximity to the London shops. "It gives me a most luxurious feeling, suggesting velvet pile and that sort of thing, which one does not expect on a staircase," she went on.

"I expect yours are the same, only that my pads being new are perhaps more noticeable."

"Pads!" Whatever have they to do with it?" asked Dorothy.

"Oh, don't you know that it is such an advantage to have a pad on each stair, under the carpet? We used to have an old stair carpet instead, at home, which does almost as well; but in our new house of course we had no old ones, so the upholsterer put down these pads. They make the carpet feel and look much thicker, and save the wear a good deal too; I have a great objection to threadbare stair carpets, but they require a great deal of care to prevent them becoming shabby; I have them moved about an inch either up or down every week. Perhaps you are not aware that stair carpets are always bought rather longer than is absolutely necessary to allow of moving them about, and the surplus piece is either

hidden under another carpet, or turned under, according to circumstances."

"Oh, yes, I did know that. At any rate, I am constantly falling headlong downstairs, and then being scolded for my carelessness in not noticing that the rods were out, and the carpets being moved."

"Well, there is nothing like an experience of that kind for fixing a fact in one's mind," rejoined Margaret, laughing. "Now I think I shall have time to try an experiment on these wax candles before we go out. I am rather anxious about them, for Aunt Annie gave them to me; she was going to use them up in the kitchen, as being too dirty and discoloured for anything else, so I begged them, as I thought I could whiten them by rubbing with flannel dipped in spirits of wine."

"Did you invent that, Margaret?"

"Oh, no. Somebody or other told me about it, but I have had no opportunity to try it before."

Margaret's aunt, being country born and bred, had hitherto had a strong prejudice against gas, and had used nothing but lamps and candles in her house. At last, the superior cheapness and convenience of gas had overcome her scruples, and she had submitted to it; at least, so far as the halls, kitchens, and bedrooms were concerned. She refused, however, to have the large ugly gaseliers hanging from the centre of the ceiling, and instead had branch lights from the walls, in various convenient spots, by which arrangement it was possible to read or work comfortably in any part of the room.

"IT'S ENOUGH TO MAKE A MAN TURN BURGLAR."

proud and sensitive, loved by nobody except her cat. The marquis shows his fiancée May's paintings, and Margaret invites the girl for a holiday in Shetland. Scarcely has the visit begun than it is discovered that Margaret and her parents have even less claim to the name of Stewart than May to that of Castle, since Margaret's grandfather had fraudulently passed off his own son as the heir to the property. Margaret's delicate mother dies suddenly before learning the truth, and very shortly afterwards the legal owner of the property, an American, arrives in Shetland with his vulgar wife and daughter. Then Margaret's fiancé, the marquis, is drowned leaving the island. Chapter XXI ends:

And that was the last that was ever seen of the bright, beautiful young Margaret, mistress of Balacluva. Next morning——

(*To be continued.*)

Chapter XXII, *After the Storm*, opens:

Next morning, Margaret came out of her room, a pale woman, with a strain across her brow and a strange light in her eyes. Her youth lay behind her. She had served God hitherto in her days of triumph and happiness and love; and whatever else was changed, He remained, though she must serve Him henceforth in solitude and patience and faith.

At the end of the story the foundling May is a distinguished painter, married to a man she met in Shetland. Margaret is living with her father, now feeble-minded, and a widowed friend, supporting herself by teaching.

She was still God's lady, though she had ceased to be the lady of Balacluva. A King's daughter does not lose her royal lineage because it is her Father's will that she should be "all glorious" only within and not without.... A story which ends by leaving a soul at the gates of heaven cannot be "a sad story". We need pity no one who has proved her birthright as "the King's daughter".

Our Bessie (1888), by the very popular and prolific Rosa Nouchette Carey, is in a lighter vein. Bessie is a typical *G.O.P.* heroine, simple, modest, sensible and bright. The theme of improvement is a favourite one in *G.O.P.* fiction; sometimes it is the principal character herself who is in need of it, while sometimes she effects it in others. In *Our Bessie*, the improvement takes place in the rich young lady Edna Sefton, whom Bessie meets when their train is held up in the snow. As a result of this meeting, she spends a holiday with Edna, her mother and stepbrother. During this period the spoiled Edna loses her fiancé as a result of her caprices, and Bessie grows to love the stepbrother, who has been starved of affection. Eventually Edna gains wisdom and humility, and regains the fiancé, while Bessie marries the stepbrother. The story is basically a sunny one, but has its pathetic side in the life and death of Bessie's young sister Hatty, who suffers not only from poor physical health but from a fretful, difficult and depressive temper which she struggles to conquer. Bessie says to her:

We can't make ourselves good, Hatty; that lies in different hands. But why don't you look on your unhappy nature as your appointed cross, and just bear with yourself as much as you expect others to bear with you? Why not exercise the same patience as you expect to be shown to you? ... Why don't you say to yourself, "I am a poor, weak, little creature, but my Creator knows that

ISABELLA FYVIE MAYO.

Far left: Dora Hope's series Margaret Trent and How She Kept House *appeared in 1882, following on from an earlier series featuring Margaret before her marriage to Wilfred Trent,* The Difficulties of a Young Housekeeper and How She Overcame Them. *Domestic advice is pleasantly disguised as fiction in the description of the young couple's establishment. Here the local constable, after disturbing a burglar at work, gives Wilfred good advice on securing the windows at night.*

ANNE BEALE.

RUTH LAMB.

Far right: the handsome and outspoken Miss Lawton, an American girl of spirit, is more than a match for the languid English Lord Beechcroft. In his loose-cut tweed suit, whose knickerbockers allow "the muscular perfection of his figure to be seen to advantage", he is said to be "as fine a type of masculine beauty as she of feminine".

too, and He bears with me. I cannot rid myself of my tiresome nature; it sticks to me like a Nessus shirt"—you know the old mythological story, Hatty—"but it is my cross, a horrid spikey one, so I will carry it as patiently as I can. If it is not always light, I will grope my way through the shadows; but my one prayer and my one effort shall be to prevent other people suffering through me"?

Another sunny story is *A Lonely Lassie* by Sarah Tytler (1891), dealing with the adventures of the seventeen-year-old orphan daughter of a Scottish country minister who comes to live in London with her fashionable relations. Scots heroines seem to appear to G.O.P. writers as essentially simple, reliable, and strictly virtuous, and here the rustic Flora is a thoroughly practical and sensible little soul, determined to hold to her childhood values in her new life. Her aunt wishes her to overcome her unmistakably Scotch accent, and Flora is hurt:

... A hundred times more hurt than if her red cheeks, which she could not defend, the fashion in which she dressed her hair on the top of her head, that her father had liked, the manner in which she disposed of her hands, or sat on her chair, had been attacked simultaneously.... Her protest was addressed to herself, and to no other. "Of course I shall try not to say Scotch words, which no one here except my aunt can understand, but as to slurring my r's and softening my a's, and 'nabbing high English', I cannot—not even to please Aunt Bennet. I should only make a fool of myself, which she would be the first person to see, for she is what father used to call nimble-witted. I could not if I would hide that I am a Scotch girl; and I shall never wish to hide it. What! conceal that I am a countrywoman of St Margaret, and Queen Mary (poor woman!), and John Knox, and Sir Walter Scott, and Burns? Never! What would everybody in Inverlochan think if they heard such a proposal?"

Later on, when she "comes out" and finds how much she enjoys gaiety, pretty frocks and compliments, Flora makes "conscientious instinctive use of the props and stays within her reach in order not to grow what she called 'silly'—properly speaking, vain and frivolous. She was not going to lose sight either of her birthright or her identity."

Serial stories with a child heroine are rare among those appearing in the Victorian G.O.P., but one such is *About Peggy Saville* (1898) by Jessie Mansergh, better known as Mrs G. de Horne Vaizey. I read this book myself as a child, over forty years after it was serialised, and I suppose it is among the best-known of the serials. Perhaps Peggy can hardly be called a child at fourteen, but she is certainly not yet a young lady, and she has an unsentimental comradeship with the boy characters in the story reminiscent of that enjoyed by Jo March and Laurie in Louisa M. Alcott's *Little Women. About Peggy Saville* was followed by *More About Peggy* in 1899.

Working-class heroines are in the minority in G.O.P. fiction, but they do appear from time to time. Ruth Lamb was an author who frequently championed the cause of the working girl. Her serial *Sackcloth and Ashes* (1892) deals very interestingly with work—the brutal, grinding work of really poor women. When the heroine first appears, though she is young and good-looking, she is so filthy that people draw away from her. A man with whom she talks on a tram gives her a small parcel which proves to be a cake of soap. Susannah decides she has been known for too long as "Smutty Sue" and puts the soap to good use. As the story unfolds,

Vol. XIV.—No. 667.]   OCTOBER 8, 1892.   [PRICE ONE PENNY.

THE LITTLE GIRL IN GREY.

A STORY OF TWO CONTINENTS.

By HORACE TOWNSEND.

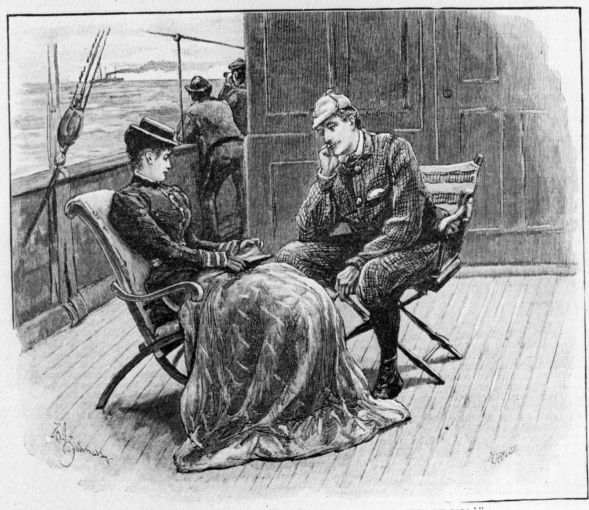

"'AH, BUT YOU'RE A LORD, AND THAT MAKES A DIFFERENCE—WITH MY PAPA.'"

HELEN MARION BURNSIDE.
Photo by Elliott & Fry.

The poems printed in the G.O.P. were often narrative in style. Two favourite poets were Helen Marion Burnside (above) and William Luff. The fiction writer, Isabella Fyvie Mayo, also contributed (below).

Far right: The Elder Sister, *a colour illustration from a painting by M. E. Edwards, which formed the frontispiece to the* Girl's Own Annual, 1883–1884. *This was accompanied by a poem, written by Isabella Fyvie Mayo, which began:*

Sis and I were alone together:
Our mother had died before I knew;
Sis remembered her dying whisper—
"Baby, Sis must be good to you!"
And every morning
she kneeled and prayed
To keep the trust
which was on her laid.

Sis learned the lessons
I'd have to learn,
She read the books
that I liked to read,
She kept my cash,
and she darned my socks,
And fed the pets I forgot to feed!
It seemed her pleasure,
and that was true:
The good heart likes
what it ought to do!

we learn that some years earlier she left her respectable country home with a gentleman who promised marriage. When she discovered his dishonourable intentions she planned to return home, but was shown by her would-be seducer a newspaper notice of her mother's death (inserted falsely, we later discover, by himself). The heartbroken Susannah resolves to do penance in sackcloth and ashes, living in squalor and choosing to earn a living by the unpleasant work of rag-sorting, until the end of the serial, when, having cleaned herself up, she is rewarded by marrying the man who presented her with the soap.

The second heroine of the story is a young lady, sunk, with her mother, to direst poverty, and earning her living by sewing. At this point, the author allows her burning indignation at the lot of the seamstresses free rein, putting it into the mouth of a woman describing the life of such workers:

"I used to get 1s. 4d.★ a dozen for making and finishing, all complete, full-sized strong shirts. These had back-linings, straight bands, five buttonholes, and seven buttons. If there were two gussets or vents put in, I had an extra penny a dozen. Buttons were found, but not needles or thread.... I knew one woman that never lay down in bed for three months, but took what rest she had sitting in a chair. She thought she should never muster courage to get up if she were once comfortably under the clothes. She had four children to keep somehow.... For handkerchief hemming a penny-farthing a dozen, or 15d. a gross, is paid. A girl I know does handkerchiefs, and gets 10s. a week or so without expenses off. One week she'd been at it nearly night and day. She was saving for a new gown. She carried in 15s. worth of work, and the master said she was earning too much, and knocked off 1s!"

(The accuracy of these figures is confirmed by Clara E. Collet's chapter *Women's Work* in Charles Booth's *Life and Labour of the People in London* (1889). "Home workers, machining a poorly paid class of shirt, can earn 2d. to 3d. an hour if at all skilled" [10s. to 15s. for a sixty-hour week]. A shirt machinist, however, did much better than a shirt finisher— "generally elderly if not aged, infirm, penniless, and a widow; she never expected to have to work for a living, and when obliged to do so, has recourse to the only work she ever learnt to do". In fact, finishers might not earn more than 4s. a week. One widow is quoted as getting 5d. a dozen for shirt finishing, doing a dozen a day, but having to pay 2d. for her tram fare. Not surprisingly, such women were usually being aided by relations, charities, or "outdoor relief". One shirt maker who won an essay competition in the *G.O.P.* could do six in a day, earning 6d. each for the better class of work.)

Clearly, *Sackcloth and Ashes* is intended to make its readers think— particularly those richer girls who might take a cue from the attitude of the third heroine, a girl in comfortable circumstances whose scruples are linked to the trials of the seamstress. While shopping, the well-off Aileen's friend praises some dainty underwear:

"They are so ridiculously cheap. It is certain they were never made for the money."

"That is just what I object to," said Aileen. "I like the articles very much,

★ See the Table of Currency Equivalents on page 108.

and I am sure my mother would. But I should be miserable every time I put them on, if I were to think that they were not properly paid for. Fancy all the stitches that have gone to each, the wearing effect on the workers' sight and health, and the miserable price paid in return for time and labour."

The serial dramatically bears out the point made in 1890 by the novelist Anne Beale in an article on *The Emancipation of Seamstresses*, dealing with the Needlewomen's Co-operative Association; she there claimed that "The buyer supports the sweating system by his or her craze for making cheap purchases."

Apart from the working-class heroines, a good many girls in *G.O.P.* serials have jobs. The heroine of *Esther*, by Rosa Nouchette Carey (1883), becomes a governess and marries the widower father of her little pupil (a plot still alive and well in magazine fiction today). In *Merle's Crusade* (1886), by the same author, Merle decides she should earn her own living, wants to work with children, but knows her appalling spelling makes her unsuited for even a nursery governess, so daringly determines to apply for the post of children's nurse, not one regularly undertaken by "ladies". She is accepted into a pleasant household, succeeds in her crusade, but gives up her post for marriage. "My harvest had come already, and yet the labourer had worked but a short time in the vineyard, while others would toil until evening. I had done so little and reaped so much."

In *Kathleen's Handful* (Anonymous, 1889) the heroine becomes a masseuse, going out to work to support her little stepsisters. "We have hardly anything to live on," she tells the family doctor, "and I very, very much want to earn money." The doctor is dismayed ("I hate to see women working for bread," he says; "you don't understand what it means to lose caste; you can't be a masseuse and a young lady"), but Kathleen is resolute. Naturally, she marries the doctor in the end.

The Annual of 1890–1891 being the first I owned, I have a special affection for it, and have selected two serial stories from this volume, both dealing with the subject of improvement.

In Evelyn Everett Green's *Greyfriars*, the improvement is effected by a young aunt who goes to look after the household of her fashionable elder sister during the latter's absence of some months. Three of the children are especially trying: Jessie, on the verge of "coming out", living for admiration; Trix, a wild tomboy; and Dacre, clever, cynical and unmanageable, kept from school and correction by his ill health. All three defy their aunt in different ways. Trix engages in a rat hunt with neighbouring boys, Jessie goes to a forbidden ball decked in her mother's diamonds, and Dacre, although disapproving of such capers by his sisters, causes his aunt (another Esther) even more anxiety than the girls, by his insolent and defiant behaviour.

However, by the time their mother returns, Esther has won the respect and affection of all her nieces and nephews, and done much to improve their characters, particularly that of Dacre, whom she has nursed through a nearly mortal injury ("though he must always be delicate, and unfit for the life of public school or college, there seemed room to hope that with time and more reasonable conduct and submission to rule he might grow up to a sufficiency of strength for the easy life of a country gentleman").

ROSA NOUCHETTE CAREY

Far left: an illustration from Greyfriars *by Evelyn Everett Green (March 21, 1891). Esther receives Everard Chester's proposal on the beach, having taken her scapegrace nephew to the seaside for his convalescence. "Can you love me enough to trust your future into my hands?" asks young Mr Chester; and she, both modest and open, lifts her face to his in answer.*

A FORTUNATE EXILE.

A STORY OF SWISS SCHOOL LIFE.

By LILY WATSON, Author of "The Mountain Path," "The Hill of Angels," etc.

Above: unhappy Honor, soon to be sent away to school, is befriended by the staid and gentle Mabel Thornycroft, a fellow-pupil (July 11, 1891).

In *A Fortunate Exile* by Lily Watson, the improvement is that of, rather than by, the heroine. This is one of the Victorian G.O.P.'s rare stories where the heroine is a schoolgirl. Sixteen-year-old Honor, coming between a poised, elegant elder sister and a precocious, appealing younger one, is the black sheep of the family. Honor's heart is sound enough and her principles need no improving, but her person does. Her mother, tired of Honor's "rounded shoulders, poked chin, large hands and feet, and masses of rough hair falling untidily from beneath her hat", and of her lack of any social graces, decides to send her away to school—presumably with a sort of Dothegirls Hall in mind ("Some exceedingly strict boarding-school"); fortunately a friend persuades her to send Honor to a finishing-school in Switzerland ("There are so many holidays in English boarding-schools"). Honor has a few difficulties at first, but soon improves her posture, learns to keep her hair tidy, and is discovered to have a promisingly contralto voice. When her family see her again, they are astonished at the transformation effected by understanding and sympathy.

LILY WATSON.

Besides the serials (running on average to 20 or 25 parts), there are frequent complete or two-part stories. Sometimes these are designed for the younger readers—*Child Island: A Fairy Tale for Younger Girls* (1886), or *Little Elsie and Her Sister Kelsie* (1887); sometimes they are little morality tales, such as Lily Watson's series based on the Beatitudes; or parables like *A Winter Garment* (1891), in which two old women both long for a warm petticoat and both receive one from a charitable source —each, not knowing that her friend has been equally fortunate, decides to present the other with the longed-for petticoat, so that in the end both have the satisfaction of making a sacrificial gift and the benefit of a warm winter garment.

In a haunting little two-part story, *Malvolia* by Alice Macdonald (1891), Janet Neal, a music teacher, receives a mysterious letter. Its author, "Malvolia", who introduces herself as a girl of twenty, says, "I want there to be one soul to whom my soul may disclose herself without the least bodily or worldly prejudice. Let me write to you as one spirit to another, without your being affected by my appearance, influence, or possessions." Intrigued, Janet replies, and a correspondence ensues. Malvolia depicts herself as young, rich, beautiful, beloved, talented, and yet unhappy. She writes of a suitor:

MRS. HENRY MANSERGH.

He is rich enough to harness my horses with diamonds if I wished it— wickedly rich, brutally rich.... I fear I was bewitched in my cradle; my mind is a very opal. I love the view of life one day that I loathe the next.... I hate my body; I want to punish it for being white, and plump, and prosperous, when I despise it so. I dream of becoming a nun.

One day she writes that she is engaged:

I won't pretend for one moment that I love him.... I may be happy—I may be wildly wretched; at any rate, it must be different, and something new.

Janet is grieved to think of the capricious, fascinating creature making a loveless marriage, and writes pleading with Malvolia to break off the engagement. Some days later when out walking, she passes an old woman who slips and falls on the ice, dropping a letter addressed to Janet herself. Questioned, the woman declares it is from her invalid daughter Emmy, and takes Janet to her room:

A narrow bed was pushed close up against the one window, and in it lay a little humpbacked figure, busy with scissors and cardboard. Janet noticed every detail with one glance—the large head set almost without neck on the meagre, misshapen shoulders, the scanty, unkempt hair, the thin dirty hands adjusting a cardboard dancer.

Janet hurries from the house to burn the letters:

Malvolia was a hideously deformed cripple, who lay bedridden in one squalid

"'LETTICE IS ENGAGED TO BE MARRIED!'"

Above: a scene from Sisters Three *by Mrs Henry Mansergh, when Hilary and Norah receive the news that their sister Lettice is engaged to be married (February 12, 1898).*

room, and made kicking donkeys and prancing ballet girls out of paper and string.

Next day she receives a pathetic scrawl from Emmy:

I used to feel myself Malvolia when I wrote to you, and beautiful and strong and rich, instead of a little humpy-dumpy in a garret. . . . I got to feel that this room, and poor old mother, and the paper toy things, were just Malvolia's dreams, and didn't matter. . . . It was quite wrong; but there wasn't any happiness that was right for me to have anywhere.

Ashamed, Janet goes back to the house, to see if she can bring some happiness to Emmy/Malvolia. But the room is empty. Emmy and her mother have gone, and all that is left of Malvolia is a crumpled and broken paper ballet dancer.

Chapter Four

DOING GOOD

The sun looked down on the night's dark frown;
'I must do good' said he.

William Luff
(1889)

AS THEY WERE.

Above and below: two illustrations taken from an article by the Marquess of Lorne, Governor General of Canada and husband of Princess Louise, describing the homes founded in Canada by "that noble lady, Miss Rye", to which orphans and destitute girls were sent from England as child emigrants (May 3, 1884).

An interest in "doing good" is something which the present-day teenager has in common with those of the eighteen-eighties and 'nineties, as the charity walks, sponsored swims, decorating of old people's houses, and conservation activities prove; but the need to rouse and activate the individual conscience in the cause of social need can never have been greater than in the era in which the *Girl's Own Paper* was born. Looking back over the first thousand issues, the Editor wrote in the February number of 1899:

Influenced, as the Editor knows [readers] to have been, in the direction of true charity by the writings of some of our contributors, they have tried in their turn to be of service to others, and through the medium of *The Girl's Own Paper* have done much useful work for the community. They have, for example—at the suggestion of the Countess of Aberdeen, who has ever taken a great interest in the magazine, notwithstanding her high public and official positions—established a working girls' home in London; also, they have re-established the Princess Louise Home for Girls, subscribing with touching readiness and liberality to each of these schemes in actual cash over a thousand pounds. They have besides made periodical grants of warm clothing for the poor, sent dolls in great numbers to brighten the dull hours of sick children in hospitals and in many other ways shown a good sisterly interest in those less happily circumstanced than themselves.

The Princess Louise who gave her name to the Home for Girls was the fourth daughter of Queen Victoria. A series of articles entitled *The Princess Louise Home*, "A Special Appeal to Our Girls", by Anne Beale, began in February, 1882. The author describes the country house, "Woodhouse", in the village of Wanstead, Essex, close to Epping Forest, where nearly eighty girls are fed, clothed, and prepared for domestic service:

It is pleasant to hear their young voices ringing through the old-fashioned and somewhat dilapidated country house in song or talk, and to realise that

ONE OF THEM AFTER TRAINING.

they are, so far, rescued from evil homes and company. For this abode, which bears the name of a queen's daughter, is also called "The National Society for the Protection of Young Girls", which implies that its inmates have been snatched from peril and placed in safety....

There are a score of vacant beds. Wherefore? Because money is needed to maintain the girls who might occupy them. In many instances they must be refused admission on account of the incapacity of friends or benefactors to pay the £13 per annum demanded for them by the Society....

The appeals for [the girls'] reception are often very pathetic, and come from Sunday school teachers, church deaconesses, and Christians of all denominations resident in various parts of England. Among those of the past year is one from a clergyman, who states that the girl is most anxious to get away from an immoral atmosphere and to "take refuge in the Princess Louise Home. She is not badly disposed, and is amenable to discipline and order," says the letter. "She must either be rescued now or, I fear, never. The only difficulty appears to be the smallness of the father's contribution towards her support. He will only contribute one shilling a month"...

The cry is now raised, both at home and abroad, of "How shall we save the girls?" and the answer is ready, "Use first the means at hand—support existing institutions; then extend them, spread them, until all our young sisters shall, if willing, be protected and prepared for the battle of life."

Not only does our well-beloved Queen lead the van in this warfare against sin, but her Royal daughters raise their standards close behind her. In days gone by, the name of the illustrious Prince Consort—of "Albert the Good"—headed the reports of the Home of which we write. Now it is the Princess Louise, of whom it is the name-child; and she is not merely a nominal sponsor. She visits the girls from time to time, examines their works, talks with them, encourages them and their teachers, and makes, both literally and figuratively, "A sunshine in a shady place".

Anne Beale takes her "youthful readers" on a tour of inspection through the airy and well-scrubbed rooms of Woodhouse, to see the girls at work:

They look bright and rosy as they stand, scrubbing-brush, broom, soap, saucepan, or pump-handle in hand, to return our greeting. But—low be it spoken—they are in sad need of new garments. Their frocks and pinafores are darned to extinction.... We shudder to think of the homes they came from, and are not surprised to hear that when they leave Woodhouse they look back upon it, and not on their previous abodes, as their *home*.

A letter from one of the "old girls" is quoted:

My dear madam, I thank you for all your kindness to me while I was in the Home, and for all your kind instructions that you gave me when you used to talk so nice to the girls at prayer-time. I always remember what you used to tell us about looking at our work after we done it, to see if we can find any little fault with it.

The Home's devoted secretary wonders whether the magazine's readers might send their handiwork to a bazaar to raise funds. "No sooner proposed than seconded," says Anne Beale, and goes off to the Home's London Office, where the suggestion of a bazaar with contributions from G.O.P. readers is very well received. "Again, no sooner said than done"; and Anne Beale hurries off to the "learned quietude" of Paternoster Row:

We are at the Religious Tract Society directly, and having mounted three flights of stairs, we have the audacity to "beard" that friend of girls, the Editor, in his very den. He can see a thing "straight off", and understands "our case"

THE SUNBEAM OF THE FACTORY.

A STORY FOUNDED ON FACT.

KATIE READING TO HER STEPMOTHER.

at once. "Yes, you may make an appeal for contributions of work to the readers of *The Girl's Own Paper*," he says, "provided I have permission to inspect the articles sent, and that each worker's gift is duly acknowledged"...

And now, my dear young friends, we have only to appeal to you for immediate assistance. Time presses, and your sisters, who are in peril of soul and body, must be saved.... We shall hope, by the kind permission of the Editor, to give our readers monthly particulars of how we progress, and we trust to be able to report that such as may not have time to manufacture even [a] "penny pincushion" ... will at least send us the penny, to expend in materials. If those who have no money will give time, and such as have no time will give money, we will somehow manage to "make both ends meet".

Above: the concluding episode of one of the shorter G.O.P. serials. Katie Morton, a factory girl in poor circumstances, is converted at a night school class to which she is taken by a cheerfully unrepentant friend, Bridget, and finds the strength to do her duty by a harsh stepmother (July 30, 1881).

Above: the work of the Thames Church Mission, described by Anne Beale (April 28, 1883). Readers made sailors' library bags ("fully appreciated by Jack Tar") and gave Bibles and Prayer books to fill them. "One likes to think of the sailor, in the intervals of his dangerous labour, taking some instructive book from its pretty receptacle, and reading maybe of his Creator."

Two years later, in 1884, comes an article entitled *What Girls Can Do to Hush "The Bitter Cry"*★. Among the suggestions made are sewing for the poor, making dadoes of Christmas cards for workhouse schools, toy-making, holidays for poor children, and teaching games in pauper schools:

They might, by regular, hearty work, turn the London play-yards into what the playing fields of Eton and Harrow are.... Among the poor and sad there is such a dearth of pleasure and play that a whole army of pleasure-creators and play-makers could not meet all their needs. There are entertainers wanted at parish and congregational parties—not people to necessarily sing, play and perform, but those who, in bright gowns and with the halo which rest and

★ *The Bitter Cry of Outcast London*, a contemporary report by a group of Nonconformist missionaries, which revealed the horrors of slum housing.

CHAPTER XX.

DURING the conversation between Hilda and her uncle on the subject of using the trust money to keep the Brinnington workpeople employed, Mrs. Oakley had remained silent. She was no uninterested listener. On the contrary, her ears were strained to catch every word, her thoughts wholly occupied with the discussion. She knew, even far better than did Hilda, how great a trial the present state of business was to her husband. She could estimate, as no other person could, the strength of the temptation presented to him by the girl from without, and seconded from within by the pleadings of his own kindly heart.

The silence was broken

Above: an illustration from the serial Her Own Choice *by Ruth Lamb (August 2, 1884). The heroine, Hilda, and her friends try to do their part in helping those who have been thrown out of work.*

refinement give in the eyes of the work-worn and rough-living, will mix among them, making the picture-book interesting with gay chat, and the game of some importance, because played against such a keen opponent.

In the same year an article called *Parish Work* shows a sympathetic and intelligent attitude to the question:

It is no unusual thing to find the lady district visitor think that she may leave all her lady's manners behind her in the drawing-room when she goes out to pay her daily calls at the cottages of her poorer neighbours. There is no greater mistake than this in the whole sphere of parish work. People of the working classes, and more especially the women who belong to them, have in their rank and degree quite as many tender, delicate places in their hearts and minds, and quite as much proud reserve as the highest lady in the land. Therefore, when a woman of position and education far above their own enters their houses pouring forth questions full of noisy curiosity, or sits by their fireside criticising freely their dress or furniture, or roams, unasked, all over their dwellings, prescribing all sorts of improvements and changes, they naturally enough either grow rude and impertinent, or else shrink into a shell of timid, injured silence.

Earlier, in Dora Hope's *My District and How I Visit It* (1880), the same point is made:

Before I began district visiting on my own account, having had no experience whatever of it, I thought it prudent to accompany a friend round her district who had been engaged in the work for some years. I knew that she was a thoroughly good woman, and was most anxious for the spiritual and temporal good of those she visited. But as we entered house after house, I noticed that her manner was as though she considered that the poor people were of a different race from herself, and that they ought to be overwhelmed with gratitude at her condescension in visiting them. She marched into their rooms without any regard as to whether it was convenient, and the inhabitants wished it or not. I think it must have reminded them of the visit of a detective armed with a search warrant. For some inscrutable reason also, she invariably raised her voice and addressed the people in a commanding tone, which frightened the children, and offended the mothers.... I learnt a valuable lesson that day, and there and then made a resolve to treat any poor people with whom I had to deal with as much consideration and politeness as I should use towards my own friends.

... The habit of promiscuous alms-giving in the street has been too often denounced to need enlarging upon here; the true way of helping such beggars is to take their address, visit them at their homes, and if their tale be true you will soon find it out, and by getting them employment, or other assistance, you may benefit them for life, and perhaps help them to become respectable members of the community, instead of encouraging them to live as professional beggars.

Below: a young helper at a village boys' club giving a lecture on botany. First introduced in the hope of quelling the noise for a few minutes by catching the boys' attention, these lectures, according to Dora Hope, proved so successful that a proper series of classes was set up, to teach the farm boys reading, writing, arithmetic, poetry, music—and needlework (February 21, 1885).

We had, amongst other things, a series of what we called "object lessons," on what the boys could observe for themselves, such as the position of the feet and legs of horses in different paces. This lesson was illustrated by all the pictures of horses we could find, winding up with some of the prints which have appeared lately in various magazines, giving the actual position taken by horses, as obtained by instantaneous photography. Then we invited the boys to notice horses during the coming week, and promised to bring the pictures again the following week that they might report their observations, and say which they considered most correct.

We found a black board indispensable, as nothing could be made interesting without illustrations; it did not matter how rough these were, but we could not do without them. In addition to drawings on the black board, we sometimes made roughly coloured diagrams on paper.

Amongst other subjects, we took very elementary

After the treatment of district visiting in these earlier articles it is rather disappointing to read the less sensitively written *On Being a "Visiting Lady"* in 1890:

With very few exceptions, one has to consider and treat the poor—the women portion at least—very like one treats children; that shrewdness and sharpness and general suspicion, which comes from early contact with the world and its wickedness, and which is so characteristic of the London poor, is in no way incompatible with the most wildly irrational reasonings, and the most wonderful and elaborate misconceptions of the simplest facts; and their determination—as it seems to the uninitiated—to take offence at the most out-of-the-way things, and twist insults out of nothing at the slightest provocation, even from relations and the very best of friends and neighbours, is as startling as it is incomprehensible.

Our Girls and Parish Work by A Middle-Aged Woman (1887) deals with some of the types of girls occupied in "doing good": the girl in a continual flutter after curates, the girl devoured by the wish to be a person of importance, the girl who is all eagerness and devotion at the start but rapidly loses interest, the girl who overtaxes herself to the extent that there is no time for any relaxation or for any activity which is not clearly parish work. The author says:

Do not be too ready to urge others to add to their responsibilities, or too hasty in condemning good women who, while manifestly adorning their Christian profession, in other respects seem backward in taking up outdoor work. On the other hand, do not, when you read this paper, run over in your minds your friends and acquaintances, and try to settle which of the characters sketched above will suit them. Consider instead if any one of them reflects yourself. If that cannot be because you do no direct work for God at all, ask yourself if there be any good reason for such a state of things. It is quite possible, as I have shown, that such a reason may exist, but it is also true that many who ought to "Come to the help of the Lord", are kept back by nothing but sloth. Self-indulgence, indolence and careless frivolity eat up many a young life, and destroy in the bud many a promising career.

William Luff, the author of the lines quoted at the beginning of this chapter, wrote the verses *Two Pictures* which appeared in the G.O.P. in 1884 and which have a heavy moral, if not a great deal else:

A lady sat in her easy chair
'Mid the odour of luxury, free from care,
Bedecked with jewels, and gems, and gold,
In embroidered satin with many a fold.
A favoured child, with a thousand charms,
She slept her life in kind Fortune's arms,
And scarcely thought of the houseless poor
Who begged in vain at her mansion door.

A maiden sat in no easy chair;
Though young, she was burdened with many a care;
Through a busy week from the dawning light
She had toiled and toiled till the shading night.
Yes, while "my lady" is taking her ease,
She will be teaching "the least of these"—
The dirty, the wayward, the troublesome, still,
Teaching them sweetly the Father's will.

"HALT!"

B EFORE offering any suggestions as to the management of village night schools, it may be as well to relate our own experience, and the circumstances which led us to begin one in our neighbourhood.

It is not at all an ideal village, a quiet peaceful spot, far removed from the living world, and inhabited by simple-minded and contented peasants; but a noisy little place, with several flourishing public-houses, and inhabited, a casual visitor might imagine, solely by a very rough and turbulent set of the youth of both sexes.

Above: Dora Hope opens her account of setting up a village boys' club, when prayer meetings in a local cottage are disrupted by local rowdies. Another illustration appears on the facing page.

Above: the opening of The Flower-Girls of London *by Emma Brewer, published on October 31, 1891.*

Lady, sit on in that easy chair,
In the odour of luxury, free from care;
Neglecting to cheer with one golden ray
The night you might change to a gladsome day.
But know in the judgment that many will rise
To the King's right hand whom you now despise:
For they in their poverty do more than you,
With your maids and your money and nothing to do.

In a series about *Gentlewomen who Devote their Lives to the Poor* (1898), there is an article on prison visiting which describes some of the experiences of workers following the pioneer Mrs Elizabeth Fry. Adeline, Duchess of Bedford, gives sensible advice: visits should be frequent and regular, visitors should keep a diary recording their cases, it is better to get to know a few prisoners well than many superficially, promises made to prisoners must be kept, confidences respected, and hope made the keynote of the work. The article goes on:

Not the least Christ-like work is taking the little children of the criminal class right away from their surroundings, caring for them and training them to be good useful members of society.

In *The Children of the City* in 1881, Anne Beale writes:

There are scenes we dare not enter, and secrets too awful for revelation, where the young soul is nourished in haunts of crime, and fed with curses; where the name of "Our Father" is unknown, and where the child lives and often dies like the brute.

The title *The Flower-Girls of London* by Emma Brewer (1891), with its romantic echoes of Eliza Dolittle, does not prepare the present-day reader for the grim content of the article:

The little ones thus employed are for the most part ragged, neglected, helpless little figures, and are as a consequence the most successful sellers; for who can withstand the pathetic contrast they present to the beautiful works of nature in their hands?
The result of this is that these children become the slaves of their inhuman task-masters, and they learn to trade on their own account, thereby losing the chance of respectable service.
The streets are hard teachers for little ones; they become old very early in life, and the cold of winter, added to the drink which, alas! finds its way to their lips, brings on sickness and starvation, and they find their way into the poor-house when Death delays its claim.

Suddenly the world of 1891, often looking so snug in the pages of the *Girl's Own Paper*, seems a much chillier place:

"I sleeps anywheres, ye know, wherever I sees a door open," replies a five-year-old flower-girl when questioned about her life. "In the mornin' I gits a swill at the fountains; and the bakers is kind, they is, an' I asks 'em for a bit o' bread." These sights are of daily occurrence in our London streets at early morning.

To anyone who assumes all Victorian social work to have been authoritarian, the insight shown by this author perhaps comes as a surprise:

Far right: the proposal to rent a seaside cottage where "many a one overburdened with incessant labour and home cares" might recuperate, was put forward by the Editor in November, 1887. Funds came in steadily through the months that followed (September 22, 1888).

THE GIRL'S OWN
CONVALESCENT HOME.

Amount previously acknowledged in No.
452 of THE GIRL'S OWN PAPER, £250 1s. 5½d.,
A. E. H., 3s., Lizzie Fell (collected), 1s.,
Ruth Mercer (collected), 7s. 3d., A. L.
Bacon (collected), 10s., Mrs. Hull (col-
lected), 10s 6d., Florence Willett, 1s., A
Friend at Nottingham, 2s. 6d., Gertrude
Eddison (collected), 10s., Miss Ball (col-
lected), 10s., Auntie, 5s., M. Fogerty (col-
lected), 7s. 6d., Mary Lee (collected), 2s. 6d.,
H. D. and Sister, 2s., Alice M. Lamb, 10s.,
Ruth S. Cove, 10s., E. Beecroft (collected),
7s., J. M., £2, Clara Collett (collected),
16s., Miss Gibbs (collected), 4s., "Fairy,"
5s., E. P., 1s., E. Pratt (collected), 10s.,
Violet, 1s. 6d., Mrs. Webster, 2s., Miss
Shaw (collected), 3s. 6d., E. Jesson (collected), 10s., Edith Yates, 2s., Annie Brooks,
Constantinople, 5s.
    Total amount received up to August 3rd,
£260 0s. 5½d.

Above: Home Parties of the Poor appeared in Summer Spices (*the Summer extra number*), 1896, with a description of a country mission to which unfortunates from the city might be brought for a peaceful day. "*The gratitude expressed is out of all proportion to the benefit rendered.*" Here a blind girl is given a breath of country air.

Far right: The Match-Girl's Dream, *a picture from the Christmas issue of 1891 which tells its own story.*

The hardships which these flower-girls undergo is beyond our power to tell. We have just witnessed the leave-taking of over a hundred missionaries, who are starting to distant parts of the earth to carry the message of salvation to the heathen. Will they find anywhere on the face of the earth vice more hideous, lives more miserable and wretched, than we can show them here ... If [the flower-girls] are to be helped, and their condition improved, it will not be by forcing them from the life they have chosen into one which is hateful to them; they must be aided in their own way and by one which does not clash with their wild idea of liberty.

In 1887 the Editor announces a plan for a *Girl's Own Convalescent Home* to send overworked girls to the seaside, and suggests that every individual supporter—estimating the readership at 250,000—should subscribe a penny. Contributions arrived quickly, and by August, 1888, nine months later, £260 0s. 5½d. has been collected. The lists of contributors are mixed indeed, including such entries as K. Linsell, 3d.; A Green Leaf, 1d.; Anon. (pink paper), 2d.; Afflicted, 6d.; Martha Chuckerbutty, 3s. 1d.; Aglaia, Euphrosyne and Thalia, 1s. 6d.; A Girl's Brother, £1.

There are other appeals, such as for *Books for Tired Girls* (1886) to equip a reading-room to be opened in the new Y.W.C.A. building in Regent Street:

Help is greatly needed in making it really attractive for those whose minds are hungry after the day's mechanical work, but who are too weary to take up a prosy volume.

The regular contributor Dora Hope (*She Couldn't Boil a Potato*) provides a series of articles in 1885–1886, headed *Stay-at-Home Girls*, in which "doing good" finds a place. Among the good causes is a boys' club, with various classes, entertainments, gymnastics, a drum and fife band, and so on. "Nannie's favourite class must not be forgotten." (Nannie is one of the girls taking part.) "This was called the 'lodgers' class', and in it she taught any young men who were in lodgings, and had no one to look after them, how to sew on buttons, patch their clothes, and darn their socks."

In 1890 an article, *Music among the Working Girls of London*, mentions the Working Girls' Club Union, with a parent club in Soho—clubs for "tailoresses, wig-makers, cigarette-makers, blacklead workers, etc., to say nothing of all the more commonly known female occupations, such as milliners, machinists, upholsteresses, and embroideresses". The author writes of the vocal talents of these girls:

> Strength of the vocal organs is evidently lacking; but voice and bodily power most often go hand in hand, and the London workgirls of 1890 are seldom very powerful specimens of humanity. In the strain and struggle for a means of livelihood it would hardly be likely they should be so.

A jocular warning is given to the earnest girl in *Thoughts on the Higher Education of Women* by A Man (1891):

> A man who concentrates himself upon one subject, while naturally less versatile than a woman, at the same time does not lose his versatility by his concentration. Let a woman, however, once concentrate herself upon one particular thing, and she loses all her natural versatility, and becomes a creature of only one idea.... I have one friend, for instance, whose great subject is the moral and social welfare of the London cabby. At first it is refreshing to know that the man who looks with disgust at anything less than double his legal fare is such a delightful character; but when you know him by heart he ceases to be refreshing, and when he is served up daily at every meal until your mental atmosphere reeks of him, and you begin to dream of him and to spend most of your nights in phantom growlers, he becomes, to put it mildly, a nuisance.

Opportunities for doing good, of course, are endless in the *G.O.P.*, and suggestions frequently made. In *What Shall We Do With Our Sundays?* (1889) the Countess of Meath describes an unsatisfactory Sunday (in which several church services have been attended, and which includes no occupation which could be called worldly). Next she describes a more satisfying one: church—brief visit to cottage invalid—luncheon—Sunday school teaching—afternoon service—reading to invalid ("We feel it to be a privilege to stay awhile with such a holy-minded woman")—tea— visit to rich *malade imaginaire* ("Could it be that Mrs B., whom we had never thought of but as an intensely uninteresting, selfish woman whom we always tried to avoid—might she be one to whom we could be of real service?")—supper—letter to absent friend. "A Sunday of 'boredom' must needs be wrong, and the cure for boredom is to be up and doing that which is worth the doing."

Sometimes comfortably-off girls are reminded that they can do good simply by taking thought. The selfishness of young ladies who are responsible for overworking underpaid seamstresses by demanding

(Drawn by M. Ellen Edwardes.)

THE BROKEN CONTRACT

dresses at ridiculously short notice is condemned more than once in these pages, and illustrated by a harrowing full-page drawing in 1885, *The Broken Contract*. This depicts a young dressmaker collapsed over her sewing-machine in front of two horrified girls, on whose party frocks she has been working.

In *The Standing Evil: A Plea for Shop Girls* (1880), the author says:

The large establishments, as a rule, are kind to their employées.... [Sadly different, however, is this from] the smaller and second-rate shops where the hours of closing are very late, the food wretchedly indifferent, and barely time allowed for taking it. No possibility of resting or sitting down the live-long, weary day, with cruel, hard rules, which must be obeyed whether the girl is well or ill, under penalty of heavy fines or dismissal. Even when not serving they are forbidden not only to sit, but they may not even lean against a counter, for they must tidy away things which have been shown to the latest customer. There are two great enemies for the shop assistant—the severe shopwalker (man or woman) and the inconsiderate lady-customer. I am sorry to say that of the two the woman is sometimes the more hard and cruel, and possessing a sharper tongue, can inflict untold pain on the helpless girl behind the counter, which, added to the physical weariness she endures, must be real torture....

Above: The Broken Contract, *another narrative picture from a Christmas issue* (Snow-drops, *the extra number for 1885*) *which points a lesson dear to the hearts of* G.O.P. *contributors.*

IF we were asked to state the most impossible thing to happen in a civilised country, we should probably, without hesitation, say, cruelty to little children.

Cruelty to the little ones, who are of all creatures the most utterly helpless, who have no voice to complain, no strength to wield in their own defence, whose only refuge is in the parents' love and devotion—cruelty to these surely would be quite impossible.

Evidently this has been the firm belief of legislators in all parts of the world, for there is no law in existence for the punishment of such a crime. No one would believe that any members of the human family, however savage or uncontrolled, would be found wantonly to inflict torture upon their own babes.

It is for this favoured land, this highly civilised age, to prove the fallacy of such a belief, and to show, moreover, that a woman can forget her sucking child and be wanting in compassion to the son of her womb; and even beyond this, that parents exist who have cast out their fatherhood and motherhood, and supplied the place with fiendish ferocity.

The intense cruelty which some of our babes and little children have suffered of late years at the hands of the parents would have disgraced savages and even wild beasts; and but for the efforts of a small band of philanthropists, headed and directed by one who has an enthusiastic love and reverence for little children, this cruelty might have continued till it had stained England's escutcheon, and lowered her in the eyes of all civilised countries.

If some of these acts of cruelty could be related here, the first impulse of the tenderhearted reader would be to utterly disbelieve them, and the next, on being convinced, to hide the face and sob like a child that such things could be done in our midst.

When once our eyes are opened to the existence of these most sorrowful scenes, we dare not shut them again, for knowledge has made us responsible. If we take no step to prevent the maiming and torturing of these little ones, we tacitly give our sanction to it.

We dare not for a day be negligent, in the hope that things will right themselves; we would not if we could, for God has implanted in our hearts a tender love for the little ones among us, and we are rightly stern and indignant with those who wrong them.

Is it not past belief that a father would take an infant of fifteen months and twice in one night cane it because it cried with the pain of teething; or that he would in a fit of temper strike his little boy to the earth with a fist that would fell an ox, and because the child cried

Above: the opening of Our Little Children, *a description by Emma Brewer of helping ill-treated children and others "bailed out" from police custody at £2 a head (September 21, 1889).*

How very rarely do we hear a lady regret or apologise for the trouble she gives when, surrounded by boxes or piles of goods, she ends by buying nothing, and yet what an amount of useless labour she inflicts on the girl who serves her!

An article by Medicus (1888) describes this practice as "cruel trifling":

This shopping hobby has of recent years become a very serious evil in this country, and ladies who adopt it . . . are guilty of doing immeasurable mischief to thousands upon thousands of their sisters who have to slave behind counters to serve them.

In *Religion: An Address to Schoolgirls* (1891) there is some equally plain speaking:

You cannot dissociate yourselves from the labouring masses, and in particular from the women and girls of England. They are your sisters; and a blight and a curse rests on you if you ignore them, and grasp at all the pleasures and sweetness and cultivation of your life, with no thought or toil for them. Their lives are the foundations on which ours rest. It is horrible in one class to live without this consciousness of a mutual obligation, and mutual responsibility.

Ruth Lamb's serial story *Sackcloth and Ashes* makes an imaginative suggestion. "Smutty Sue", talking to her friend about the use of public parks by poor folks, remarks that the parks are free. He answers:

But the poor workers are not free to come. They cannot afford to lose half a day's work, and those that want it worst can only get the fresh air by going without a meal. Stop work and you stop bread. Go out, and you get a better appetite without anything to satisfy it. . . . The park has to be given twice. It has been done well once. Now we want gentle, kindly ladies to go into these women's homes and buy them a day's freedom to enjoy a place like this. What enjoyment is there for the poor soul who has dragged her body here and left her heart behind at the wash-tub or the sewing-machine? who has her work along with her, calling to her all the while, because she has taken a pleasure she cannot rightly afford?

Help in distributing the publishers' tracts is naturally encouraged. DOROTHY, in 1891, is told:

If you wish to do good service, over and above your family and natural duties at home, we suggest that you can procure packets of nice little books, and the Holy Gospels—each in separate form—from our publishing office, and when you travel, by land or water, or even take a drive in any hired vehicle, you can leave them to be found—under a seat-cushion; for remember that many of the lower orders feel insulted by the offer of one—a result of which you should beware, so as not to defeat your own object.

Dear Dorothy! Did she follow this advice and leave surprises of nice little books in cabs? And did she do good by it?

The "family and natural duties at home" of which Dorothy was reminded are the subject of a little fable in 1889 called *A Society for the Prevention of Cruelty to Mothers.* Marion is giving a finishing touch to her essay "The Development of Religious Ideas among the Greeks" before setting off to her French History class, to be followed by a guild meeting and a German lesson. The tired mother she has no time to help falls asleep over her sewing, and Marion sees two angels, the Angel of Life and the Angel of Death, bending over the sleeper:

WORKING FOR THE BAZAAR.

"GIRLS! come here," called out Jeannette Mayhew, as she heard her sisters coming in from a walk one morning. "Who do you think has been to call while you were out? But I may as well tell you, for you will never guess—Lady Cargle, of Cargle."

"Oh, I wish we had been in!" exclaimed both the girls at once. "What did she come for? It could not have been only a friendly call, for people say her visiting list is so extremely select she will not know a creature in the neighbourhood."

"No, it was not pure friendliness that brought her, but she is going to have a bazaar

"Those grey hairs" [says the Angel of Life] "come from overwork, and anxiety to save extra money for the music and French lessons. Those pale cheeks faded while the girls were painting roses and pansies on velvet or satin.... Those eyes grew dim sewing for the girls, to give them time to study ancient history and modern languages; those wrinkles came because the girls had not time to share the cares and worries of everyday life. That sigh comes because their mother feels neglected and lonely, while the girls are working for the women of India."

[The Angel of Death laments] "This is indeed sad—loving, industrious girls giving their mother to my care as soon as selfish, wicked ones."

[Marion waking from her dream soliloquises] "I see we might have lost the best of mothers in our mad rush to be educated and useful in this hurrying, restless day and generation.... Until she gets well restored I will take charge of the house, and give up all the societies except one—that I'll have by myself, if the other girls won't join—a Society for the Prevention of Cruelty to Mothers."

Above: The Girl's Own Annual, 1885–1886, contains Dora Hope's tales of the projects undertaken by "the Stay-at-Home girls" (Elsie, Nannie and invalid Jeannette) who cheerfully engage in good works, from staging a grand bazaar to setting up a penny savings bank.

An extract from an article by the animal-loving Gordon Stables (Medicus of the health and beauty features), *The Debt We Owe to Birds and Beasts* (1889), might surprise any who imagine "conservation" a cause entirely of our own day. It deals in part with general concern for animal welfare, and includes a denunciation of the fashion of wearing birds in women's hats; the *G.O.P.* regularly crusaded against the pathetic ornaments. The article continues:

The same wanton and thoughtless extravagance goes on in the fur world, and in that of ivory and wild beasts' skins. Already the very noblest of our larger animals that dwell afar in forest or jungle are becoming woefully scarce; sacrificed they all will be ere long at the shrine of fashionable folly.

It will surely be a poor sort of world to live in when neither buffalo nor bison roams in the wilderness or prairie; when the roar of the king of beasts awakes no more the echoes of African hills; when the elephant, the seal, and the bear can only be met with stuffed in museums; when coals have gone down, and heat and power can only be obtained from the earth's dark depths, or from the heaving breast of ocean; when the woods shall be silent in spring, and the only notion of bird-song shall be that handed down or preserved by the phonograph.

I suppose it is something to be thankful for that the fears of the eighteen-eighties are not—quite yet—the facts of today.

Left and facing page: the inside front cover and the back cover of each monthly issue of the G.O.P. were used for advertisements. Many advertisers, notably Beecham's Pills and Cadbury's Cocoa, repeated their bookings faithfully, month after month. The illustration on the facing page shows the inside cover, March, 1894. The column on the left appeared in April, 1902, and is perhaps surprising in its range of items.

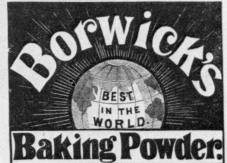

EMBROIDERED SWISS MUSLIN OR
ZEPHYR DRESS.

*Above: an illustration from June, 1887,
showing embroidered Swiss muslin made up
into a dress for summer garden parties.*

*Far right: the girl on the left demonstrates
the style of wearing figured and plain sateens
in the summer of 1882. Her gown is
trimmed with newly-fashionable string-
coloured lace. Her companion wears "a
pretty walking dress of striped and plain
materials. The Paris dress from which it
was copied was of black cashmere, with
black striped satin and moiré."*

Chapter Five

DRESS

HIS WIFE'S BONNET: A young man in a train was making fun of a
lady's hat to an elderly gentleman in the next seat to him. "Yes,"
said his neighbour, "that's my wife, and I told her if she wore
that bonnet some fool would be sure to make fun of it."

Varieties
(1890)

Although beauty articles as we know them received comparatively little
space in the Victorian *Girl's Own Paper*, fashion was the subject of a regular
feature; throughout much of the epoch this was headed *Dress: in Season
and in Reason*, by A Lady Dressmaker. Extra articles appearing from time
to time dealt less with the season's vogue than in a practical way with
some special aspect of dress, such as budgeting, the trousseau, or clothes
for sport or travel. There were no photographic illustrations to the fashion
pages, and no coloured sketches—only line drawings. However, the latter,
with their clear sharp outlines, probably gave a more reliable impression
of a garment than many of the wilder flights of a modern fashion photographer. Often several figures were depicted under headings such as *At
Ventnor, In the Park*, or *A Rainy Day Visitor*.

Delicious names of colours glow in these pages—rose-cendré, blush
pink, yeux de chat, souris-agitée (agitated mouse?), cowslip, mignonette
(or réséda), mirror-grey, dragon, lizard green, artichoke, pineapple,
poinsettia, cigar ash, serpent, winter grass.

Materials, too, have tempting names. Some may be mysterious to a
modern reader, and where unusual ones appear in excerpts quoted in
this chapter, brief descriptions have been added.

Writing in the late 'eighties, the Lady Dressmaker declares:

It is perhaps a little difficult to know where to begin in the early autumn
months to describe the dress of the moment, for we are still, and unavoidably,
in doubt as to the final selection. Fortunately, of late years we have become
more free to choose, and a dozen fashions are worn at once, instead of one
only, as was the case some fifty years ago.... We have many new cloth
costumes for autumn wear; and green cloth of various hues seems still in
favour. Amongst these watercress, walnut, and fir greens seem the prettiest.
The long redingote [long double-breasted coat], and the Empire skirt and jacket
bodice, seem both equally popular, and the "accordion" pleated skirt, with a
vest [waistcoat] and plain bodice, will probably be one of the features of the
winter dresses. One of these skirts, made in a dark green woollen material,

was a great relief to an economical friend of ours, the other day, who instantly decided that her last year's parasol should do for this year also—after being brightened up by her own careful fingers, and decorated with a few yards of cheap black lace.

Stockingette jackets are much used, and are very desirable indeed for the chilly and dubious days of April and the early part of May. They are tight-fitting, and made quite plain. In many instances, when for indoor wear, they are covered with coloured beads on the fronts and backs. Black silk and taffeta gloves will be again used this year. They are made very long on the arm, and the most favourite colour, after black,

will be a very dark green. The *gants de Suède* are cheaper than ever, and will be much used in tan-colour and yellow.

Stockings form the next subject, which is likely to be of interest to our readers. Black is still the correct colour, and very good well-dyed stockings in both cotton and Balbriggan can be had at reasonable prices. Self-coloured clocks are more fashionable than

coloured ones, and the very elaborately embroidered fronts are no longer in vogue. For young girls, ribbed stockings are the most worn, and dark colours are always selected.

In speaking of capes, I should have mentioned that the young lady with her back towards us in the picture of hats is wearing one of the prettiest shapes in which the capes are made, *i.e.*, with a yoke-like gathered top.

NEW DRESSES.

Above: the three summer fête dresses described on August 30, 1884 as "not beyond the skill of the home or the country dressmaker to produce".

was shown to me lately, having eight rows of black satin ribbon round the skirt, about an inch in width, and placed respectively half an inch apart. This was the sole trimming of the skirt. The bodice had a vest and revers, which were of black satin, and the smaller buttons were also black.... The military and tinsel thread embroidery now used so much on the jackets seen in the shop windows was not to be seen on the jackets of H.R.H. the Princess Louise of Wales★, and the quieter-looking the jacket is, and the more simple in every way, the less it will show its age and date—a matter of considerable economy. Dresses, jackets and redingotes, trimmed with bands of fur, will be one of the characteristic features of the season of 1889 and 1890.

Many of the fashions illustrated in the *Girl's Own Paper* were designed for girls with money and leisure. For instance, an issue in 1884 illustrates three delightful "summer fête" dresses:

The dress made with "accordion" pleats and a puffed overdress is the plainest of the three. It may be made of nun's veiling [thin, soft, loosely woven fabric], of the Nagpore or Corah silk, or of the new écru muslin, with white brocaded designs upon it. The first two present a large range of colour from which to choose—white, tan, primrose, water-green, beige, nankeen, maize, mustard; indeed, any of the beautiful Oriental colours in which the silks made in India are sold. The hat is of white lace, mixed with the same.

★ Eldest daughter of the Prince and Princess of Wales (later to be Edward VII and Queen Alexandra)

Here is a description of another summer outfit from the same year:

The centre figure in the group of three wears a very charming washing-dress made of sateen, or of foulard or washing-silk. The skirt, of poppy-red sateen or silk, made in "accordion" pleats; and the pleated front is of the same, while the polonaise [cut-away overskirt] is of maize colour, with flowers of green and poppy-colour. The hat is of white straw, with poppy-coloured velvet and flowers.

In the eighteen-eighties and 'nineties, a woman would as soon have appeared out of doors bare-footed as without a hat, so of course millinery plays an important part in the fashion articles:

Grey hats and grey feathers; black velvet hats and white feathers; and cream felts, trimmed with iris or violet velvet, are the usual afternoon hats this autumn. [October, 1883]

Save for very young girls, bonnets are more correct and ladylike than hats, the latter being only used in the early hours of the morning. [December, 1883]

Now I am on the subject of bonnets and hats, I cannot help expressing my regret that the poor birds are again called on to pay tribute to the follies of fashion. Follies they really and truly are, for nothing so horrid has yet been seen as the miserable deformities we are asked to admire, and, what is worse, to wear, as birds in our hats and bonnets.... I do hope our girls will avoid encouraging this needless persecution of our poor little winged neighbours, and choose velvet or ostrich tips for a trimming. [December, 1883]

Above: an early illustration (May 21, 1881) which opens an article on seasonable dress. "Everything hangs in graceful folds, and more drapery is used than has been seen for some time past." The Lady Dressmaker particularly praises long, close-fitting jackets, in black, grey, navy or drab, as "becoming and simple" for out-of-door wear.

HATS AND BONNETS OF 1888.
MID-WINTER.

DRESS: IN SEASON AND IN REASON.
By A LADY DRESSMAKER.

Above: an array of millinery from January 28, 1888. Cloth hats and bonnets, trimmed with velvet or cock's feathers, were popular at this time, with muffs to match them.

Very bright scarlet feathers are worn on black velvet bonnets, and there is any amount of the most horrid things of Parisian origin, the last being a small kitten—not real, I am glad to say, only an excellent imitation. [February, 1884]

The subject of the slaughter of birds for decorating hats is returned to again and again in these pages. In 1887, the Lady Dressmaker writes:

One step in the right direction was taken a few days ago, at a meeting of ladies in Bond Street. It was convened on the subject of dress, and it was decided that "the plumage of small birds should no longer be considered a fashionable trimming for either robes or mantles". I hear also in connection with the same idea that some of the principal ladies' hatters of London have declared their intention of not using the plumes, wings and skins of wild birds in future, for the decoration of either hats or bonnets.

There is no limit, however, to floral trimmings:

The flowers used for both hats and bonnets are those of the season—violets, narcissus, Lent lilies, auriculas, hyacinths, cowslips, phloxes, and some water-grasses and weeds. A great deal of lilac is used, and sprays of syringa flowers. [May, 1886]

One of the changes worthy of notice this season in London is, that hats [as distinct from bonnets] are now worn so much more in town than they used to be, and on occasions when no one would have thought of wearing one.... Most of the hats worn are extravagant in shape and style, and look as senseless and as unlike head-gear as it is possible to imagine. [June, 1886]

By July, 1889, readers are being informed:

One of our recent introductions is the "collapsible bonnet".... It will fold up without injury, can be carried in the pocket or the handbag, does not crush the hair, is a boon to people when travelling, is extremely light and comfortable, will not collapse on the head, but is firm as an ordinary bonnet and, lastly, when folded, it can be used as a fan.

BEIGE AND NUN'S VEILING COSTUMES.

MANTLE AND JACKET.

"Fair-headed girls look better in paler tints than their dark sisters," announces the writer of *Hats of Today* in October, 1896, going on to say:

Soft, artistic shades of blue, réséda, heliotrope, and rose, all as a rule suit a girl with a fair complexion and light hair; while stronger tones, such as poppy-red, some vivid shades of green, orange and yellow show off a clear, dark skin and brown hair. Cornflower-blue is becoming to most people, and the girl who has red shades in her hair, and the very fair complexion that generally accompanies that colour, will find most green tints, eau-de-nil, lettuce-leaf, even grass-green, eminently becoming; also all shades of brown.

But while the main fashion features are written with that Olympian assurance so characteristic of the fashion writer, informing readers of the styles, fabrics and colours either gone out or come back in, the supplementary articles on dress regularly discourage excessive frivolity. The writer of one such article states in 1885:

The fewer gowns we possess, the less our worries and the greater our comforts as a rule. A well-made and well-fitting serge or tweed, a handsome black silk or satin, and a thinner grenadine [fine, loosely woven fabric, usually made of silk or wool, sometimes mixed with cotton] with silk, is enough for the

Above: the girls on the left model light woollen dresses for the summer of 1883, with matching silk-lined mantles, to be worn if the weather is chilly. "When one thinks that muslins were really worn in the summer once upon a time in England, it seems difficult to credit the fact, so much have our seasons altered." The third girl wears an Olivia bonnet without strings, and a gauze mantle, "one of the new shapes suitable to young married women", while her companion has one of the new costume coats (May 26, 1883).

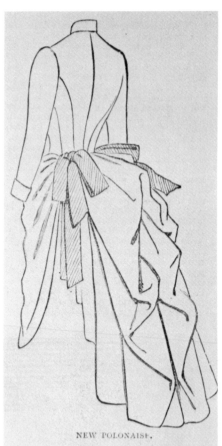

NEW POLONAISE.

The paper pattern selected for this month is one of the new polonaises, which promise to be so much worn during the coming year. It is simple in make, is buttoned up the front, and partly open. The pattern consists of nine pieces. The back is draped in Bedouin pleats, and the polonaise takes from eight to nine and a-half yards of material, according to the width of stuff; price 1s.

Above: a paper pattern for a new polonaise, obtainable by post from The Lady Dressmaker (September, 1887).

Far right: an array of caps illustrating an article of May 21, 1892. Figures 1, 2 and 3 show caps worn by nurses, "so clean and dainty"; 4, 5 and 6, caps for morning wear, or for servants; 7 and 10, caps for older ladies; 8, a fancy cap in blue tulle and velvet, for a stall-holder at a bazaar; and 9, in lace or chiffon trimmed with velvet ribbon, one for evening wear.

dress of an ordinary married woman. For a girl, if she go out much, or play tennis, a tennis-gown and white lace or afternoon garden-party gown must be added.

In 1886, Isabella Fyvie Mayo writes in *A Vexed Woman's Question:*

The tight-laced, be-flounced, be-trained damsel proclaims to the world her utter unwomanliness. The nursery would soon make havoc in her finery. Let us hope she would never carry it into a sick-room, and in the kitchen it would be a nuisance, and a bad example.... Of material we should buy the best and most durable within reach of our purse. We have no right to keep people employed in weaving and making up useless and perishable shoddy articles. It is a dishonour to them to do such work, and if they are forced to do it that they may get bread to eat, we are keeping them in the worst kind of slavery. That we pay them for it does not make it any better, any more than if we paid them for any other degrading and wasteful service. We insult them by taking their industry and trampling it underfoot, as if they had no concern in their work, but only in their wages.

Articles about dressing on a small income are frequent—sometimes on a *very* small income, and here we are in the realms of severe practicality. In a feature in 1883, called *Girls' Allowances and How to Manage Them* by Dora de Blaquière, a list of dress expenses for one year is given. (The table of currency equivalents on page 108 may be helpful.)

	£	s.	d.
Four pairs stockings (lisle thread, 2s. 10d.)		11	4
Four pairs woollen stockings (3s.)		12	0
One dozen handkerchiefs		5	0
One pair black stays		10	6
Two pairs house shoes (4s.)		8	0
One pair boots	1	1	0
One pair walking shoes		8	6
Gloves		15	0
Winter dress of serge and toque (3s. a yard)	1	10	0
Nuns'-cloth dress (1s. a yard)		16	0
Linings, etc.		3	6
Washing-dress		10	0
Bonnet		6	0
Summer hat, covered with muslin and lace		3	0
Ulster	1	1	0
Winter jacket	1	1	0
Fur cape		12	6
Umbrella (en tout cas)		7	6
Undervests, winter and summer		4	6
Two flannel petticoats		10	0
Underlinen (each year, 10s.)		10	0
Sundries	1	0	0
Winter petticoat		10	6
	£13	6	10

——but my calculations make the total £13 16s. 10d.

The prices on this list appear almost unchanged at the end of the decade, giving an idea of the stability of the cost of living.

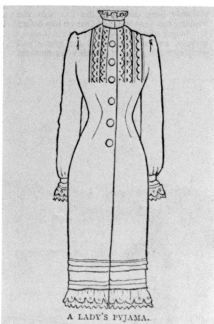

A LADY'S PYJAMA.

All paper patterns are of medium size, viz., thirty-six inches round the chest, with no turnings; and only one size is prepared for sale. They may be had of "The Lady Dressmaker, care of Mr. H. G. Davis, 73, Ludgate-hill, E.C.;" price 1s. each. If tacked in place, 6d. extra. The addresses should be clearly given, with the county, and stamps should not be sent, as so many losses have occurred. Postal notes should be crossed, but not filled up with any name. *Patterns already issued may be always obtained*, as the Lady Dressmaker selects only such as are likely to be of constant use in making and remaking at home, and is careful to give new hygienic patterns for children as well as adults, so that the readers of the "G.O.P." may be aware of the best methods of dressing themselves. The following in hygienic underclothing have already been given :—Combination (drawers and chemise), princess petticoat (under-bodice and petticoat), divided skirt, under-bodice instead of stays, pyjama (nightdress combination). Also housemaid's and plain skirt, polonaise with waterfall back, Bernhardt mantle, dressing-jacket, Princess of Wales jacket and waistcoat (for tailor-made gown), mantelette with stole ends, Norfolk blouse with pleats, ditto with yoke, blouse polonaise, princess dress or dressing-gown, Louis XI. bodice with long fronts, Bernhardt mantle with pleated front, and plain dress-bodice suitable for cotton or woollen materials. New tea-jacket, or *après midi*, for indoor wear; Garibaldi blouse with loose front, new skirt pattern with rounded back; bathing dress; new polonaise.

Above: another paper pattern, designed for ladies who wanted "comfort and hygienic advantage" in their lingerie (October, 1886); and a list of some of the patterns available to readers.

In *Passing Rich with £40 a Year* (1890), the dress allowance is only 2s. 6d. a week:

I am of opinion that on the sum available—2s. 6d. a week—a gentlewoman of ability and taste can dress becomingly and suitably. I take it for granted that she is able to do plain dressmaking, and knit a stocking.... One gown, £1 5s. 0d. Three gowns are quite enough to have at one time; the new one for best, the previous year's for second best, and a former one, sponged and repaired, into a respectable third.

Clearly, if a girl could afford but one gown a year she had to forgo primrose silk and poppy-red sateen.

Readers often wrote with enquiries about washing or cleaning dresses and, since few of these were easily washable, and bearing in mind the far dirtier atmosphere of large cities at the time, a light-coloured dress was an extravagance.

A recipe for cleaning white or very light silks is given in 1887:

Take a quart of lukewarm water, and mix with it four ounces of soft soap, four ounces of honey, and a good-sized wineglass of gin. Unpick the silk and lay it in widths on the kitchen-table. Then take a perfectly new common scrubbing-brush, dip it in the mixture, and rub the silk firmly up and down on both sides, so as to saturate it. Rinse it in cold water twice, until free from soap, and hang it on a clothes-horse to drain, until half dry; then iron it with a piece of thin muslin between it and the iron, or it will be marked on the ironed side. Keep the silk quite smooth when laid on the table, so that every part may come under the brush. White silk requires a little blue in the water.

Old black or coloured silk, readers are told in 1888, may be renovated with potato-water:

Grate five or six raw potatoes into cold, soft water, allowing one large potato to each quart. Five or six quarts will clean two dresses. Wash and pare the potatoes, leave the mixture undisturbed for two days, then pour off the clear liquid only, and dip the silk into it, without rubbing or creasing it. Hang each piece of silk on a clean [clothes] horse to drip, and then lay them on a clean cloth and wipe with a clean towel. Lastly, iron, if needful, on the soiled side, with a cool iron.

The trousseau, of course, is always a popular subject. A fascinating article in 1890 is *Hints on an Inexpensive Trousseau*, in which Aunt Margaret advises Queenie, the bride-to-be, how to spend the £30 which can be afforded for her new clothes.

"Let us begin with nightgowns," says Aunt Margaret briskly, "of which I think you may find nine enough." ("So I should think!" the reader is tempted to reply.) The nightgowns are to be made of calico, by Queenie herself, also the same number of calico combinations and half a dozen camisoles for summer wear. In addition the bride has four flannel petticoats "embroidered with flossine", two white petticoats, a summer underskirt and a winter petticoat, one pair of white "bridal" corsets and one pair of black, four pairs of black spun silk stockings at 2s. 6d., four lisle thread pairs at 1s. 11d., and eight black cashmere pairs at 2s. 6d. Dresses recommended are "one of the charming boating-gowns of navy serge which look so well on cold summer days", a vieux rose zephyr dress, and, for evening wear, a pretty black Russian net skirt and bodice,

HOLIDAYS BY THE SEA.

and "a perfectly plain lizard-green velveteen, without a morsel of trimming, cut low back and front".

Having dealt with all this, Aunt Margaret comes to the wedding dress, and suggests one suitable for smart afternoon occasions, rather than for evening wear:

"I have rather set my heart on a cream-coloured Indian muslin made with a plain skirt, edged at the bottom with three rows of narrow satin ribbon worked over in silver thread in this manner—a row of silver crosses webbed over the ribbon. The bodice made with a full waistcoat of silver embroidery or cream and silver gauze, and a line of the silver on the cuffs. Your hat must be made of the cream muslin, a Vandyke shape, with a bunch of silver wheatears and pale blue cornflowers, and your bouquet must be tied with blue and silver

Above: a bathing scene, published on September 27, 1884. The bold sash worn by the girl on the left is in turkey-red twill. "The tiny maiden in the foreground was sketched from life on the beach at Ramsgate."

95

TEA-GOWN:
THE DRESS OF THE FUTURE.

Above: the tea-gown was warmly recommended by the G.O.P. (February 25, 1888) as becoming, artistic and hygienic, although The Lady Dressmaker felt this particular "bag-front" model might look better tied with ribbons at the waist.

Far right, above: "Spring", a simple flowery picture which, with a companion piece, "Summer", appeared in May, 1894.

Far right, below: a wedding "At Home" illustrating an article on afternoon weddings (October, 1897). The guests are to enjoy sandwiches, patties, biscuits, cake, fruit, and sweetmeats, with tea and home-made lemonade to drink.

ribbons. You must wear tan gloves and shoes, and I rather think you will please Walter's fastidious taste in this rather fetching 'get up'."

"It sounds lovely!" cried Queenie, clasping her hands ecstatically.

Also practical. The Victorian bride expected to get full use from her wedding gown.

In *What to Do with a Wedding Gown* (1891) the writer says:

During the short time that a bride is being fêted and honoured, and is taking precedence of more staid matrons at parties and dinners, the white satin gown is a thing expected by everyone, and much admired and regarded as a matter of course. For a bride without her finery is like a peacock without its tail—an anomaly.

She goes on to suggest ways of adapting the gown later:

Cut the bodice either low all round or square back and front, and also cut the sleeves off quite close to the shoulder. Then trim the top of the bodice with some handsome gold embroidery about an inch deep, which will cost about 1s. 2d. a yard; and if the bodice has been cut in the fashionable long shape, convert it into a short one by taking away the basque and putting a deep edge of the gold all round the hips, nearly up to the waist, the trimming in this case being four or five inches in depth. This arrangement will form a sort of band, and give a smart finish to the bodice. Then fill in the sleeves to the elbow with gold-spangled net, put in rather full, and drawn tight just above the elbow with a narrow line of gold embroidery.

When the ex-bride is tired of this dress, she can adapt it further by removing all the gold, making a train of black velveteen, covering the front of the skirt with fine black lace, and veiling the bodice with the same lace, finished off by narrow braces of velvet from the waist over the shoulders.

Working girls, however, are recommended by their mentors to avoid white wedding gowns and choose something more practical. DAISY is told she "had better get a 'nun's cloth' trimmed with satin for her wedding dress. A light shade of the colour called 'London smoke', the bonnet and gloves to match, and a white bouquet." This advice may, of course, be directed at readers of mature age or widowed status; but it sounds very much the sort of bridal outfit which the G.O.P. would favour for a working girl. "A wreath and veil would not be very expensive, but would be very useless purchases for a poor woman," readers are told in an article on wedding dresses in 1887. In 1891 an article appears entitled *A Servant's Wedding Outfit*. It seems safe to assume that the personality of Nellie the parlourmaid, who tells her tale in the first person, is a fictional one, and somewhat idealised, but for all that it makes engrossing reading.

Nellie is twenty-six at the time of her marriage, having saved £50 in the Post Office Savings Bank, although she has never earned more than £16 per annum in her life. She started her career at not quite thirteen, a maid-of-all-work at the greengrocer's, for 1s. a week, and her master opened the account for her as a thirteenth-birthday present. Nellie's description of her career is full of little nuggets of advice for other young servants; she never puts herself forward for tips, for instance, and when she contemplates laying out several pounds of her savings on a sewing-machine she discusses the purchase beforehand with her mistress. She is, in fact, the very model of a Victorian parlourmaid, and her wedding dress is just as prudent and modest as could be supposed; grey cashmere and a grey bonnet, trimmed with bows of narrow pink velvet. She spends £9 on her trousseau (and like her social superior Queenie, she has a practical blue serge dress). The article also deals with Nellie's purchase of blankets, sheets, cutlery and other household necessities as her contribution towards the matrimonial home.

Among the articles on wedding clothes, bridesmaids' dresses are not forgotten. Those suggested for winter weddings in 1890 sound more original and practical than many modern ones:

At a recent naval wedding the bridesmaids wore navy blue serge, faced and piped with white silk, and felt hats of blue and white. Another very pretty choice was grey "ladies' cloth" and grey astrachan; the toque hats, muffs, and jackets being all of the same. On this occasion the bride's travelling dress was the same as the bridesmaids' dresses. Grey cloth is also employed with silver embroidery, and also blue cloth with gold.... When white is used for the bridesmaids' gowns, white flannel seems very naturally in more request than anything else, and is a very useful selection in view of future occasions.

Those dresses do not sound likely to languish in the wardrobe after the first wearing.

In *Wedding "At Homes" for People of Small Incomes* (1890) a suggestion is made which seems more artistic than realistic:

My idea is, that the hostess should give a hint to those near relations who are quartered in the house that the wedding is to be a heliotrope one, or a "vieux rose" one, as the case may be; so that in buying their gowns the ladies might be guided as to the colour, and so be in a certain sort of harmony. Thus a very pretty, harmonious wedding would be where the bride was in white silk or muslin; the bridesmaids in white gowns, with pale mauve trimmings; the bride's mother in silver poplin or dead grey silk, with a bonnet composed of pale lilacs; the bridegroom's mother in deep heliotrope velvet; and the rest of the relations in harmonising colours, with posies and ribbons all alike—of lilacs, violets, or heather. Even if the dresses have, of necessity, to be of the cheapest materials, let the cashmeres or alpacas blend artistically. With the present fashions, and the present shades of colouring, bad and inartistic dressing is quite an unpardonable sin.

It sounds, indeed, enchanting—assuming that the bridegroom's mother did not take exception to a hint that a heliotrope velvet dress would be a more harmonious choice than the nut-brown satin she had in mind.

On a sadder note comes the question of mourning. A generation earlier, in 1861, Queen Victoria's intense and lasting grief at the death of the Prince Consort had plunged her into black, unrelieved even for the wedding of her second daughter, Princess Alice, seven months later. (The bride had a black trousseau, and the bride's mother clung to crape and a widow's cap.) The extravagance of some mourning fashions led to the establishing of the Mourning Reform Association, mentioned by the Lady Dressmaker in a G.O.P. article, in 1887:

Mourning dress follows very much more closely than it used to do in the steps of the fashion of the day. Tucks have gone out of favour, and crape is usually put on in panels, wide or narrow, as the case may be, and the depth of

Above: in January, 1888, The Lady Dressmaker wrote about widows' mourning: "After the first six months few people wear the long veil, and some widows never wear the cap at all, or at most for a month or two; while the weepers and large muslin collar are always used by widows for the first year. The more simple the drapery and quiet the style of the widow, the better taste and feeling she shows."

Far left: a charming bride with four bridesmaids in pink lawn with tulle hats.

Above: a little boy wears a simple frock, with a princess top and kilted flounce; the girl (shown front and back), spotted serge with a huge velvet bow; and the toddler, dressed to withstand the cold, a fur-trimmed grey pelisse cape and hood, with snug gaiters (January 26, 1884). In the same article The Lady Dressmaker *recommends "Kate Greenaway" styles for little girls, and the pelisses and bonnets she illustrates do indeed look charming—so simple to cut and sew, she says, that they may easily be made at home.*

mourning requires. . . . A perfectly plain dress of Scarborough serge, with no crape trimmings, yet looks very deep in its dull black tones. The same may be copied in crape-cloth, and is suitable for an everyday dress in the deepest mourning. . . .

There is no doubt that the efforts of the Mourning Reform Association have done much to shorten the period and reduce the depth of the mourning worn, with great advantage to everyone, and yet never were the lost more sorrowed over nor mourned than just now, when we are reducing the outward signs of grief. In the old days, when the excess of mourning was the rule, it is melancholy to remember how the fashion added to the deep trouble of the time, by entailing a large expenditure of money when perhaps half the income was gone, thus plunging a household into debt and difficulty.

Despite the efforts of the Association, however, the subject was one which still preoccupied readers and Editor:

J.M.—The length of time for which mourning is worn much depends on yourself. A widow would wear deep mourning for one year, lightening it the second a little. A year for father or mother, six months of which would be deep crape. For an uncle or aunt it would be a six months' mourning. [1880]

ELIZABETH J.—Very little children are not regularly "put into mourning", as it is termed; that is, very little crape is used for their dress, none in fact, save on the hat. Black ribbons on white dresses, and little black dresses and white pinafores, would be suitable for your little sister. [1880]

Nearly all the fashion pages deal with the clothes of grown-up young women, and it is rarely that the adolescent is catered for. However, the Lady Dressmaker writes in 1884:

Some months ago, I went to see a young girl at school who had arrived at that difficult period, between twelve and fourteen, when, even with the greatest attention, all girls look ungainly and awkward. My girl is no exception to the rule, for she is very tall, and, of course, looks just now more legs than body. Her dress, a large check of many colours, very short, with a gathered

HOME AND SCHOOL DRESSES.

waist and band, added to her ungainly appearance. My idea of a pretty dress would have been a plain red or dark blue cashmere or serge, made with a flounced skirt, a polonaise, and full front; for girls of that age should have no waist, and the princesse dress or polonaise is the best thing for them.

A MARCH ELF (1886) sounds like a young teenager, since she is told on the correspondence page that she "should wear her hair in a plait at the back, tied up with a bow of ribbon and curled a little in front. She is too young to need steels in her dresses."

In 1897 came a series of articles for mothers of little girls, entitled *The King's Daughters: Their Culture and Care*, by Lina Orman Cooper. One of these is devoted to dress:

Above: dresses for teenagers (January 24, 1885). "The quieter and plainer they are, the more ladylike the wearer." There is no end to the ways of tastefully and ingeniously "freshening-up" old dresses, with new overskirts cunningly concealing the worn-out fronts of girls' gowns.

I.—A BONNET TO SUIT ANYBODY.

Above: a bonnet in fancy straw and black lace, trimmed with yellow velvet and a bunch of nasturtiums (November, 1896).

Far right: lingerie, December 1899.

Below: a jaunty but practical tricycling gown with matching hat (August, 1887).

TRICYCLE GOWN.

The clothing of our children should be as light as possible; as warm as possible; as cool as possible. Wool alone will work the miracle. So the first garment our six-year-old girlie should don must be a woollen one.... This combination garment should button on the shoulder, not down the chest, and should cover the thighs. Over this porous envelope, a corselet should be buttoned. No bones must be allowed in it. On this matter I feel very strongly. We are dreadfully shocked at the cruelty of Chinese mothers in binding up their children's feet to prevent growth. Yet—can it be believed?—I have seen little soft-growing bodies—belonging to girls of seven—encased in buckram and whalebone!... One petticoat of flannel and one of cambric is sufficient.... A mother's love for fine needlework and many tucks may be displayed in the white petticoat. It should be made very full, neatly gauged and gathered into a bodice of the same, trimmed with insertion and edged with frills of torchon [rather coarse handmade lace]. This bodice should button at the back. The drawers worn by our little daughter should be equally beautified. Valenciennes [narrow cotton or linen lace] makes a pretty frilling above the knee, or Cashe's cambric frilling looks well. Let the leg-hole be cut amply large and plenty of room for kicking about and running. The frock or overall will be, of course, always a matter of taste. But as long as possible, let it be white.

The *G.O.P.* was keen on what it called "hygienic underclothing" and patterns were offered regularly for "combination (drawers and chemise), princess petticoat (underbodice and petticoat), divided skirt, underbodice instead of stays, pyjama (nightdress combination)". In 1883, it recommends "dress drawers":

... to do away with the weight of petticoats, and their pressure at the waist, and to produce more warmth for the limbs, while avoiding the fatigue produced by the long skirts flapping against the ankles.

The subject comes up again in 1891:

The casting-off of underpetticoats is no novelty during the present winter. I have met several ladies who do not, and have not, worn them, using warm knickerbockers of red flannel, or of the material of the gown if in serge, instead, and finding great comfort in the change, which at the same time is perceptible to no one. The divided skirt has also many adherents, and so have the American dress drawers, both of them made of the material of the gown.

In 1897 the *G.O.P.* states:

The ordinary underdress of so many women at present consists of a woven combination and a pair of knickerbockers only.

An interesting aspect of the trouser question is raised in a *Dress in Season and in Reason* article, in 1887:

I daresay some of our girls have been looking with interest on the struggle of the poor "pit-brow" women to keep their work at the pit bank. These women, by the most trustworthy accounts, seem model workwomen: industrious, respectable, and often supporting their families ... and setting an excellent example in every way to their brother working men who, I fear, are seeking, in the abolition of the "pit-brow women", a rise in their own wages. The complaint brought against their work is, that they have to perform it in trousers and tunic, thus adapting their costume to their work.... Our brave sister-women don the most suitable, decent dress.... It is from the women themselves—not from men—that complaints should come.

Advice on a suitable outfit for tricycling appears in that ever useful serial of Dora Hope's, *She Couldn't Boil a Potato* (1887). The heroine,

FIG. I.—BOLERO SHAPED AND PLAIN UNDER-BODICE.

FIG. 4.—CHEMISES OF NAINSOOK AND FIGURED BATISTE.

is concerned, so that the body might be kept warm evenly; and we have learned the respective advantages of cotton, wool, and linen. Though the rage for woollen garments has, in a measure, passed off, we have learned from it more of our real requirements than we should have otherwise learned. A great good has followed, namely, that the subject of underclothing has come to be dealt with personally by each wearer, and hence the diversity of opinion which I mentioned above at the beginning of my article, for everyone seems to have certain requirements which she must meet. So we have every kind of mixture in the way of garments.

Years ago the underlinen formed the largest portion of the trousseau. It was prepared by dozens, and a small trousseau would have from a dozen to a dozen and a half of each article. In Germany the numbers seemed fabulous that were thought needful, and included the houselinen as well. Even in England I have known women who, after thirty years of wedded life, still possessed remains of their trousseau, marked with their maiden names. Even those immense outfits for India are greatly pruned down, to the saving of our purses and the amount of our luggage.

The reason for much of this reduction may be found in the universal adoption of woven undergarments of wool, silk, cotton, and thread, or any two of them mixed together. Their popularity seems unbounded, and the

origin lay, in some degree, in the Jaeger craze; but certainly in hot countries and in others where the heat of the summer is great, the wearing of these woven silk, cotton, and thread vests was found far more satisfactory than cotton chemises next the skin. And so we find them used everywhere as well as in England, where, united with the knicker-bockers, in either coloured cotton, alpaca, or serge, they seem to form the chief apparel. There is a diversity of opinion about the drawers of cotton and nainsook, but if the woven combinations be worn, they are very generally omitted, as not being at all needful.

The flannel petticoat is another garment about which there is some discussion, but not much, for it is very generally dismissed from all our wardrobes, as we do not in the least degree require its added weight, when we wear combinations of any kind; and it was the one inequality in our clothing, to avoid which we wear the drawers or combinations which certainly supply its place completely. It was the source of much over-heating when it was worn, especially to girls and children. Now, for the summer, we do better without it, and in the winter its place is occupied, where petticoats are concerned, by a silk, alpaca, or moirette skirt, lined with flannel, flannelette, or alpaca, the latter an excellent material for a lining. Otherwise, we use the ever-useful knickers, which can be purchased in any material, from cotton, drill, alpaca, and Oxford shirting, to serge, tweed, silk and satin. Galatea is a favourite material with many ladies for both knickers and combinations.

The subject of petticoat bodices, and indeed of all forms of stay and neck coverings, and other kindred garments, is a very large one, and as, to my mind, it is closely connected with the comfort of dress, I intend to give the fullest consideration to it, for they are very needful articles, even if you do wear combinations high to the neck. Many girls have left them off for this reason, judging that they were not wanted. The old-fashioned

petticoat or slip-bodice, made of cotton, high to the neck, with a little edging at the neck, seems to have been succeeded by a woven stockingette bodice of much the same shape, in either cotton or silk, and these seem worn. There are also several forms of low necked bodices (see Fig. 1), which are popular, but I fear many girls do not wear anything, if they use, as I have said, the combination high to the neck. Of course, where the muslin or cambric blouse has a slip-bodice, it is not needed; but otherwise, nothing can exceed the ugliness of the appearance, and the untidiness also. The very best thing for ordinary wear is a tiny kind of Bolero jacket (see Fig. 1), made of muslin and lace, which meets with a button or ties in front over the

FIG. 2.—UNDER-BODICE WITH CROSSED FRONTS.

FIG. 3.—DRAWERS TO MATCH.

SINGERS IN DEBATE.

Ella, is to be introduced to the sport by two new acquaintances and observes:

Their tricycling dresses were made of rather thick grey homespun, with well-fitting but not tight Norfolk jackets fastened with a belt, and with a convenient outside pocket for a handkerchief and whistle. The skirts, to Ella's surprise, were neither long nor wide, in fact Joan's, which answered very well, was barely longer than an ordinary walking-dress, and measured hardly three yards round the bottom; and Doris said she must take a perpendicular tuck in hers to reduce it to the same measurement, as the extra width caught in the wheels. The skirts were perfectly plain at the sides, and the necessary fullness was supplied by one or two box pleats in front and behind. For the rest of their costume they wore soft felt hats, or on sunny days, when there was no wind, straw sailor hats, and either tennis or ordinary walking-shoes.

What Joan and Doris forget, unfortunately, is to warn Ella to wear flannel or merino underclothing for tricycling, so she catches cold after her first ride. Characteristically, Dora Hope has cloaked her practical instruction in fiction.

Dress, in fact, is often an important element in G.O.P. fiction (as in so many stories written for young females—Meg March's wardrobe in *Little Women*, for instance). In the first of all the G.O.P. serials, *Zara, or My Granddaughter's Money* (1880), the description of seventeen-year-old Zara's costume tells us something about her:

[She] came into the room with a flounce and a fluster, the long train of her pale green flimsy dress sweeping far behind her on the grey carpet, the glitter of her large gilt earrings, her brooch, and chain, lighting up the place with a faint glory.

This does not prove that Zara is bad-hearted (and indeed she is not), but it certainly is intended to indicate that she has not been properly brought up. "Flimsy" is always a significant adjective in this context. In contrast, Annis, the hero's true sweetheart, is described in her "neat, well-fitting, blue serge dress, and her blue hat to match, looking, as she always did, a nicely-dressed, ladylike girl". Serge is very much an approved fabric —as are alpaca and cashmere.

Here are the Miss Hayters, in *A Lonely Lassie* (1891), a pair of shiftless girls, again not bad-hearted, but with no other object in life than to wait for something to change their futile existence without the least effort on their part:

The fault of their somewhat flimsy heliotrope and réséda thin woollen frocks was that they aimed more at prettiness and fashion than at what was serviceable and lasting, and they were totally out of place in their surroundings. Such puffings on the girls' shoulders, such standing collars at the back of their little necks, and such elaborate rows of curls, combed and pinned, extending, at a cursory glance, from the nape of the neck to the arch of the eyebrows, Flora had not seen in London town.

Nun's cloth, or nun's veiling, is a fabric that only a good girl in a story is permitted to wear. Apart from the purity implicit in its name, it is economical. *Our Bessie* (1888) shows us the heroine faced with the serious matter of suitable clothes for her visit to the rich and fashionable Miss Edna Sefton. However, she reassures her anxious mother that she can cope perfectly well:

SERGE DRESS TRIMMED WITH BRAID.

Above: a dress in serge, a fabric much in favour with the G.O.P., with braid trimming to soften its serviceable look (December, 1884).

Far left: an illustration which shows the different style of drawing introduced into the fashion pages in the eighteen-nineties. The standing girl wears a vicuna cloth dress, its skirt made in one piece, with a seam at the back, to give a long simple line. The hat is buff-coloured straw trimmed with black lace, jet, and crimson roses ("yellow, or malmaison, of the colour of the straw, or toning with it, would perhaps be in better taste"). The girl with the song-book has a dress with a bell-skirt in dark shot silk. "The double and treble bell-skirts will continue to remain in good style, as their correct cut and set are not attainable by the inexperienced."

IN THE AUTUMN DAYS.

Pale grey cashmere, with yoke of orange satin covered with lace band of same on skirt, large butterfly bow of pale green silk with black velvet on the edge.

Above: an autumn gown to welcome in the new century (September, 1900). Greys, browns and greens are the fashionable colours. The Lady Dressmaker praises a vivid Parisian yellow, and a rich autumn red for millinery—hats and bonnets being much trimmed with fruit, especially cherries and plums.

"I have my grey dress and hat; and father thinks they are very becoming; and there is my Indian muslin Uncle Charles gave me for best occasions, and if you will let me buy a few yards of white nun's cloth, Chrissy and I will contrive a pretty dinner dress. I like white best, because one can wear different flowers, and so make a change."

Edna Sefton, after changing for dinner while Bessie puts on the white nun's cloth dress, is revealed as "looking like a young princess" to Bessie's dazzled eyes. Her gown, earlier said to be "old", is in fact "a delicate china blue silk", "trimmed in a costly fashion", and at her throat Edna wears "a locket with a diamond star".

(I am much too fond of Rosa Nouchette Carey to want to laugh at her, but I did catch an echo of Daisy Ashford's Mr Salteena here!)

Within Sight of the Snows (1884) is fiction, but includes early in the narrative a description of the heroine's wardrobe for her Swiss holiday. As this is not particularly relevant to the story, it was evidently intended as a guide to other travellers. "My wardrobe was very limited," says the heroine, a young music teacher, "and I usually wore black for economy's sake." She goes on:

"My equipment consisted of a travelling dress of soft silky black alpaca, and a black silk gown that had seen much service, but was lissom and becoming even in its decadence. I put in one or two lace collars for evening wear, and a card of cream lace for tuckers. One shady hat with a broad but graceful brim, that I purchased at a sale at one of the West End shops for a shilling or two, prettily trimmed with wheatears and poppies, went into the portmanteau; and I intended to make the black straw that I prepared for travelling serve for all occasions when that was unsuitable.... I added two large square handkerchiefs of cream Indian muslin, trimmed with lace, which I made myself, and intended to wear out of doors to brighten up my black gown if the weather were very hot."

It sounds a singularly modest wardrobe, and the portmanteau need not have been very large to contain it all. At the opposite extreme in advice to travellers is that given in *On the Purchase of Outfits for India and the Colonies* by Dora de Blaquière, in 1890, where a really formidable collection of trunks must have been required.

The outfit required by a lady on such a journey would probably be a travelling gown of beige [natural undyed fabric], serge, homespun, cheviot [rough-surfaced, all-wool fabric] or ladies' cloth [fine flannel in plain weave], not necessarily new, to be used on sea voyages, with jacket either to match or to go with it, made simply—preferably tailor-made. There must be a hat or bonnet to match, a veil of gauze or grenadine, a hood for travelling and at sea, of black or coloured silk; warm ulster [long belted overcoat], cloak, or fur cloak; good rug, and one with waterproof side; tailor-made gown of tweed to land in, and a lighter gown of the same kind to wear on ordinary occasions; jackets to match; a washing-silk, surah or pongee; two cottons—one dark and one light; a black silk with high and low bodice; a black lace with ditto; several blouses in silk, cotton, flannel, and elastic material; a mantle for dressy occasions; two dust cloaks made of washing or tussore silk, made up so that they can be worn without the bodice of dress [sic]—a great comfort when the weather is hot on long railway journeys; one dozen and a half of stockings—thread, silk and wool; handkerchiefs, gloves, veils, and a workbox or bag, with cottons, silks, needles, and all the requisites for working.

AT A GERMAN RAILWAY STATION.

The picture of an indomitable Victorian lady traveller is completed by the list of articles she is recommended to include in her travelling outfit:

An indiarubber folding bath, an Etna or small spirit kettle, and a bottle of spirits; some tea and a little sugar; a bath towel or two; an air cushion, or a pillow; a small drinking-cup and flask; soap; a pot of Liebig or Bovril; matches and candles; medicine; some potted meat for sandwiches; insect powder and mosquito netting; vaseline, lip salve, camphor, sal volatile, seidlitz powders, mustard leaves, chlorodyne, and eau de cologne.

The Lady Dressmaker in an article in 1887 gives another useful hint to the traveller:

Above: the middle lady wears "one of the new spotted foulard dresses"; her companion is in embroidered tussore, with a dark blue tulle bonnet; and the new arrival wears a travelling dress in plain and cross-barred wool, with matching hat (September 25, 1886).

CHILDREN'S DRESS.

DRESS:
IN SEASON AND IN REASON.
BY A LADY DRESSMAKER.

Above: a group of children's dresses February, 1888

"We women are very slowly growing more sensible," says The Lady Dressmaker in this article, "and, I daresay, with each year we shall become more and more capable of disdaining the decrees of the milliner and dressmaker."

One of the pleasantest corsets for travelling is of the new knitted kind. They fit the figure when stretched upon it and fastened and they expand with every breath, and appear to gain in popularity every month.... A short stay is always desirable in journeying abroad, and many ladies like riding-stays for that reason as they can drive, climb, or mount on a mule's back with ease and comfort, not dreading broken stay-bones—the most miserable of all events to happen on a journey....

Perhaps she has the last word on late Victorian dress later in the same article:

Some day, when we progress towards the acquirement of common sense, how we shall look back to many a foolish opinion and childish fashion which we have erected into a Juggernaut car to make our lives wretched, and to ruin our health and spirits, merely because we "must do as other people do". Tight boots and pointed toes, tight stays, large dress improvers and huge horsehair pads, will all be smiled at as foolish, and even wicked folly, when we know better in the far future.

Chapter Six

FEATURES

No matter what a girl's tastes or needs may be, on looking into *The Girl's Own Paper*, she will sooner or later find what she is in want of.... There never has been in this country, or indeed in any other, a storehouse of material by means of which girls can make the most of their lives, at all to be compared with it.

Editorial in the Thousandth Issue
(February 25, 1899)

I have included under this heading a selection of the very varied material which does not fit tidily under any other. "How To" articles were frequent: *How to Play the Harp* (1880), *How I Taught Myself to Read the Greek Testament* (1887), *How to Drive* [a horsedrawn vehicle] (1891) *How to Start and Manage a Mothers' Meeting* (1897), *How to Form a Girls Cycling Club* (1898).

Below: the heading from an article of December 14, 1895.

Articles on *How to Budget* were as popular with the Victorian reader as they must be now with the social historian. For the wages and prices in these articles to have any meaning, it is necessary to know their equivalent in today's currency. Before the old system (£. s. d.) was superseded by the decimal system in Britain (1971), each pound (£1) was divided into twenty shillings (20s.) and each shilling into twelve pennies (12d.).

£. s. d. system			Decimal system	
Pounds	*Shillings*	*Pennies*	*Pounds*	*Pence*
		1 d.		$\frac{1}{2}$ p.
		6 d.		$2\frac{1}{2}$ p.
	1 s. *or*	12 d.		5 p.
	2 s.			10 p.
	2 s. *and*	6 d.		$12\frac{1}{2}$ p.
	5 s.			25 p.
	7 s. *and*	6 d.		$37\frac{1}{2}$ p.
	10 s.			50 p.
	12 s. *and*	6 d.		$62\frac{1}{2}$ p.
	15 s.			75 p.
	17 s. *and*	6 d.		$87\frac{1}{2}$ p.
£1	*or* 20 s.		£1	*or* 100 p.

The smallest coin was the farthing, equivalent to one-fourth of a penny. In common use was the half-crown, which was worth 2s. 6d. There was also a two-shilling piece, called the florin. Twenty-one shillings (£1 1s.) made a guinea.

To buy in 1979 goods and services which cost £1 in 1880 (leaving aside the difference in standards) we should need to spend £19·65. Prices remained remarkably constant during the late Victorian period. They fell slightly from 1880 to 1890, but were still at the 1890 level in 1900, so that £1 in 1890 or 1900 may be considered as equivalent to £21 in 1979. (These figures were kindly supplied by Lloyds Bank Ltd.)

In 1885 an article entitled *How to Live on £100 a Year* budgets for a man, wife and two children; *£60 per Annum and How I Live on It* for a single girl in 1888. In 1893 there is *How Two Sisters Live in the Country on a Pound a Week*, and in 1899 *Three Girl-Chums and their Life in London Rooms*:

The incomes of our three friends amounted altogether to £270 a year. In the winter months the accounts for the rent of the rooms, coal, gas, candles, and similar expenses came to £1 3s. 6d. each week, as the following accounts set forth:

Rent of rooms	12s.	0d.
Abigail's wages	2s.	6d.
Gas-stove	1s.	0d.
Oil for lamp		4d.
Candles ($\frac{1}{2}$ pound at 6d. a pound)		3d.
Coals for sitting-room	1s.	10d.
Washing-bills (personal)	3s.	0d.
Washing-bills (house linen)	2s.	7d.
£1	3s.	6d.

(Drawn by F. S. Walker.)

"The riders pass, with a well-slacked rein,
While whispering trees sing their soft refrain."—*A Summer Ride.*

"Marion's food expenses for the week" totalled 18s. 1¾d. "With this account of her expenditure she was perfectly content. Her aim was to keep the money spent on food below ten shillings a head, and this week she was well within the margin."

Passing Rich with £40 a Year (referred to on p. 94) appears in 1890:

A dwelling must be chosen in the country. A love of rural life must be innate or engrafted. There must be a rigid line drawn between wants and needs. Every need must, as far as possible, have its definite allowance. There must be no mistiness over accounts. There must be no tardiness over paying bills, be they ever so small. There must be no leaving details to fall out as they list. There must be no helplessness over plain needlework and cutting out. There must be no indolence over small domestic duties. There must be an intelligent attitude towards the economics of cookery, dress, and the other incidentals of outlay. There must be the high thinking of a lady. There must be contentment of spirit. There must be loving sympathy.

. . . Let us begin by setting aside 1s. under the head of charity—collections at church; a few pence to buy wool to knit a pair of warm cuffs, or a muffler, for poor rheumatic old Joseph; or to get a tiny packet of tea to gladden feeble, bedridden Sarah; or a bit of flannel to make a small petticoat for the baby of some needy, overworked mother. . . . Next we set aside 1s. as provision against

Above: a drawing to a poem by Edward Oxenford (July 31, 1880):

There is converse gay
 'mid the chatt'ring throng
As they urge their thoroughbred
 steeds along,
And a laugh, that speaks
 of the lack of care,
Uprises and floats
 on the summer air.

Above: a splendidly sober artist considers his work in an illustration to the serial story, Bound to Earth (*November 4, 1882*).

sickness. It may seem rather much out of 15s.; but, O the comfort and freedom from anxiety that spring from the knowledge that there is a little sum laid by against a time when so many extra expenses come! It is worth making an effort to get the restful assurance....

One large, or two small, unfurnished rooms can be met with in almost any remote village for 1s. or 1s. 3d. per week.... The best and usual way is to pay so much for rooms, attendance, laundress, and vegetables; and from personal knowledge, I am sure that 3s. per week would cover all these expenses. (If the rooms are furnished, most likely 1s. a week more would be charged.) Then there is fire and light; and here, again, I have positive evidence that 1s. per week would be ample allowance for both. For food we will set aside 5s. 6d., which with methodical outlay would be equal to all demands in this direction....

A snug, peaceful little home; nourishing, enjoyable food; comfortable, lady-like clothing; some knowledge of the outer world and things literary through

a good magazine and weekly newspaper; extensive landscapes and skyscapes, finer far than any on the Academy walls; flowers, or gorgeously tinted foliage for the gathering all the year round; free high-class concerts in spring, summer, autumn, and even in winter often; pure air; hearty, unsophisticated friendships; time for thought (rare privilege these days!): and opportunities for doing good. Surely, with these blessings, any woman might be "passing rich".

Another contributor is inspired to write a feature with the same title a few months later:

I have one good-sized room in the house of a gardener living near a London suburb.... For this room and the sweeping of it, which is all the attendance that I require, I pay £8 a year, which includes the use of the kitchen for my cooking when I wish. Food is a large item, but 5s. a week affords plenty of nourishing and tempting food.

Finance is also dealt with in *What to do with your Savings* (1892), sub-titled "A Paper for Working Girls":

A girl of eighteen, earning fair wages, and having no-one but herself to care for, ought to be able to save 2s. weekly, or £5 4s. 0d. per annum. I would advise such an one to place her savings in the Post Office Savings Bank, in preference to other banks.... By the time she is twenty-five years of age, her savings, and the interest thereon, would amount to £42, or thereabouts. This sum, combined with the savings of her prospective husband, should prove amply sufficient to commence housekeeping on her own account.

To those readers who have neither the need nor the desire to look for paid work, an article called *Between School and Marriage* (Anonymous, 1886) is directed:

Every girl ought to "make the most of herself" and gain accurate and general information on the subjects that interest intelligent people. Why should she give up study at eighteen, just at a time when, having got beyond the rudiments, the work of teaching herself would after some time become so enjoyable that it would in many cases be continued even after marriage? When books are looked upon by a girl on leaving school as instruments of mental torture, she is stopping her education just when she has reached its most interesting phase.

But mind and body are co-partners, and while cultivating the one a girl must not injure the other. In after life she will require all the health and vigour of body she can obtain from riding, swimming, tennis, rowing, and the gymnastic exercises which have now been made to suit girls....

To scrub floors, scour saucepans, blacklead and clean grates, to black boots, to clean plate, to wash and iron—all these things may be done in a right or a wrong way, and it is only by learning how they ought to be done that a woman can teach others.

To set beside this, there is an article with the intriguing title *Our Brothers —in Training for Husbands* (1892). It is pleasing to learn that "while yet a little bare-legged boy" a son "should be watched in the companionship of his sisters, and any overbearing treatment of them should be, so to say, nipped in the bud. Feelings of tenderness and love for them cannot be too early instilled and cultivated by every means that the trifling incidents of nursery life may offer." The writer (anonymous) considers the "fagging" system in school brutalising to boys—"the meanest, most cowardly system of oppression and positive cruelty.... Were there a little more care expended by mothers on the early teaching of boys, and were the abuse of the powers of fag-masters reformed, we should cease to see such painfully-suggestive books as that entitled, *Is Marriage a Failure?*"

Stories which conceal in the jam of a narrative the healthful powder of instruction (*She Couldn't Boil a Potato*) have already been mentioned. In 1900 a similar system is applied to the rules of polite society in *The Law of Order; and How Beryl Came to Observe It*. The Beryl of the title is a naive young lady who requires to be instructed in the social graces by her more sophisticated cousin, who tells the story. While Beryl is walking about the West End in her best clothes she is addressed by a strange man; aghast, she goes home and consults her cousin:

"Beryl," I said, "to begin with, you should not walk about the Strand or Regent Street and Piccadilly by yourself in the afternoon. It is an understood thing that it is not advisable to do so, and in any case if you are obliged to go into any crowded regions unaccompanied—and you can nearly always avoid it by taking an omnibus—then you should be as quietly and unobservably dressed as possible. Indeed you should aim at that whenever you are in London by yourself."

Far right: an illustration from Inside Passengers; or The Wonderful Adventures of Luke and Belinda, *by A London Physician (described on pages 116–117).*

Even more caution, however, is needed in Paris. In 1889 Evelyn Upton's article *A Week in Paris for £6* is published. (The £6 includes the return fare.) The author warns:

Although I only give the scale of expenses for one person, I do not for a moment propose that one lady—least of all a young lady—should spend a week in Paris by herself. It would, indeed, be the height of impropriety. In fact, every young woman, whether she be of gentle or humble birth, who visits Paris, cannot remember too often that more discreetness of behaviour is necessary there than in any other city in the world. This I can vouch for from my own observation.... For the sum of ten francs, or eight shillings per day, you secure bedroom, lights, and service, plain breakfast and table d'hôte.

The *G.O.P.* features occasional articles on the life of girls in other countries: *The Arab Girls of Algiers, Lapp Girls, Japanese Girls*. In *Belgian Girls* (1884) we learn from Darley Dale:

Many Belgian families are unfortunately very much the reverse of well regulated; the *mauvais ménage*, as it is called, is more common than with us. Now a *mauvais ménage* means a household in which the husband and wife live apart, either from incompatibility of temper or for other causes, and it can easily be understood such a state of affairs can have only a bad effect on the children, so that if we find Belgian girls have very grave faults we must not forget that their home influence is often the very reverse of what it should be and happily generally is among our English girls.

However, Belgian girls "are generally very amiable, bright, good-tempered, cheerful and affectionate".

In *French Girls* in 1883, Anne Beale writes:

We could wish to see many changes in the manners and morals of French girls. We should like to see them reverence the Sunday, instead of keeping it as a *jour de fête*. They think us *triste*; we think them irreverent, because we would "Remember the Sabbath-day to keep it holy", while they dance, attend spectacles, and otherwise divert themselves, after their early Mass. Sunday in Paris, with its races, operas, cafés, work and worldliness, is, to the thoughtful mind, a melancholy sight.... Long may God preserve to us our English Sabbath!

However, she goes on to say:

The more we make excuses for one another (not for ourselves), and the less we pass judgment on our neighbours, whether native or foreign, the better.

Articles on travel are quite frequent. Two London Bachelors describe *Our Tour in North Italy* in 1886, and in the following year we have *The Bachelors in Central Italy*. The British tourist is dealt with severely in *A Holiday in Norway* (1888):

Many of the English one meets in Norway are a disgrace to their country, and have to be shunned by their more respectable compatriots. Having travelled in France, Germany, Switzerland and Italy, I had come to the conclusion that Britons abroad had been much maligned, and were as a rule by no means the egotistical, objectionable, and narrow-minded beings represented by our satirists of the last generation. But if when the Continent was more or less new to them, and when travelling was a little more arduous than now, they behaved in the manner that so many of the tourists one meets in Norway do, nothing that has been said of them is sufficiently severe.

Far left, above: The Supper Table, *illustrating a feature on entertaining, from* How I Keep House on £250 a Year. *The Author sends out fifty invitations; makes everything but the cakes and biscuits at home; hires a few extra chairs and one waitress to pour out tea and coffee (on the landing); and does it all for a cost of* £5 5s. 0d.

Far left, below: You Have Brought Me to Life Again, *a richly romantic presentation colour plate, published in the* G.O.A., *1890–1891.*

NOTICES OF NEW MUSIC.

NOVELLO AND CO.

The Syrens of the Sea. Song for soprano solo, female chorus, and orchestra. Music by Florian Pascal. — We heartily recommend this song, which is in reality a scena, as being one of the most graceful things of the kind that we have ever come across. The voice parts are simple, but the accompaniment, a digest of the orchestral score, naturally makes greater demands upon executive skill. However, the graceful arpeggios and passages, and the fairy-like modulations, fully merit the trouble and study required to reproduce their Melusine-like beauties.

Scènes Poétiques. By Benjamin Godard.—Best known to us as a French violinist and writer for his instrument, M. Godard is here introduced as a writer for full orchestra; for the charming *scènes* before us are transcriptions by George Pfeiffer, either as solos or duets for pianoforte, from the full score. Of the different numbers we prefer No. 1, "Dans les Bois." Good as the arrangements are, they are essentially orchestral, and therefore difficult as solos for piano. The other numbers, "Dans les Champs," "Sur la Montagne," and "Au Village," are published separately.

J. AND J. HOPKINSON.

Sylvan Echoes. Composed by Oliver King.—A book of duets for female voices is always a welcome publication nowadays, and these five duets will prove an interesting addition to the fast-increasing *répertoire.*

METZLER AND CO.

Christmas Album. — We specially call attention to the

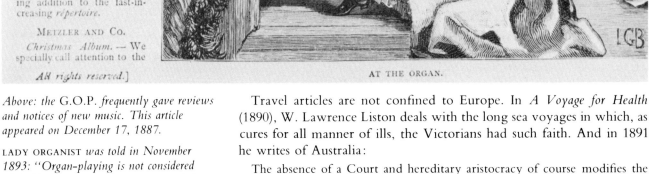

AT THE ORGAN.

Above: the G.O.P. frequently gave reviews and notices of new music. This article appeared on December 17, 1887.

LADY ORGANIST *was told in November 1893: "Organ-playing is not considered advisable for women. Strong, unmarried, middle-aged women may play the foot-keys without suffering from the unsuitable strain on the back and loins; but it is a risk if the instrument be a large one."*

Travel articles are not confined to Europe. In *A Voyage for Health* (1890), W. Lawrence Liston deals with the long sea voyages in which, as cures for all manner of ills, the Victorians had such faith. And in 1891 he writes of Australia:

The absence of a Court and hereditary aristocracy of course modifies the social conditions considerably, but I do not know but what, after the ridiculous exclusiveness and reserve of certain classes in England, it is not refreshing to come among a people speaking English, and with social independence.

In *A Summer Trip Across the Sea,* our old friend Medicus writes in 1889:

*Above: a charming picture of a Victorian
family at home (September, 1894).*

It has always seemed to me strange that so few health-seekers ever think of crossing the Atlantic from our country, seeing that so much pleasure and benefit may be derived from such a trip. American ladies come here by the score and by the hundred. Have they more sense than English girls? It would really seem so. They are assuredly more independent, both in thought and actions; precocious is perhaps the only adjective that will meet the requirements of the case, or, in more poetic language, let me say that a charming precocity pervades the nature of the true-born American girl. And this is true enough; a New York miss is out of leading strings long before a London or Glasgow lassie has given up wearing bibs. When in America last I met some very delightful children, but many of them were so wondrously wise for their years that I was really afraid to mention lollipops or dolls to them, for fear of giving offence; and the policy of the American Government on the Canadian fishery question several times suggested itself as a more appropriate theme for conversation, than the merits of the different brands of chocolate creams.

According to the author, the price of a return ticket on one of the best ships, including everything except wines, is thirty guineas. He continues:

Everything in America is on so extensive a scale as to astonish one. The word "free" is peculiarly applicable to the United States, for here the very soul has

OUR TOUR IN NORTH ITALY.

By TWO LONDON BACHELORS.

LECCO, LAKE COMO.

Above: an account to correct any romantic ideas of Italian travel—the Two London Bachelors find themselves in a dingy pensione, which turns their thoughts to tales of murder. After searching the bedroom floor for secret springs, they push the bed across the door and unstrap their umbrellas "which would have to do for want of more effective weapons" (May, 1887).

room to expand. External surroundings have really a great deal to do with the modelling of one's mind, and life in New York makes you feel just a little ashamed of the little cramped and crabbed village in Blankshire, where you live at home, with its shabby dwellings, its narrow-mindedness, and perhaps cant as well as hypocrisy. You won't forget your native land all the same, but you will wish the good folks at home could all travel for six months in America, then go back with enlarged minds and live happy ever after.

A rather different journey is the subject of a curious feature in 1885, which seems well worth a mention. It is entitled *Inside Passengers; or The Wonderful Adventures of Luke and Belinda*, and is designed to instruct in a most original fashion. Luke is a young surgeon and Belinda his fifteen-year-old sister, and by a set of improbable circumstances involving vanishing cakes they are reduced to microscopic size and swallowed by their uncle. Conveniently, Luke has on him some waterproofing powder, so that the moistness of Uncle's interior does not prove too great a problem, and equally conveniently, he has some "Hospital Full Diet Pills" with which he and Belinda may stay their own pangs of hunger while themselves being digested. The pills alone provide food for thought, each being equivalent to 12 ounces of bread, 8 ounces of potatoes, 6 ounces of roast beef and 1 pint of porter.★ (The author adds, "See Diet Table, London Hospital, 1882". Reference to the London Hospital, Whitechapel, in 1979, confirms that this robust fare was indeed the "Full Diet for Men" at the time when Luke and Belinda were travelling in the interior; women, however, received only 4 ounces of meat and half a pint of porter. In 1888 porter was replaced by milk unless otherwise ordered.) Belinda reminds her brother that as one who wears the Blue Ribbon of the Temperance Movement she is not permitted porter, but is assured that in pill form it is all right.

At the start of their journey through Uncle, the two find themselves in:

... a sort of little cave, formed wholly of ivory.... The roof was of pure and unmistakable gold. From Luke's position it could be seen that the cave was but a recess high up in the side of a cavern of such huge dimensions that its further wall was only dimly visible.... The whole roof, sides, and floor of the cavern consisted of a red material somewhat resembling granite, which was everywhere excessively moist, not to say extremely damp. The floor was in almost incessant tremulous motion.

They are, of course, in a gold-filled tooth in Uncle's mouth, and measurements are 100 yards to 1 inch (90 metres to 25 mm).

Some time later:

Luke gazed with awe at the altered aspect of his uncle's throat. The vast fleshy curtain dividing it from the mouth in front, raised by some unseen power, stretched horizontally just level with his head, reaching back to the posterior wall of the pharynx, and cutting off all communication with the nose above, and, indeed (but for being a little more raised on his side), with the eustachian tubes as well, while the whole of the cavity of the mouth, which he could now plainly see, together with the pharynx, was filled with a tossing, whirling stream of turbid water, that, reaching nearly up to his feet, was rushing and eddying like a maelstrom down the dark abyss at the rear.

This gruesome description in fact refers to Uncle drinking beer. One wonders with a slight shudder, during the progress of Luke and Belinda through Uncle's anatomy, just where and how it will all end. Perhaps fortunately they are restored to the outside world and full size before the digestive processes are more than half completed and Luke and Belinda decide that it has probably all been a dream.

Hobbies are frequently and more predictably the subject of features: knitting, crochet and embroidery (needlework was particularly prominent in the first year), painting, photography, wood-carving, fretwork,

---

★350 grammes of bread, 250 grammes of potatoes, 180 grammes of beef, ½ litre of beer.

Above: Girls at Hockey *appeared on December 20, 1890. "We are quite sure that hockey will grow in favour as a winter game for women."*

pigeon-keeping (*Doves' Down; or Pigeon Life*, 1889); poultry-keeping (*A Recreation and Source of Income for Girls*, 1888); bee-keeping (*A Girl's Own Apiary*, by Bee Orchis, 1890).

Sport is dealt with, too; skating is the subject of one of the earliest articles. Serious sportswomen may perhaps have been shocked by the somewhat frivolous account of *A Girls' Cricket Club* (1888), in which, armed with bats, the girls play a team of men wielding broomsticks. ("I know a good many people regard cricket as a most unladylike and improper game for girls to play at; but it has always seemed to me that if the girls behave quietly, and only have friends for spectators, there can be no serious objection. I would like further to explain that we knew all the gentlemen very well indeed.")

In a feature on golf (to be pronounced "goff") in 1890, readers are told that the "fair ones" were willing, "except in a few cases", to leave driving to the men, and confine themselves to putting. Black golf balls are, we learn, in use on courses where daisies abound, and red ones when there is snow about. *Girls at Hockey*, a few months later, sounds more energetic; even though a tennis or light cork ball is, according to the writer, customary for ladies' matches, there is still the risk of a blow on ankle or shin. Later in the same year, in *Some Types of Girlhood; or, Our Juvenile Spinsters* (1890) S. F. A. Caulfeild deals with a variety of "types", of which the Muscular is one:

Lawn tennis has become a "rage" with both sexes alike; amongst a minority even hockey has been annexed from the exclusive proprietorship of the stronger sex; and by others, the dangerous and most unfeminine sport of polo. Who knows but that football may not follow in due course? Some day in the future we may even blush to see, in a struggling, writhing heap of prostrate human forms, piled in confusion, one over the other, the soiled (once dainty) skirts of these muscular sisters of ours, and the long tangled locks in wild disarray, floating over the cropped heads of their masculine playmates. . . . I find no fault with fencing, nor even boxing, if not a public exhibition, nor engaged in with male companions. I once enjoyed the gloves, the foils, and single-stick myself, but only with my brother in the privacy of home.

In early issues the tricycle seems to be mentioned more frequently than the bicycle, but in *Our Girls A-Wheel* in 1896, an ecstatic article in praise of the "fascinating, health-giving, and educating" pastime of cycling, the two-wheeler is clearly favoured:

As our memory recalls vividly the antiquated, heavy three-wheeler, and compares it with the dainty, beautiful, and light two-wheeler of today's fashion, we are filled with respect and wonder concerning the grand old pioneers, who so bravely fought the way towards cycledom.

(These "grand old pioneers" were those of a mere twelve or fifteen years earlier.)

In the magazine's first year, *A Girls' Walking Tour* by Dora Hope appeared. The girls in question number six, the eldest of them being twenty-four, and one evening they are apparently sunk in sad reflections:

. . . mourning over the various pleasures that girls are debarred from, just because they are girls, and not men, who can do anything they choose without anybody being shocked or scandalised. We spoke of the delights of cricket, some sighed for football or paper-chasing, others acknowledged a hankering

DOVES' DOWN;
OR,
PIGEON LIFE.

By EMMA BREWER.

CHAPTER III.

THE CARRIER PIGEON.

"I felt like the messenger pigeon flying home."—*Jane Eyre*.

THE habits and manner of life of the dove appeal to us all. Everything about it is interesting—whether it be the beauty and purity of its plumage, the swiftness of its flight, its love of home, its gentleness, its travels, or its attachment and service to man; and yet we knew scarcely anything about this bird until old John Moore, the friend of Pope, published his "Columbarium" in 1735. It is a curious old book, and so rare that I think only one original copy exists, and that is at the British Museum; it is quite worth seeing. Since its publication, however, it has been the delight of many to seek for knowledge concerning the habits and varieties of the dove, and to dot down their experiences.

At what period man added the dove to his list of domestic feathered retainers is not accurately known, but it must have been at a very remote period. What we do know is that we English have to thank the Romans for teaching us how to build our dovecots.

In varieties outside the carrier pigeon, between whom and man an intimate relation has always existed, people did not formerly very much interest themselves; it is otherwise now; we have learned that each variety has its own interesting features and characteristics.

In former days it was a privilege of noble birth to keep a dovecot. In Provence, for example, in the time of Louis XIV., no one of inferior position could possess one. A seigneurial tree at the gateway, a weathercock on the chateau, and a dovecot, were each and all signs that a family was ancient and of high birth.

In Ispahan a dovecot is still looked on as a great privilege. There are at the present time above three thousand in that city, but they are the exclusive privilege of the natives; no Christian may possess one.

THE PRINCESS OF WALES FEEDING THE PIGEONS IN THE PIAZZA OF ST. MARK, VENICE.

after rowing or canoeing, which latter girls certainly cannot indulge in without being considered "fast", unless it be in private waters.

Inspired by the resolution of one of their number, they decide to make a tour together ("without a single gentleman or *chaperones* to interfere with us"). They agree to provide themselves with a kind of uniform:

Above a chapter from Doves' Down, *showing the Prince and Princess of Wales in the foreground.*

Supposing that you propose making your luncheon in the carriage, and that it consisted of cold chicken and ham, do not set aside the habits of civilised life, because you have to lay a napkin on your lap instead of a large cloth on a table. It is quite disgusting to any spectator to see how some travellers gnaw and tear their food, and grease their fingers, looking like so many ghouls! Divide the fowl before leaving, and prepare the meat in sandwiches. If unprovided with a folding knife and fork, hold the end of a joint with a piece of white paper, and use the pocket-knife in such a way as to keep the hands clean, laying small pieces of fowl upon neat little scraps of bread—as you eat cheese. Leave no greasy paper nor eggshells about the carriage nor crumbs on the seat. Why should you behave like a savage because you are on a journey?

It may be that you have to travel at night, and cannot afford the luxury of a sleeping-carriage, and moreover that your *compagnons de voyage* are not of your own sex only. In some former article I told you that etiquette absolutely forbids gentlemen and women to lie down in each other's society, with the sole exception of the exigencies of steamboat travelling or of a railroad journey by night. Of course, in cases of sickness, "Necessity has no law" in any place or at any time. Supposing that a gentleman occupies a seat in your carriage, you must observe a certain amount of formality and reserve in both word and action. You could not sit upright all night, but you and your friend should take your rest in turns. Lie with your face outwards and cover yourself with a rug, tucking it in well under your feet; then let your friend sit close against them and wake while you sleep; her turn can follow, and you can do the same for her in return. But by day nothing could be more unseemly, in persons of either sex, than to put up their feet along the seat in presence of each other, and on the part of a man it is a mark of great disrespect. It is quite as impertinent to perform any office of the toilet, such as cutting or cleaning the nails in presence of each other—a disgusting practice of which we are sometimes spectators.

Above: an extract from one of Sophia Caulfeild's articles on etiquette, the subject in this case being good breeding shown when travelling (November 17, 1883).

Right: sitting on the Hog's Back in Surrey, the girls of the walking tour party prepare their picnic luncheon of poached eggs, bread, marmalade and tea, with a slice of cake to come—but their president, terrified of cows, bestows the cake on a helpful drover instead (June 12, 1880).

Dresses of thin olive green serge, made quite short, and waterproofed to save carrying cloaks, quiet-looking hats of the same, and gloves to match, which, however, were generally discarded, except on occasions of ceremony; light, but strong, boots and, *of course* woollen stockings. One of the party who, fortunately for the rest of us, looked much older than her years, was set up with a cap and spectacles, and would have looked quite an imposing chaperone had one been needed; but, as it happened, in every hotel we had the coffee-room to ourselves.

Some readers might have felt it probable that any stray visitor, discovering six girls clad uniformly in olive green serge and one wearing cap and spectacles, would have beat a hasty retreat anyway.

The girls cover 96 miles, an average of 16 a day, which seems good enough going, and the total expenditure for the whole party during six days and five nights is £8 4s. 6d. (an average of £1 7s. 5d. each), which seems better going still.

Medicus turns up, under his own name of Gordon Stables, as the author of articles on pets—particularly on cats (*Our Mutual Friend, Puss; The Domestic Cat; Friends in Fur*):

I have proved over and over again that plump, well-fed and carefully tended cats are the best for killing mice. For the art of mousing requires great patience and that is a virtue in which a starved cat is singularly deficient.... Cats are very cleanly in their habits and natures. They are soon taught to behave themselves well indoors, but gentleness and firmness should be used towards them, and in no case do they deserve beating, nor even chasing out; treatment of this kind is certain to demoralise them, and cause them to hate instead of loving you. If your pussy has been absent from home all night, you should kindly welcome her return in the morning, and show your forgiveness by presenting her with a nice dish of warm milk sweetened with sugar.

Medicus also believes that a cat can be taught to shake hands, play dead, retrieve like a dog, jump through hoops, and move rhythmically to music—with some reservations, however:

Tabbies are par excellence the Englishman's cat. They are good-natured, brave and noble, fond of children, and very fond of their offspring.... I should never expect a white cat to do anything *very* clever.

"SUDDENLY THE PRESIDENT SCREAMED."

The Romance of the Bank of England, or, The Old Lady of Threadneedle Street by Emma Brewer runs through a number of issues in 1886–1887. A serious note is struck with Black and White Heroism: Stories from the Abolition Crusade by Ascott R. Hope (1890). Two Ways of Looking At It (1892), by A Middle-Aged Woman, is an amusing little piece consisting of two letters home written by twin sisters—fair, graceful Ethel and dark, merry Flora, both paying a long visit to London, to have music and drawing lessons, and "see the sights". Ethel remembers only that their journey to London was in a crowded and noisy railway carriage, while Flora's letter describes breaking the journey by an enjoyable visit to Canterbury; Ethel relates how whiffs from the stables and the cooking odours from a neighbouring boarding-house float through the window, Flora mentions musk, sweetpeas, and the hayfields at Hampstead; Ethel remarks that the illuminations at the Naval Exhibition were very pretty, Flora gives an ecstatic description.

In the Golden Jubilee year of 1887, Anne Beale wrote an article in the G.O.P. called What We Saw at the Children's Jubilee Fête. According to this, the Daily Telegraph and School Board marshalled thirty thousand children in Hyde Park. Each child received a jubilee medal and a paper bag containing a meat pie, a bun, a piece of cake, and an orange. Memorial mugs were distributed at four o'clock, disappointing some children by their lack of handles. When the Queen appeared, cheerful cries of "Don't she look pleasant!" and "Isn't she nice!" mingled with the loyal applause.

Articles on the Royal Family were as popular with Victorian readers as they are with those of today. The Girlhood of Queen Victoria, featured in the very first issue of the G.O.P., is followed throughout the period by frequent articles on some member or aspect of Royalty. The supplementary Summer Number of the Golden Jubilee year (1887), called Victoria's Laurel, is largely taken up with The Girl's Own Life of Queen Victoria, by James and Nanette Mason ("Her life is certainly a pattern for girls in every station.... The Queen's quiet and simple pleasures everyone can make her own").

Our Princess Alice (1884) reviews the life of the popular and exemplary Princess, Queen Victoria's second daughter, who had married Prince Louis of Hesse. With her little daughter May ("the sunshine of the home"), she had died of diphtheria in Darmstadt six years before. The article begins:

One of the characteristics of the age in which we live is the utter absence of mystery in the domestic life of Royal persons. The veil which separated kings and queens, princes and princesses from the people in former times has been gradually drawn aside; not by means of vulgar curiosity, but by the hand of Majesty herself.

There are quotes from the Princess's letters to the Queen, which had recently been published in a book:

What will young mothers think of a princess who writes, "I have made all the summer walking-dresses, seven in number, for the girls from beginning to end. I manage all the nursery accounts myself, for we must live very economically." Our princess soon made her mark in the country of her

> The etiquette to be observed in meeting an acquaintance requires the lady to bow first, as she has the right to look another way, and avoid meeting his eyes (if, for any motives of prudence, and to escape from unacceptable intrusion, she should prefer to ignore his presence, and avoid an interview). In this case, again, the above-named code of rules provides for a woman's defence. At the same time she must beware of appearing to "cut" any-one by allowing them to see that passing them without a bow of recognition was intentional. This would be an act of exceedingly bad taste, and actual rudeness.
>
> Should a stranger be walking with your gentleman friend, when you bow to the latter it is the duty of that stranger to raise his hat to you likewise, but while so doing he should look down, and not meet your eyes during that bow, because such a formal act of respect does not involve you in any acquaintance with him, nor should it lead you to think he means to intrude himself on any subsequent meeting, when no bow on either side should be made. Of course, however, at the time that your friend raises his hat, in acknowledgment of your recognition of him, you should extend your bow, and look towards his friend (if he raise his hat) in return for his salutation.
>
> A foreigner, and an English highly-bred man, will raise his hat on meeting a lady in a hall or passage, or in a narrow path, bringing him closer to her than otherwise he needed to be. This he does merely to set her at ease, and prove that she is in the company of a man who knows how to show her all due respect. But, as in the former case named—if a bow from a stranger—a gentleman should not look at the lady when so raising his hat; but there should be a marked gravity and reserve in his manner and his general bearing.

Above: another extract from an article by Sophia Caulfeild, Etiquette for All Classes (November 5, 1881). First, she firmly tells maid servants that "etiquette forbids any man presuming to introduce himself to you; that it is a gross act of impertinence, and shows that he thinks you of little account". Next, she turns to girls in more comfortable circumstances, and deals with the vexed questions of meeting and greeting. Every small point, from donning one's gloves to coping with the hat of a gentleman visitor, is dealt with in a calm and decided tone.

adoption. Societies for helping the sick and needy sprang into existence; hospitals were visited; education was fostered, and ladies who would never have dreamed of interesting themselves in labours for the poor were attracted and fascinated by our princess, who invited them to her afternoon coffee parties and drew them with loving, gentle words to join her in work.... Are not you English girls proud of such a woman having sprung from your midst?

The marriage of the Queen's youngest son to Princess Helena of Waldeck in the spring of 1882 was greeted by the *Girl's Own Paper* with a rose-framed portrait of the bride, wearing fresh flowers in her hair and a large plain cross as her only adornment. Mrs Linnaeus Banks wrote a poem of welcome (*For Leopold of England, Good Albert's noble son, Fair Helena of Waldeck, Has truly wooed and won*), and 26,000 maidens, including many readers of the *G.O.P.*, presented the bride with "The Maidens' Bible", bound in purple and crimson, with tastefully chased clasps.

Girls in the higher social reaches might hope to be presented at Court, making their formal curtsey and kissing the Queen's hand. In one *G.O.P.* feature, *How I Was Presented at Court* (1896), the author, signing herself La Petite, gives a detailed insight into the experience which readers of today may find as intriguing as those of the period surely did. "Of course," she says, "I had always known it would happen some day, and used to watch my mother go, and wonder how I should look in that sort of costume, but somehow I could never picture myself in a long train with plumes on my head." Unmarried girls wore two white plumes, and married women wore three; walking backwards with a long train was an alarming prospect ("You really hardly have to do this at all," an earlier article had said reassuringly, "it is a crab-like sideways movement you have to execute" [1880]). La Petite was taken off to the Court Dressmaker so that the style and material of her presentation dress might be chosen (the colour was always white).

My costume was to be a wonderful mixture of satin, crêpe-de-chine, tulle and lilies of the valley, and my mother's was heliotrope velvet and silk, yellow satin, orchids and big yellow marguerites, all of which was not arrived at without long and mature deliberation. After this Mamma, deciding (as all mothers do) that nothing was too good for her child, settled not to present me herself but to ask a titled lady of high rank (herself a contributor to our dear "G.O.P.") to perform this office, and, the request being made and granted, the next step was taken....

Our names had been submitted to the Lord Chamberlain in due form, and copies of the regulations were sent us, together with two pink cards on which my name and that of the lady presenting me must be written....

The Court curtsey had to be practised with the peculiar glide sideways which accompanies it, but I found it easier to master than might have been expected....

At length it came to a week before the important day, and we went for the final trying on of the costumes. This was literally the most trying of all, for every detail was attended to, plumes, veil, flowers and train, and I got thoroughly tired out. In fact presently I collapsed altogether in a little heap of white satin, and the dressers had to run for water and smelling salts while I was propped up on the floor and brought round!...

At length all was ready, and the only disappointment in connection with it was that the Queen was not going to hold the Drawing-Room in person. We did not know it for certain till the night before, but it made an important difference to me, as *débutantes* kiss hands if the Queen be present, but simply curtsey to any of the Princesses. I felt rather injured, I fear, and did think the Queen might

Far right: After The Presentation (*"from a sketch made at Buckingham Palace"*), *published in December, 1896.*

WALKING DRESS—*then.*

than we were, sitting, often cross-legged, I fear, in our dear window seat, with our dolls and our patchwork. We read our Rollin and our Chambaud too, mind you, and could do a rule-of-three sum with the best of you. But we were not above a game of hide-and-seek, or trap-bat and ball, or follow-my-leader. I am not talking of babies. We were children, you know, till we were fifteen; wore our pinafores and our arms and necks bare; and were slapped, too, soundly often, as I have said, till we were seventeen. And we were "girls" till twenty.

We had no croquet, no Badminton, no rinks, no GIRL'S OWN PAPER, no sewing machines, no female "colleges," no lady "professors." But we were very happy.

For one thing, when I was a girl, we saw more of our parents. Our fathers lived nearer their business; they could not run to and fro to London so easily. There was less visiting, more home life; so our mothers were with us more.

I fancy the presence of the cupboard tells a good deal. These were all over the house. They pervaded it. In every room they were to be found—book closets, china closets, store closets, china cupboards, corner cupboards. They had strong locks, and bright finger plates on the doors; and within, such stores of good things! Our mothers were not above looking to all domestic matters. You see shops were few and far between; every house had to provide its own supply to some extent. Housekeeping was a reality and a thing to study in those days.

I sometimes wonder whether the girls of to-day fare as wholesomely, on the productions of Messrs. Mixum and Pestum, as we did in my time, on the home-made stores of those dear old cupboards, whose very aroma seems again to fill the air, as it did when a certain jingle of keys announced to us that mother was at the store closet; and what a rush followed to get a glimpse into the mysteriously dim recesses and their hidden treasures!

When I was a girl caps were believed in. Not the pretty little knots of ribbon and lace which have lately come into fashion, but real structures, built up of net, blonde,

EVENING DRESS—*then.*

have made an effort when she knew I was coming, but I was consoled on hearing the Princess of Wales was to hold it, and decided to make the best of it.

She went to bed early and next morning was made ready for her *début*. At noon the carriage drew up outside, the coachman and footman wearing huge bouquets of yellow marguerites. A crowd began to gather. After a hurried lunch, the ladies put on their wraps, which were large soft shawls of finest muslin edged with lace—anything heavier would crush their finery—and emerged:

A crimson carpet was put down over the pavement and we walked out through what I fondly hoped was an admiring crowd and entered the carriage, our trains being arranged on our laps after we were seated and filling up all the available space. I was still waiting for what I supposed was the inevitable fit of nervousness, but I may as well say here that it never came, and I thoroughly enjoyed myself from beginning to end.

They drove to the palace and were taken to a side-room where the Queen's dressers arranged their veils. Some of the *débutantes* were already white and ill with nervousness.

When we were pronounced ready our trains were deftly folded lengthwise into three and laid over our left arms, so that we could carry them without injury or trouble, and we sailed up the grand staircase.... On we swept through many rooms all brocade, mirrors, and exotics, looking out on the gardens, till we came to one filled with rows of chairs, where we sat down and waited. A barrier divided it from the next room, guarded by an officer, a certain number being admitted at a time, and here we remained for half an hour....

One poor bride (presented on her marriage) was leaning up against the mantelpiece shivering in spite of the fire that was almost scorching her dress, and muttering at intervals to her husband, "How much longer will it be? Will it never be over?"...

A girl, nearly crying with fright, was almost incapacitated altogether by her mother who, to hide her own nervousness, kept whispering sharply, "You are stooping dreadfully. Do hold yourself up properly. Don't tread on my train whatever you do. Mind you remember what I said about your curtsey!" and so on till we sympathised heartily with the unlucky daughter whose misery was pitiful to behold.

At last her turn came. Two pages took the train which she had been holding over her arm all this while and spread it out behind her. It was longer than she was tall, and the shining, spotless folds were heavy as she drew them after her.

I stepped on solemnly and gave my second pink card ... to the Lord in Waiting, who called out in stentorian tones, "To be presented. Miss —— by Lady ——", and it seemed to me as if all London would hear him.

The next few minutes passed like a whirlwind. I found myself sinking mechanically to the floor while the sweet face of "our own Princess" flashed a smile back at me.... The Royalties were all standing side by side across the room and, facing them, stood a row of soldiers....

When Mamma joined me she comforted me by saying I had done very well, though I had made only six curtsies and ought to have made eleven, as there were five princesses and six princes present, but still very few people manage to curtsey to every individual royalty, so I did not mind...

I was so happy and enjoyed it all so much, only I could have wished it had lasted longer, it was so very soon over! Of one thing I am certain, namely, that however often I go I shall never forget How I was Presented at Court.

In pleasing contrast to La Petite's spontaneously youthful and vivid style is an article from an early issue, retrospective and nostalgic. Browsing today through this feature, *When I Was a Girl*, it is curious to think of those Ethels and Alices, in the full tide of their youth and modernity, dressed in the latest fashion, smiling affectionately over the quaint doings of *their* great-grandmamas.

When I was a girl [writes the anonymous author] we wore our frocks off our shoulders and our arms bare. How odd it would seem to the Beatrices, Mauds, Ethels and Louises of the present time, to adopt this style—in ordinary, you know, in the house, and all day long. "Keep your shoulder in your frock!" was the constant admonition; those unfortunate shoulders had such a habit of pushing off the top of the dress—low on one side, while the other would be unduly covered. More often than not the culpable shoulders would receive the chastisement.

Going on to the joys of turning out her mother's cupboards, finding the spencer and poke-bonnet Mama wore when *she* was young, she says:

The Mauds and the Ethels were not in vogue when I was a girl. Betty, Jane, Maria, Amelia, Harriet, Caroline, were the customary names bestowed at birth. Charlotte and Rose were favourites, Eliza by no means despised. Indeed, I should not be surprised if revolutions were to be effected in this direction ere long. We have really a surfeit of Victorias, Alices, and Ethels.

(The lists of successful *G.O.P.* competitors reinforce this remark. The popular Christian names of the period—Florence, Annie, Alice, Edith, Gertrude, Emily and Clara—all appear regularly.)

The anonymous writer gently concludes:

You see, dears, when I was a girl, a little of everything went a long way. We did not live so fast. Folks, old and young, were contented with smaller pleasures, and things which would seem to you all very small matters for rejoicing over were with us the ultimate of our desires.

WALKING DRESS—*now*.

you received one from some absent friend it cost you at least a shilling. Fancy that! having to pay a shilling to the postman every time you get a letter now!

Of course it followed that people did not write unless they had something worth saying. So when one did receive a letter one knew it meant real news, and we were eager in proportion. A letter then was composed of a large thick sheet of paper, written closely upon every one of its four pages, hardly room left for the address. We had no envelopes, the letter was sealed with red wax and a fine seal. We girls used to beg seals off the letters, and save them up, just as some of you save up used postage stamps nowadays.

Perhaps you would fancy, dear girls, that the days were slow, that time hung heavy on our hands. Indeed it never did. We had our own little interests, small you may think

EVENING DRESS.—*now*.

them, but they were nearer home, and **very** dear!

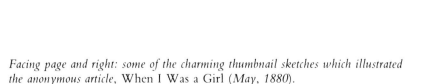

Facing page and right: some of the charming thumbnail sketches which illustrated the anonymous article, When I Was a Girl *(May, 1880).*

M. S. T.—1. To make a "corn dodger," pour boiling water on one quart of Indian meal till all be wet, but no water about it. Add two tablespoonfuls of flour and one teaspoonful of salt. Mix well and spread it smoothly on a plate or pan previously heated and oiled. Then set on the fire, and as soon as able pass a knife under the paste to turn it; and lastly, stand it up before the fire to toast. 2. "Imperial" is very easily made. Take of cream of tartar ½ oz., lemon peel ¾ oz., white sugar 4 oz., boiling water 3 pints. Mix all together, cover, and leave it to cool. It is a good beverage in cases of fever, or for ordinary use in hot weather.

LOTTIE.—"Frumenty," otherwise called "furmety" and "fromenty," is popular in other counties besides Lincolnshire. It consists of wheat boiled first in water and then in milk, with a little admixture of flour. Sugar and spice are added, and sometimes currants, raisins, eggs, and lemon peel.

JEMIMA.—To make lemon-kali, use of powdered white sugar ½ lb., tartaric acid and carbonate of soda of each ¼ lb., and 40 drops of essence of lemon. Add the latter to the sugar, and mix well. Then the other powder; and having dried it well, pass through a sieve, and keep in a closely-corked bottle. A teaspoonful will suffice for a small tumbler of water, until it concretes into small grains, like salt of tartar; and pearlash is of the same nature. Your writing is not at all well formed, and we should imagine that you have been more in the habit of writing in the German character.

KITTY.—Water and cream ices are of many kinds respectively, and one example of each must suffice. A strawberry water-ice is made thus: Pick 1 lb. of strawberries and 4 oz. of red currants; bruise all together, with a gill of syrup, in a basin with a wooden spoon, and rub the fruit through a hair sieve into another basin. Then add a pint of syrup, freeze, and set up. To make the same fruit into cream-ice, bruise a pound of them with 8 oz. of sifted white sugar, rub through a hair sieve, add the pulp to a pint of thick cream, freeze, and serve. To make currant and raspberry cream-ice, bruise ½ lb. of red currants and ¼ lb. of raspberries, with 10 oz. of sifted sugar; stir in a sugar boiler on the fire until it begins to simmer; then rub the fruit through the sieve, mix the pulp with a pint of cream, and freeze it.

Above: answers to readers' queries about cookery, September 11, 1880.

Chapter Seven

THE DOMESTIC ARTS

A poetical woman, who found the cords of Hymen not so silky as she expected, once gave vent to her feelings in the following touching stanzas.

> When I was young, I used to earn
> My living without trouble;
> Had clothes and pocket-money too,
> And hours of pleasure double.
>
> I never dreamed of such a fate,
> When I, a lass, was courted—
> Wife, mother, nurse, seamstress, cook, housekeeper,
> chambermaid, laundress, dairywoman, and scrub
> generally, doing the work of six
> For the sake of being supported.

After Marriage
(1889)

The early issues of the *Girl's Own Paper* contain more articles on housekeeping, cookery and other domestic subjects than might have been expected of a magazine designed primarily for girls in their teens. The first number started the feature *Our Cookery Class* with an article on roasting—an extract from which reminds one of the complications of Victorian cookery:

A good cook is very particular about her fire. She first pokes it well underneath, to clear it thoroughly from the dust and small cinders which will have settled at the bottom, pushing the live coals to the front of the range. She then puts fresh coal on the fire, choosing for her purpose not large blocks of coal, but what are called "nubbly" pieces. She does not throw these on from a scuttle, but arranges them with her fingers, protected by an old glove, so that they shall be packed closely, yet leaving room for a draught of air to pass between the lumps. She then sweeps up the hearth, collects the cinders, and places them with some coke or damped coal-dust at the back of the fire. A fire made like this will last a long time. As soon as the front part is clear and bright it is ready for the meal.

This is followed by *Gravy for Joints*, which ends with the statement:

It is very safe to conclude that where meat is served regularly with good brown bright gravy, perfectly free from fat, some one in the house knows something of cookery.

Articles on boiling, baking, the frying-pan and the gridiron follow at intervals.

Recipes appear regularly; also useful features such as *How to Make the Most of Cold Meat* or *Economical and Wholesome Dishes Made Without Meat.*

In 1887–1888 Mary Pocock produced a series of articles entitled *When Going to Market.* This opens with "The Butcher's—How to Distinguish Joints, and Advice on Purchasing", with diagrams showing how an ox and a calf would be cut up for the London market. A list of prices is included, to give an idea of the relative value of the different joints. The author says, "I am aware that the prices are lower than many butchers', but they are cash prices (no booking or calling for orders), as I invariably go to the butcher's and pay for what I order." Among the prices are:

Above: from Phillis Browne's article on cookery for the poor (December 2, 1882), with cheap and nourishing recipes: ox-cheek stew, cow-heel, pig's fry, stewed giblets, scrag of mutton, toad-in-the-hole, and similar dishes.

Beef, sirloin		11d. per pound [450 grammes]
Steaks, rump	1s.	2d.
Flank, prime		9d.
Gravy beef (neck or leg)		7d.
Silverside		$8\frac{1}{2}$d.

The second article deals with mutton, lamb and pork; 11d. per pound is given as a likely price for legs of mutton and 9d. per pound for the best end of necks. Later articles deal with buying fish, poultry, groceries and so on.

Over a number of years Dora Hope produced several "serial stories" designed to instruct readers in the domestic arts. A very early one, in 1880, is *The Difficulties of a Young Housekeeper and How She Overcame Them*. The heroine, Margaret, is the younger of two motherless sisters who finds herself obliged to take over the role of housekeeper for her father and brothers when the elder sister, Joanna, leaves the home to get married. Dismayed and nervous at first, she learns to manage through trial and error, and with occasional timely advice from Joanna. At the end of a year, and the end of the serial, she has found her confidence—and competence. "A year's experience had taught her so much."

Graduates in Housekeeping and How They Qualified (1883) opens with the aristocratic and impoverished St Adrian girls sitting at a meagre breakfast with their papa and receiving a letter from their Aunt Gwendolyn, offering the elder daughter, Narcissa, a post in her school:

I have waited till Narcissa's twenty-first birthday, as I thought, when she became a woman, she might possibly see the folly and sin of the worse than idle life she is leading, and might strike out some line of usefulness for herself. But this is hardly to be expected of a girl who has been brought up as you, brother Adrian, have brought up yours, teaching them that because they bear an aristocratic name, they must look upon industry as vulgar, and because they come of a good old family, must prefer penury to earning a competency by honest work.

However, the girls feel the sting of poverty sufficiently for Narcissa to persuade her father to let her go to work at her aunt's school. The Headmistress, Miss Gwen, says bracingly:

I like girls as a class, I love them with their kind young hearts and generous impulses; but as a rule they are born without *gumption*, my dear.

She aims to teach them gumption by plenty of practical education:

All the girls learn how to dust a room and make a bed; to cut out, make, and mend their clothes; and those above fourteen years old learn how to arrange, cook, and serve a dinner; to keep accounts, to black a grate and light a fire.

A similar story, in 1887–1888, is *The Brothers' Benefactor*. This begins with Eleanor Lawrence "going home for good" from her boarding-school, and as she is the only girl among five boys she anticipates plenty to do. The first paragraphs include the puzzling sentence, "Her father and mother had been millionaires in India", shortly followed by the statement that "the education of five sons, and other heavy expenses, made it needful to live very economically, at least for a time". (Was a millionaire in India different from the usual kind?) Eleanor is not entirely delighted by the prospect before her, preferring "Greek to making shirts, and mathematics to mending socks":

However, her own likes and dislikes must be put aside in the new life, and with a sigh for herself and a hearty little prayer for help, Eleanor resolved to be a model sister and daughter, and to exert the best influence over her brothers.

Eleanor begins her career as a model sister by a long and grim-sounding

Far right: an illustration to a poem by Isabella Fyvie Mayo, printed in December, 1883. A tender-hearted girl brings Christmas gifts to a blind cottager:

*"To homely boons of food and fire
She adds the dainties and the flower."*

session of cleaning and mending her brothers' clothes. That done, she turns her attention to making neckties:

With the unsparing candour of brothers, Mark told her that it would be much cheaper and better to buy the ties if they only lived near decent shops; though really for a girl her work was very good, and he should not at all object to wearing her handiwork. This was meant for high praise; but, as Nell remarked to her mother, "Brothers' compliments take some time to penetrate" ...

Nell's work for her brothers did not consist only in mending their garments, making them dressing-gowns, or doctoring chilblains. She soon found there were other things to be done and difficulties to be met. Among a group of five boys who had grown up almost strangers to each other, and had not enjoyed the softening influences of home, there were sure to be many rubs and jars. . . . On the whole the six agreed very well together, but still there were sometimes cross-tempers to be smoothed and impending quarrels to be averted; Roger's over-particular and critical spirit to be remembered and soothed; Will and George to be trained out of their rough, rude manners and boisterous practical jokes; Frank to be coaxed out of his sullen moods and protected from the young ones' mischief; and last, but not least, Mark to be thought and planned for, to be made happy and content at home, and to be kept in remembrance of that home when at college.

Although these stories impart information pleasantly, Dora Hope's *She Couldn't Boil a Potato—The Ignorant Housekeeper and How She Acquired Knowledge* (1886–1887) is much more fun to read. "She" is a young girl called Ella, who is sent to take charge of her sick aunt's household—not such a terrifying task, perhaps, since the aunt has two servants and a trained nurse, but alarming enough for inexperienced Ella, who wails:

"I am sure I shall never manage. Why, I can't cook, and I can't keep accounts, and I have no idea how many pounds of meat people want for dinner. I shall order a tin of Australian meat, and just have it at every meal till it is finished, and then get another."

Dora Hope manages to fit in instruction even before Ella leaves home for her aunt's house: a suitable dressing-gown for a sick-room, the right way to strap up rugs for a journey, and a packed lunch to eat in the train, are dealt with in the first chapter. Once there, we learn with Ella how to make nourishing light dishes, lay fires, feed the fowls, and even how to give a tactful Christmas present to maiden ladies "as proud as princesses and as poor as church mice".

More dramatically, one evening Ella finds Annie, the housemaid, rushing about the room with her dress in flames and shrieking wildly for someone to save her, while the cook is crouched in a corner with her apron over her head. Luckily for Annie, the nurse appears in time and is more successful than Ella in extinguishing the flames; another useful lesson being learned. However, the escape from burning does not sober Annie, who is discovered not long afterwards having a beano late at night in the dining-room with the cook, two men friends, and the contents of the cellaret.

Housemaid and cook are sent packing next morning, and Ella has the task of engaging new servants. Rather interestingly, one promising applicant's former mistress informs Ella that, though honest, sober and competent, the girl is disobliging and pert, but Ella is so struck by the lady's

Far left: Christmas in the West Indies, *the colour plate for December, 1898, taken from a painting by Helena Maguire.*

much reason to wish their method had been different.

When the picnic basket was opened on the day of which we are thinking, the first thing to be seen was a white damask tablecloth, neatly folded to cover everything. This was spread on the grass, and a stone was put at each corner to keep it in its place. The cloth spread, knives, forks, spoons, tumblers, and plates were soon taken out and set in order. These trifles made a goodly show when laid on the grass, but the basket did not look appreciably different because they had been removed. On further investigation it was found that the following articles had found a place within it.

The eatables consisted of a beefsteak pie, large enough for four persons to have one wedge each, but no larger; a fine lobster, the shell of which had been thoroughly cracked though the meat had been left inside; a galantine of chicken, which was placed in a jar with a lid; a cos lettuce, which had been trimmed of the outer leaves, cleansed, made quite dry, and torn into pieces (the lettuce was wrapped in a napkin); six small rolls of bread; a little delicately stewed fruit, which had been put into a wide-mouthed French plum bottle with a screw lid; a pint mould, containing a somewhat stiff apricot cream; three tiny packets of twisted white paper, one of which contained salt, another pepper, and another sugar; three small bottles, one full of salad oil, another full of French vinegar, and another containing mustard; a white china jar with small balls of butter, and a tiny branch of parsley; three tea-cakes, and a small tin, which everyone supposed was Swiss milk, but which proved to be a shilling tin of cream. The cream had been ordered by Mabel from a Dairy Company, and it had reached her by post an hour before starting. This cream was a great

success. It was thick, sweet, and good; in quantity it was sufficient for the needs of the whole party, and it was a great addition to the stewed fruit brought in the French plum bottle.

In a separate hamper were a large jug of cold water, four champagne bottles, and a kettle; also a small box in which were packed cups and saucers and other requirements for afternoon tea. There was a mysterious little case, too, which was put on one side and left unnoticed: it was not wanted for the luncheon. The sight of the kettle did not appear to be altogether delightful to the young men of the party. "You have brought a kettle?" one of them said. "I thought that the last time we had a picnic we decided that even a cup of tea was scarcely worth the trouble of collecting sticks and lighting a fire." This remark the girls appeared not to hear; at any rate they did not reply to it.

It is not at all improbable that at this stage two readers of this paper, judging it from opposite standpoints, may feel disposed to criticise our picnic provision rather unfavourably. The first critic will say, "Were all these provisions intended for four people only? What profusion! What extravagance! Surely here would be enough food for a crowd!" The second critic would remark, "Was a luncheon like this pronounced 'the finest lunch on record'? I should call it a most commonplace affair! The food was homely to a degree!" To the first critic I would reply, "I should be very sorry for you, my friend, if you had to make a meal off what was left when these four hungry, hearty young people had finished." To the second, "If during the course of your life you are never called on to sit down to a meal inferior to the one here described, you will not do badly.

Our poor sisters and brothers would think themselves in luxury if they had food one-tenth as good."

The critics may say what they like, however; our young folks were satisfied. They enjoyed their lunch, and considered it a triumph of skill and good management. After an argument which lasted a minute or two, they were contented even with the contents of the champagne bottles, and declared that after this experience they should never care to have anything stronger than they had this day, because the lemonade was so refreshing, and the ginger beer was so superior. For it must not be supposed that the champagne bottles contained champagne. Nothing of the kind. One of them was filled with delicious lemonade, made not of citric acid, but of plenty of real lemon-juice, sugar, and water; one was filled with lime-juice and water; and the remaining two with brisk, sharp ginger beer, made by Barbara herself. The explanation of this surprise was that these two young friends of ours, Mabel and Barbara, had taken the subject of champagne and claret cup into their serious consideration. They had noticed, even in their young lives, that some of the cleverest and most agreeable of their friends were not quite so agreeable nor quite so respectful after they had had one or two glasses to quench their thirst; therefore they resolved that they would do what two young girls could to remove danger out of the path of all with whom they were acquainted. They promised one another that never would they say a word to induce anyone to take what might be harmless, but which might be worse than poison. I think they did right. It is probable that at no period of their lives have girls greater influence than just as they are approaching womanhood. If at this period they would do

"OPENING THE PICNIC BASKET."

disagreeable manner that she decides she probably asked for it, and gives Sarah a trial. The author then gives some guide-lines as to what may reasonably be expected of a servant, mentioning that Ella's aunt "had a very great objection to clandestine 'followers' but saw no reason why servants should not be as openly engaged to be married as their young mistresses":

As soon as she found that the new maid, Sarah, had a "young man", whom she ascertained to be a thoroughly respectable young mechanic, she told her she might invite him to the house once a fortnight, and to begin with, he might come to tea and go to church with her the following Sunday, but she must invariably come straight home after church.

Life below stairs is full of perils in this household. Sarah is bitten by a dog and both she and Ella are terrified of hydrophobia, but the doctor scorns their fears and strongly advises against having the animal killed, since he cannot possibly say whether it had rabies or was only out of sorts. Mercifully, the latter proves true.

Eventually, happier and wiser, Ella returns home, and says to her mother:

"I hardly feel like the same person that I was a year ago. I never shall forget how unhappy I felt when I heard the servants saying with such scorn what an ignorant housekeeper I was—that I couldn't even boil a potato."

A little article which also appears in 1886 is *Dinners for Two*, probably designed for the bride. It gives twenty-four dinners, with recipes for many of them. The first seven are as follows:

1. Mulligatawny soup
   Fillet steak with mushroom ketchup
   Baked batter pudding

2. Flounders water souchet
   Piece of best end neck of mutton roasted
   Steamed semolina pudding, lemon sauce

3. Potato soup
   Steak and kidney pudding
   Apples stewed in syrup

4. Filleted plaice (dressed white)
   Veal cutlets, bacon and baked tomatoes
   Cheese fondue

5. Lobster salad
   Stewed breast of mutton
   Cake fritters

6. Brown onion soup
   Roast fillet of beef
   Spanish rice

7. Slices of cod fried
   Toad-in-the-hole
   Melbourne pudding

Anyone who assumes that all Victorian meals were on the "take a dozen eggs" scale may be surprised at the comparative economy of these menus, although fish appears regularly as a first course.

HOUSEKEEPING.

ANXIOUS LITTLE MARTHA.—You do not give enough particulars of what you have to do with your £83 income. Are clothes included, or, as your father owns the homestead, is it only to be expended in food, light, and heat? The expenditure of £1 a week for four persons for that would be much as follows: Meat, 6s. 6d.; grocer, 5s. 6d.; baker, 3s. 6d.; vegetables, 1s. 6d.; coals, and wood, and light, 2s. 3d.; milk, 1s. If you could bake at home, the bread is cheaper and better; and if you have a garden you should not have to buy vegetables. As you are so young, we should certainly advise you to have a charwoman in once a week to help; she should do the washing and all the heavy cleaning and scrubbing. The new American way of washing would save you much labour. The way employed is as follows: Fill an ordinary sized copper half full of water, put in half a pound of soap, and add one and a half tablespoonfuls of paraffin; heat till the soap be dissolved, then put in, without steeping, the linen of the ordinary wash. Boil well for half an hour, then lift out and rinse through one or two clean waters, as the case may be, and the washing is done. Flannel and coloured things cannot be washed in this manner. The clothes are kept a better colour washed in this way, and all odour of the paraffin disappears when they are dry.

AVERN.—We thank you for your contributions to the Girls' Convalescent Home, and your recipe for home-made wine. We give it hereunder:—Parsnip wine.—Add 3 lb. of parsnips (well washed and thinly peeled) to every gallon of water; cross the parsnips, and boil till quite tender. Then remove from the furnace and strain them through a hair sieve; and to every gallon put 3 lb. of lump sugar. Boil it again for three-quarters of an hour, then put in a tub, and when about milk-warm work it with barm, spread on a piece of toasted bread; stir several times a day during four days, and then pour it into a barrel. A little brandy should be put into the barrel before the wine is poured in, to make it keep, and the fermentation should have stopped before it is "stopped down." Let it remain in the barrel during one year, and then bottle it for use. The best season for making this wine is during March and April.

DAWKINS.—Lemonade for a number of people may be made as follows: To five gallons of water add one quart of lemon juice, one pint of grated or tinned pineapple, four oranges and four lemons sliced; add sugar to your taste.

MARY.—It may be necessary for you to send the feather bed and pillows to be baked, so as to destroy the moth. In fact, if you attempted to clean them out yourself you would fill the house with them the more rapidly. They deposit their eggs in May and June. Brush all woollens very carefully.

A MOTHER.—(1.) We very much doubt whether you could go through the process of re-lacquering at home. Try cleaning the brass with a little cream of tartar. An old recipe for re-lacquering is—1 oz. turmeric, 2 drachms annotto, 2 drachms saffron, and 1 pint of alcohol. Shake for a week, occasionally; filter into a clean bottle through a piece of clean blotting-paper, and then add to the mixture 3 oz. of clean shellac, and shake up the bottle occasionally during a fortnight. Apply with a soft brush, having warmed the brass articles first. (2.) To clean marble and slate, make a thin paste of whiting, soda, and pipeclay, rub it on and leave it to dry. Then rub off and polish with a little oil.

LIZ and GREEN HAG; TOOTSIE and OTHERS.—The white marks are made by the hot dishes and plates that have been placed on the tables and trays. Take 2 oz. of tripoli (powdered), put into a basin with just enough water to cover it, then take a piece of white flannel wet with the tripoli and water, and rub the tables and trays gently. Clean off with a little oil.

Above: some of the answers to housekeeping queries, given on August 11, 1888.

Far left: Rosemary, the Summer extra for 1889, includes an article by Phillis Browne describing a picnic lunch for four. Mabel and Barbara, practical, sensible girls, even include an oil stove for making tea. "The finest lunch on record!" is the verdict.

MY WORK BASKET
A PRETTY AND EASILY-MADE PEN WIPER.

CUT a piece of black or any coloured cloth in the shape of a small tea-pot cosey; turn in the edges and hem them without taking the stitches through to the right side; then either braid it with very narrow gold-coloured silk braid, or work it in chain stitch with netting silk. Sew the two sides together, and neatly hide the seam with the narrow braid, making a little double loop at the top to hold it by. Make a thick tassel of wool, or narrow strips of black cloth, and fasten it inside the cosey at the top; this should fill it up without showing below the bottom. This forms a very excellent wiper for the pen, and is an ornamental addition to the writing table.

BED POCKET.

A very novel and inexpensive bed pocket may be made of coloured sateen to match the bed furniture. Cut the shape, which is composed of four pieces of stiff cardboard; cut the sateen to cover the fronts of the pocket much larger than the actual size, and fasten it down in small puffs all over the cardboard, turning the edges over to the back, which is to be covered plain with the sateen; then neatly join the pieces together with a twisted cord or narrow quilling of ribbon. The inner pocket may be divided to hold the watch and small book or letters. A long double strip of sateen is attached to the back, by which it is suspended to the bed.

SOFT BOOTS FOR DRESSING-ROOM.

The slipper is made of soft kid or merino, and the upper part of silk the colour of the kid.

Above: one of the handicraft features from My Work-Basket *(February 14, 1880).*

Far right: a narrative poem by L. G. Gardiner, illustrated by Marian Gardiner (October 10, 1885).

To open 1887 comes *The Bride's First Dinner Party*. Mabel, with one young maid, wants to entertain six guests for £1. After discussing with a more experienced hostess whether the entertainment should be high tea or dinner, and comparing the costs, Mabel decides on the following menu:

Potato Soup

Tomatoes Farcies

Rolled Loin of Mutton and Sour Plums

Mashed Potatoes, with Brown Potatoes round

Stewed Celery

Ready-made Pudding; Orange Jelly

Macaroni Cheese

Dessert

Coffee

This, for eight people, costs 16s. 4d. (about 82p.), a sum which surprises even Mabel by its cheapness. Ready-made pudding, incidentally, turns out to be a dish made with flour, sugar, milk, eggs, sherry, and nutmeg, which sounds rather pleasant, as do the sour plums.

Some years later, in 1891, we have *Madge Vaughan's First Dinner Party*. Madge has two servants to Mabel's one, although the younger is only fourteen. Her menu is somewhat grander, and we are not told the cost:

Julienne; Mock-turtle soup

Cod and oyster sauce; Filleted herrings; Dutch sauce

Herrings' roe and mushrooms on toast

Madras curry

Boiled leg of mutton and caper sauce; Roast chicken

Orange jelly; Raspberry cream; Pineapple trifle

Cheese straws; Olives on toast; Dessert

I pondered over "Dutch sauce" until I realised it was simply anglicised *Sauce Hollandaise*. Both Mabel and Madge serve orange jelly, but Mabel makes her own from gelatine, while Madge's is a Clarnico jelly. Mabel's guests presumably drink water; Madge's are served "a very pleasant 'Hochheimer', purchased from a well-known firm at a shilling a bottle", and "a sound claret at 1s. 9d. which would not be ruinously extravagant. The after-dinner wines were to be a delicate claret at 3s. 6d. a bottle, and port at 5s."

The domestic arts are represented not only by cookery. Needlework is not forgotten. In 1880 there are articles on the basic principles of plain needlework, and one on "Swiss darning", claimed as being not only imperceptible, but so smooth that it cannot be felt by the most delicate touch. *My Work-Basket* appears from time to time—in 1880, for instance, girls are told how to make a lace antimacassar, a gentleman's cravat, and a case for visiting-cards. In 1890, examples are a child's jacket in crochet, an embroidered umbrella case for travelling, and embroidery in white cotton for house linen, underclothing, etc.

LEAVING HOME.

To her first place poor Jenny goes,
Wondering what life may now disclose
Of sharp or sweet, of good or ill,
Mid faces strange, hearts stranger still.

She "like a woman" heard it said
She must go forth for daily bread;
Even heard it with some pride,
And strove all doubts and fears to hide.

She'd learn, aye, all that could be learned,
Send home to mother all she earned.
Bright hopes, thank heaven! give rainbow gleams
Even to poor plain Jenny's dreams.

So bustling talk and cheerful face
Bade brave good-bye; she'd not disgrace
Her fifteen years with sigh or tear,
Though leaving all to her most dear.

But the train moves, and now, alack!
The child's heart yearns. Would she were back!
The lessening view and farms upstart
Bigger to her—they fill her heart.

She "has her feelings." Who has not?
And tearful eyes strain for the cot
Where rough but happy youth was spent,
And nights were calm and days swift went.

Oh, "missuses," if Jennys come
Across the threshold of your home,
Adrift from theirs, give kindest heed
To ignorant faults, to ignorant need.

You have the 'vantage ground; you stand
'Twixt toiling Marthas and the Hand
That beckons nearer angel wings,
To raise you both to higher things.

L. G.

Above: an illustration from The Drawing Room *by Mme de Lorraine (March, 1881). Mabel and Nora plan to give the drawing-room of the new vicarage "refined and home-like charm", staining the floors themselves, enamelling the walls, and doing the upholstery.*

Articles on household decoration appear occasionally, such as *How to Decorate a Girl's Sitting-Room* (1887). Even in the eighteen-eighties some girls apparently attempted to hang wallpaper and paint woodwork.

Mistresses and Maids (1888) contains sensible advice, but "Be very kind but very strict, and never let them gain the upper hand. Remember they are merely grown-up children, and treat them accordingly" must surely have caused some wry faces among the domestic servants in the *G.O.P.*'s readership. One is pleased to read, however, Medicus's comment in

"TURNING THE COVER WELL UP."

"HE PUTS HIS GLASS ON IT."

another issue, that it is the duty of the mistress to behave towards her maid "as if she really were a sentient and sensitive human being". Another sympathetic view is expressed in *A Novel Holiday* (1888), where four girls spend a holiday in a cottage without servants, to the great amusement of their friends and relations. They decide they will play cook, kitchenmaid, and two housemaids, turn and turn about. (The kitchenmaid's place soon proves to be much the hardest.) The author writes:

For those who are inclined to criticise the work of their subordinates without understanding its difficulties, I would strongly recommend a holiday week of this kind, which I can promise them will prove enjoyable and instructive, for we all felt that we came away wiser though certainly not sadder women.

Laundry is not neglected in these pages. In 1885 ALICE is told:

Washing at home is, of course, the cheapest plan; and, in addition, you have the comfort of not being stinted. For a small family of two or three persons, you should wash every fortnight or three weeks, having a washerwoman in. She would probably take two days only if your servants did the folding and hanging out and helped in the ironing. 2s. and 2s. 6d. is paid by the day, the latter for ironing. A washing-machine and a wringer simplify matters, and save in soap and time. About a bar of good old soap, four pennyworth of soda, and a quarter of a pound of starch would be enough. The clothes should be put in soak overnight.

Above: two of the illustrations from How To Wait at Table *(April 30, 1887). The parlour maid helps the guests to seat themselves ("It is otherwise very awkward for a lady with a great deal of skirt to get a heavy dining-room chair up to the table"), waits while Grace is said, and after serving soup or fish, takes the joint to the carver, turning the cover well up to catch any condensation drips. On the right, she is serving a guest with draught ale. He places his glass on the silver salver and she fills it from the jug.*

Examples of the Victorian washing-machine may be seen at the Science Museum in London. To use one of the lever-operated washing-machines and mangles, made in about 1880, the washerwoman placed the clothes in a wooden box filled with hot water, and pulled a lever which rotated a roller, fitted with smooth wooden perforated blades, thus agitating the clothes. Morton's Patent Steam Washing-Machine, made in 1884, incorporated a gas stand. The clothes were placed in a metal drum, water was poured into the boiler, the lid was put on, and the gas jets were lit. When the water was hot, the handle was turned so that the clothes tossed about inside the drum. A similar machine, Howarth's Patent Steam Washer, was advertised in the late eighteen-eighties for £6 10s.

Dryers also existed, called hydro-extractors; one is described in *The Art of Washing* by Dora de Blaquière in 1892:

This is a round basin-like kind of machine, having an inner openwork cage, in which the linen is placed. The machine is then set in motion, and the cage flies round and round, whereby the air is forced through the wet linen, while the water is forced out; with the result, that the drying is more than half accomplished when the clothes go into the hot closet. This is not, however, very generally available in private houses and amongst people with small incomes; and it is not to be expected that they will have more than a wringing-machine, or perhaps a washer and wringer combined.

Dora de Blaquière recommends a washing-day every couple of weeks:

The day before the washing it is also advisable to make some arrangements about the dinner on that day. Have a small roast of beef, which can be eaten cold, with pickles; and if you have mashed potatoes, they can be put into a greased bowl and baked until they are of a nice light-brown colour all over.

The sweet course can also be arranged for by having some stewed fruit—apples or pears in winter, rhubarb in the spring and summer, and any summer dainty that is in season. This, with a mould of rice or cornflour, can be prepared the previous day. By the time of late dinner your maid will have finished her washing, and will be dressed and tidy, and ready to lay the table, if you have not already partly laid it yourself.

One might perhaps not have expected a magazine designed for girls in their teens to carry articles on mothercraft, but the *Girl's Own Paper* did. In 1896 Lina Orman Cooper contributed a series called *Queen Baby and Her Wants*. Mothercraft writers of our own time tend to describe a baby as "he", probably because it provides a conveniently distinct pronoun, and it is interesting to notice that this eighteen-nineties infant is not "King Baby"; interesting, too, is "One diet table for Queen Baby when she had completed her first year":

7.30 a.m.	A slice of stale bread with a breakfast-cupful of new milk.
11.00 a.m.	A cup of bread and milk.
12.30 p.m.	One egg beaten up and baked into a custard with a cupful of milk. A couple of rusks.
4.00 p.m.	Arrowroot biscuit and milk.
7.00 p.m.	A breakfast-cupful of prepared food—Neave's or Benger's.

Of course changes should be rung on the above table.

But no mention of meat, fish, vegetables, or fruit.

Lina Orman Cooper follows this series with another, *The King's Daughters: Their Culture and Care* (1897), dealing with the upbringing of "Queen Baby" after she has reached childhood and girlhood.

There are nine things at least wanted to keep the bodies of the King's daughters in health: (1) Plenty of air, (2) Plenty of light, (3) Plenty of sleep, (4) Plenty of warmth, (5) Plenty of food, (6) Plenty of exercise, (7) Plenty of work, (8) Plenty of play, (9) Plenty of Love.

The harshness of the Victorian parent is a subject the popularity of which shows no sign of decreasing (and I sometimes feel the term "Victorian" is used today to cover everything between the accession of

Below and overleaf: That Luncheon, *a characteristic blend of domestic advice and easy narrative, which appeared on April 1, 1899.*

"THAT LUNCHEON!"

A YOUNG HOUSEKEEPER'S DILEMMA.

"NELLIE dear," said Mr. Vernon, the principal solicitor in Riversmouth, to his nineteen year old daughter and housekeeper, " I have just run across to tell you that young Squire Laurence is riding over to consult me this morning, and I should like to bring him in to lunch at half-past one. Can you manage it ? "

For a moment dismay ran riot in pretty Nellie's heart. Nearly ten o'clock already, nothing to speak of in the house, and a smart luncheon to provide, as well as the schoolboys' early dinner! However, she must do her best, and answered cheerfully to that effect.

" It need not be grand, you know," added her father encouragingly, "so long as every-thing is nice and tasteful, as you so well understand how to make it."

Nellie had been on her way to practise, but she now returned to the kitchen, and, resuming her big apron, surveyed the larder for the second time that morning. Ten minutes earlier, yesterday's underdone leg of mutton re-roasted, with some vegetables, and the remains of yesterday's pudding, with the addition of a homely roly-poly, had been deemed sufficient for the one o'clock meal, and as Mr. Vernon was dining out that evening, the butcher had been dismissed without orders. Economy was a stern necessity to Nellie, whose house-keeping allowance was not unlimited.

Accustomed to making " something out of

nothing," the cold remnants did not look as hopeless to her as they might to some young housekeepers. A cold whiting, the badly-roasted mutton, and a bowl containing about half a pint of tomato sauce, represented absolute riches to Nellie's mind at that moment, and she quickly collected her materials and set to work in the kitchen.

The menu she drew up was as follows :—

Fish Scallops.
Cold Salt Beef. Cannelon and Tomato Sauce.
Potato Chips. Salad.
Hot Apple Tart. Lemon Creams.
Custards.
Cheese. Biscuits.

The maid was despatched with orders for

the milkman and greengrocer, and a basket in which to bring back a pound of cold salt beef in slices from the pastrycook's, half-a-dozen scallop-shells, and two lemons.

In the meantime Nellie began the creams, which she knew must have plenty of time to cool, and for this reason decided to make them in cups. There was only a quart of milk in the house; a pint of it she put into a bowl with half an ounce of gelatine, and left it to soak for half an hour, whilst she made the rest into a custard, and stood the jug containing it in cold water to facilitate its cooling.

She next prepared a small bowl of bread-crumbs, and finely flaked the whiting, removing the bones. Then Mary having returned with the things, Nellie peeled a small quarter of one of the lemons very thin, and put milk, gelatine, lemon-peel and five ounces of white sugar into a lined saucepan on the fire.

During the time it took to bring it to the boil, she buttered the scallop-shells and proceeded thus :—A layer of breadcrumbs, a layer of fish, salt and pepper to taste, a layer of breadcrumbs, sprinkled with small lumps of butter, and so on, taking care to heap the materials well up in the centre of the shell, and to scatter the last layer of breadcrumbs liberally with butter ; the scallops were then placed on a baking-sheet ready for cooking, twenty minutes being sufficient to brown them nicely.

After boiling for five minutes, the contents of the saucepan were strained into a jug with a lip, and when sufficiently cool to prevent curdling, the well-beaten yolks of two eggs were stirred in. The directions, Nellie knew, were to pour constantly from one jug to another till nearly cold, but she had to content herself with doing this occasionally, whilst making the pastry for the tart.

A ring at the bell announced the arrival of the greengrocer with the apples and lettuces. As Mary was busy in the upper regions, Nellie answered the door herself, returning quickly to prepare the apples, which she quartered and cored before peeling them, to keep the pieces whole.

By this time the lemon-cream was cool enough for her to add carefully the strained juice of the lemons, stirring briskly the while, after which it was poured into the cups, and these were surrounded with cold water to set the cream quickly.

"Now for the mutton," said Nellie to herself, proceeding to cut up the joint. "No wonder the boys said it was like 'old boots,' and I fear its toughness isn't entirely due to under-cooking ! Well, 'cannelon' is a splendid way of using tough meat," she thought, first reserving several thick slices to be converted into mock cutlets next day, and then grinding the rest in the mincing-machine. The minced meat was well seasoned with salt, pepper, parsley, thyme, and a soupçon of finely-chopped onion, half a cupful of breadcrumbs and a well-beaten egg. She made the mixture into balls rather larger than a walnut, and placed them, wrapped in oiled paper, on a tin, to be baked in a moderate oven for half an hour. The tomato sauce was put in a lined saucepan ready to be heated, and the potatoes which Mary had peeled for that "early dinner" she cut into slices to be fried crisp and brown.

Mary was a tolerable plain cook ; therefore, after directing her, Nellie was free to arrange fresh flowers in the dining-room, and to make the necessary additions to her toilet, before laying the luncheon, which she did herself, in order to send the handmaiden up to dress at a quarter to one.

The salad was soon made and prettily decorated, the beef arranged tastefully on a dish and garnished with parsley, and then Nellie whisked the whites of two eggs with a little sugar to a stiff froth, piling it in snowy billows amongst the golden creams, previously turned out into a glass dish. To this the custards in dainty little cups made an excellent vis-à-vis, the salad occupying a central position on the table.

Mr. Vernon, entering the dining-room with the guest, was abundantly satisfied with the result of Nellie's busy morning. Spotless damask, bright electro-plate and glass, go far to making up for costly dishes or priceless silver, and the luncheon-table, decorated by an old gold centre-piece, with sprays of fiery virginia creeper, and vases of citron chrysan-themums, was a picture. He could not but observe the quick look of admiration his daughter called forth when he presented Mr. Laurence.

She presided at lunch with a gentle dignity, conversing with the visitor, her father and the two boys, and betraying no anxiety about the arrangements, which insouciance Mary tried to deserve by changing the courses as deftly as she could. Mr. Vernon, perhaps for the first time, realised what a treasure he possessed in one who, at such short notice, could provide a luxurious meal, and have house, servant, herself and her little brothers, looking the pink of neatness to do honour to any friend of his.

Possibly Mr. Laurence was clever enough to read between the lines, for the lawyer's modest circumstances were well known; at any rate, the luncheon-party, which Nellie triumphantly assured her father had only necessitated the outlay of four shillings, was the means of introducing the Squire of Templemeade to his future wife.

George III and the end of the First World War), but the work of this, admittedly late, Victorian writer indicates that they were not always as harsh as is often suggested. Mrs Orman Cooper is no advocate of Spartan training:

Delicate, sensitive, shrinking little bodies have been trained to the ordeal of a daily plunge in ice cold water, under the mistaken notion that it was good for them … the little, dark, coffin-shaped bathrooms in most modern dwellings are simply ice-houses! Let Dorothy and Phoebe and Rose take the chill off, and liver, lungs, and heart will thrive. Sweet little King's daughters! We would not condemn you to one pang, one shock, one fear that is unnecessary.... I think many a cold and cough might be nipped in embryo, if a little fire was thought necessary to undress by. The cosy feeling of welcome warmth, the flicker of a cheerful blaze, often makes "going to bed" a pleasure instead of a pain.

One wonders if Medicus approved of such advice.
Elsewhere she says:

Mother's arms should always be open. Her bosom their refuge. We must also realise that a false delicacy often stands in the way of a little girl mentioning ailments. A false delicacy which we ourselves have fostered by strained ideas of maidenliness.... Our sweet, beautiful women-children should know no shame.

"I WAS CONDUCTED TO THE NURSERY DOOR."

God has made them goodly and fair. Every function of their bodies are part of His great scheme [*sic*]. I cannot write more definitely of what I mean—guardians of the King's daughters will understand.

And again:

The secret of all home influence is

LOVE, LOVE, LOVE

Nothing succeeds like Love. Begin with it, go on with it, you will never finish it. Take your sweet, obedient, truthful, good-tempered little girls in your arms and love them much for being good. Take your unruly, sulky, deceitful little girls into your arms and love them into being good.

In *Higher Thoughts on Housekeeping* (1883) Alice King asserts:

Even the literary woman and the female artist need to know something of housekeeping; it is a branch of knowledge which cannot be left out of any woman's daily life unless under the most peculiar circumstances, and which, therefore, no girl's education can be complete without.... It is a very wrong and false notion that a literary woman or a female artist cannot make the best of wives and mothers; there is not the smallest reason why she should not stand at the head of the list as both.

Above: a drawing of a nursery scene, from the first instalment of the serial Forlorn, Yet Not Forsaken, *"The true story of a nursery governess" (October 3, 1885).*

139

STINGS FROM BEES OR WASPS.—Chalk wetted with hartshorn is a remedy for the sting of a bee, also table salt kept moist with water. A raw onion is an excellent remedy for the sting of a wasp, also poppy leaves bruised and applied to the part affected will give almost immediate relief.

SICK HEADACHE.—Two teaspoonfuls of powdered charcoal in half a tumbler of water generally gives instant relief. Another remedy is, when the first symptoms of a headache appear, take a clear teaspoonful of lemon juice fifteen minutes before each meal and the same dose at bedtime; follow this up until all symptoms have passed, taking no other remedies, and you will soon be free from your unwelcome pain.

SILK pocket-handkerchiefs and dark blue cotton will not fade if dipped in salt and water while new.

SAL VOLATILE, or hartshorn, will restore colours taken out by acid. It may be dropped upon any material without doing harm.

OLD LINEN should be carefully preserved, as it is always useful in sickness; afterwards it can be washed and then scraped into lint.

POTATO PUFFS. — Chop and season well some cold meat or fish. Mash some potatoes and make them into a paste with an egg. Roll it out, and cut round with a saucer, put your seasoned meat on one half, and fold the other over like a puff. Fry a light brown, and serve hot.

Above: some of the Useful Hints *which were a regular feature of the G.O.P., taken from the issues for 1883.*

A poem by Catherine Grant Furley, entitled *A Girton Girl*, appears in an issue of 1887:

Why, sir, should you seem so startled
　When you chance to come on me
Talking silly baby-language
　To the child upon my knee—
To this happy, crowing urchin,
　While his peasant mother stands
Watching us, while she is wiping
　Thick-flaked soapsuds from her hands?

When you met me first, at dinner,
　At the Hall the other night,
You were seated on my left hand,
　The professor on my right;
And you saw I cared to listen—
　Saw it with a scornful mirth—
To the facts that he was telling
　Of the strata of the earth.

And again, when of the Iliad
　My companion chanced to speak,
You were less pleased than astounded
　That I quoted Homer's Greek.
And beneath my half-closed eyelids
　I observed your covert smile,
When our hostess spoke of Ruskin,
　And I answered with Carlyle....

Over-wise! Nay, it were folly
　If I cherished in my mind
One poor fancy, one ambition
　That could part me from my kind—
From the maiden's hopes and longings,
　From the mother's joy and care,
From the gladness, labour, sorrow,
　That is every woman's share.

Not for all life's garb of duty
　In the self-same tint is dyed;
I must walk alone, another
　Shelters at a husband's side.
Yet I claim her for my sister,
　While—though I must stand apart—
All her hopes, her fears, her wishes
　Find an echo in my heart....

Chapter Eight

COMPETITIONS

Even if a girl neither receives a prize nor a certificate, the work itself will prove a reward, and she may console herself with thinking that doing her best this time will certainly lead to doing better on a future occasion.

> A competition announcement
> (April 26, 1890)

"DEAR ME, WHY DID NOT *I* JOIN IN THE LAST PRIZE COMPETITIONS. I SHOULD CERTAINLY HAVE TAKEN THE FIRST PRIZE."

Above: a cartoon from the Answers to Correspondents, *June 4, 1881. In this issue appeared the results of the prize competition for an essay on a famous Englishwoman of the seventeenth century. The Editor pointedly disqualified "foolish and careless entrants" who chose Lady Jane Grey, Grace Darling and Queen Victoria. It is interesting to note the name "Georgina Hamilton" among the winners (see page 13).*

Reviewing the progress of the magazine in its thousandth issue (February, 1899), the Editor said of the competitions:

By means of [the many competitions], we have from time to time tested the ingenuity, taste, accomplishments, skill, and perseverance of our readers. These have occasionally roused a remarkable degree of enthusiasm. In one of the most successful, we well remember, the papers came in such numbers, that the Post Office had to send a special van with them, and one sackful took four men to carry it upstairs. A large amount of money has, from first to last, been distributed amongst the winning competitors, and a great many certificates of merit have been granted to those who, whilst failing to get a prize, obtained a certain percentage of marks. These certificates have been much valued and not a few have been found serviceable as testimonials to painstaking and ability, when girls have had to make their way in the world.

A competition typical of the earlier years of the magazine is one set in 1885. Competitors were required to submit:

A collection of quotations illustrative of conduct and character drawn from various authors, and arranged under the fifty headings given below. Eleven prizes of one guinea each will be awarded, a prize of one guinea being given to the most successful competitor of every age from thirteen to twenty-three.... THERE ARE MANY ADVANTAGES TO BE GAINED, even without taking into account the prizes and certificates. Those who engage in it will remember it all their lives with pleasure. The mere turning over books will enlarge their mental horizon, and the Sayings of the Wise thus brought home to them cannot but have a good, wholesome, and improving effect on their own conduct and character.

Examples of the fifty headings are: Affectation, Ambition, Bashfulness, Courage, Economy, Fidelity, Gratitude, Honesty, Innocence, Kindness, Modesty, Punctuality, Purity, Vanity, Virtue.

Towards the end of the century, competitions tend to rely on "puzzle poems" or the précis of stories, but the earlier ones are designed to do good to the competitors, either by enlarging their mental horizons, as described above, or by causing them to exercise practical benevolence.

One of the very early ones was for a nightdress, the work to be bestowed on children's and other hospitals; and another, still charitable but less utilitarian, invited water-colour paintings on the subject of springtime. These were sent, after the judging, to children's hospitals, "to brighten the plain walls and to cheer the sad hearts" of the patients. The flower paintings were highly praised, but the candid Editor admitted:

Most of the figure paintings showed a lack of knowledge of even the elements of painting or drawing from life, and it is surprising that the painters of these should have sent them on the chance of gaining a prize or certificate. However, we do not wish to discourage anyone, but to nerve them up to better work.

What would he have said if he *did* wish to discourage someone?

In 1887, the Editor instituted a competition for plain needlework:

In view of the prevailing distress among children at the Board schools and throughout London, especially for clothes.... The work, after being judged, will be carefully distributed, either through the children's hospitals in the poorer quarters of London or through the mistresses of Board schools.

The articles to be submitted for the competition were boys' unbleached calico shirts, girls' unbleached calico chemises or drawers, and winsey or flannel petticoats with plain stay bodices. The price limit recommended for materials was 1s. or 1s. 6d.

The prize lists are always interesting, and give an idea of the age of the G.O.P. subscribers and their geographical location. In this competition alone there were winners from Australia, New Zealand and South Africa among the 400 entrants. One competitor was aged nine, one ten, and one eleven; there were 11 twelve-year-olds ("Work generally good") and 12 thirteen-year-olds ("Hemming particularly good"); 34 competitors gave their age as seventeen ("Work not so good as the girls of thirteen years of age"), 31 as eighteen ("Work fairly good"), 31 as nineteen ("At this age the best we have seen"), 32 as twenty ("The button holes generally very faulty"), 33 as twenty-one ("Button holes still faulty; hemming and stitching extremely good"); the eldest was twenty-nine ("Work excellent"). The "well deserved" Champion Prize Golden Jubilee Brooch, for the very best needlewoman, was won by Elizabeth Lucy Marsh of Aldershot, aged twenty-two.

A teacher from Battersea duly wrote to thank the Editor for the garments her school had received and which she had distributed, on a bitterly cold day in January, to the poorest and most deserving of the children. One recipient was "a little girl of eight years, who is only of the same size as a properly-fed child of four ... her chemise was the colour of mahogany, with filth"; dressed in the warm undergarments, she "was so comfortable she scarcely knew herself".

Another practical competition was that for knitting for the Mission to Deep Sea Fishermen (1888). Patterns for sea-boot stockings, steering-gloves, comforters, caps, guernseys (thick sweaters), and so on were sup-

Far right: the prize-winning drawings selected from some 150 water-colours in the second prize competition (December 4, 1880). The winner was Eva Webb, aged eighteen, with her idealistic treatment of Summer as a human figure. Second came the landscape with sky and meadow (top left).

ow sweet to rest

er on my Saviour's breast

plied. Two of the competitors were six years old! There were two aged seven, two aged eight, and nine aged nine. "The pair of stockings sent in by Agnes Knight are quite wonderful for her age." In spite of the fact that the magazine was, according to its title, designed for "girls", a substantial number of the competitors, on this occasion at least, were over twenty-five, and two of them were aged thirty-two. (The very earliest of the *G.O.P.* competitions, however, were confined to girls under nineteen.) The Editor wrote:

> Several of our girls knitted with crippled hands, and two of them had been called to a happier home of rest and peacefulness before they had completely finished the work they had commenced for the benefit of the toilers of the sea. In both cases the work laid down by the poor lifeless fingers was finished by the sorrowing mother, and sent in to the competition.

An essay competition, *My Daily Round*, set in 1896 for "All Girls Who Work with their Hands", produces some interesting information. The first prize of five guineas was won by a locomotive-tracer; lesser prizes went to a pottery-painter, a shirt-maker, a lace-maker and a general servant.

The "daily round" of these hundreds of brave courageous girls comes as a revelation to those who, having the good things of life, have no need to work with their hands; it illustrates the ennobling results of enduring hardness, and sows the seed of good deeds; it comes as a help and encouragement to those who have lost heart in the battle of life; it acts as a stimulant to those who are standing shoulder to shoulder in the struggle; and it is a lesson to every one in whatever rank they may be to see what these handworkers get through cheerfully in their twelve or sixteen hours of daily toil.

The prize essays were printed in the magazine without alteration.

A competition for "Professional Girls" followed; the prizes were smaller than those presented to the hand-workers. First came a hospital nurse ("downright hard and earnest work"), second a folklorist in the Highlands (knowing little Gaelic when she started), and third, a music teacher struggling in an overcrowded profession.

Not all the competitions have an end-product designed for charitable purposes or the motive of praising honest industry. The very first was for the two best essays on the life of any one famous Englishwoman born in the nineteenth century. The number of essays received was 1,221 (compared with only 125 water-colour paintings entered for the second competition). The life of Charlotte Brontë was the subject of the greatest number, Grace Darling coming next. The essays on the latter, however, "almost without exception, were found to be lamentably faulty". Florence Nightingale, not surprisingly, was a popular subject, and so was Queen Victoria. Fame, however, is an uncertain commodity. How many teenagers today could say who Frances Ridley Havergal was? In fact she was a writer of religious poetry and hymns (*Who is on the Lord's side? Who will serve the King?*) and had died in the previous year. In 1880 her life was the subject of the essay which won the two-guinea prize, sent in by a girl at Longnor Vicarage. The guinea prize, for an essay on Queen Victoria, was gained by a girl from Egglestone Vicarage; and six other clerical addresses appeared in the list of winners. But who were

Far right: "Good-Bye!"—the colour presentation plate which appeared in the first twentieth-century Girl's Own Annual, *1900–1901. A Grenadier guardsman, leaving for the Boer War, says farewell to his wife.*

Grace Aguilar, Sarah Martin, Agnes E. Jones? All were sufficiently celebrated to inspire an essay:

The subject set for an essay competition some months later was the life of some famous Englishwoman born in the eighteenth century. The first prize was won by a girl of twenty from India for an essay on the life of the religious reformer and author, Hannah More. Felicia Dorothea Hemans, however, was the subject of most of the essays in this competition. After her, in point of numbers, came "good Mrs Fry, the prisoners' friend". While in a similar essay set today Elizabeth Fry might well stand high on the list (though perhaps not before Jane Austen as she did in this competition), it seems improbable that Mrs Hemans would appear at all; indeed the poem for which she is mainly remembered, *Casabianca*—"The boy stood on the burning deck"—is generally associated with Victorian recitations, and the fact that she was born in 1793 and died two years before Victoria came to the throne is forgotten.

A few months later again an essay was set on a heroine from the seventeenth century. "The life most extensively chosen by the contributors was, of course, that of the beautiful, virtuous, and unfortunate Lady Russell." Of course? It is shaming to discover that the name of the lady on whose life 137 of the 620 competitors chose to write their essays hardly rings a bell with at least one twentieth-century reader. The winner was an Oxford girl of nineteen.

Results of two competitions published in 1884 show a vast difference in the number of entrants. The plain needlework prize competition, for a nightdress, received only 77 entries. (The judges, surprisingly, noticed the fault of "over-neat work, shown by taking too small stitches".) On the other hand, the competition to write biographical notes on a hundred famous women listed by the Editor produced 4,956 entries and readers were informed that the weight of them was not far short of a ton; laid end to end they would have reached from London to Brighton, and one sack delivered by the Post Office took five men to carry it upstairs. (This was the competition referred to by the Editor in the thousandth issue.) The ages of winners ranged from eight to twenty-eight.

It is exceedingly gratifying to us to say that the quality of the tables is quite as respectable as their number. The greatest pains, as a rule, have been taken, and we have finished our task as examiners with a high opinion of the patience, research, industry, and neatness of almost all who have taken part in the competition. . . . Of course our tables contained many remarkable errors, not only in regard to dates, but facts, as when one girl set down St Cecilia as the "daughter of William the Conqueror", and another made out Sarah Trimmer to be "a famous actress". But few on the whole seemed to have written at random, and praiseworthy efforts were made in many cases to settle the truth when authorities were found to differ. Now and then the information given was exceedingly meagre. Surely we might have been told more of the Princess Amelia than that she was the "daughter of George III"? or of Miss Proctor, that she was the "author of 'Legends and Lyrics'," or, as another has it, "a young English poetess"? . . . Mrs Godolphin was often omitted; but that was no girl's fault. In the list supplied she was accidentally inserted just a century too late. One girl tried, we noticed, to settle the matter by saying that Mrs Godolphin was the wife of Mr Godolphin; but that did not add much to anyone's information.

Far left: an illustration from Courtleroy, *a serial story by Anne Beale (May 22, 1886). Horace has been summoned by telegram to rejoin his ship, which is ordered to the scene of war, off the coast of Africa. In the trim and pretty shrubbery, Mimica gathers a nosegay of spring flowers which she gives him as a last remembrance.*

PRIZE COMPETITION
IN
STORY WRITING.

THE Editor is anxious to possess, for the purpose of printing, a short original story, in which the scene given in this illustration shall be faithfully introduced.

The story must not be longer than would occupy four columns of this magazine.

Prizes of Five Guineas and Three Guineas respectively will be awarded to the two most successful writers. The MS. must be written upon foolscap paper, and only on one side, and be fastened together at the left hand top corner, and the name and address of the writer must be clearly written upon the back page of the MS. There must also be added a certificate from a Clergyman, Teacher, or Parent, assuring the Editor that the work is that of the competitor only, and in her own handwriting.

No letter should accompany the story sent by each contributor.

The story should be sent by book post, with the words "Story Competition" written outside; and in no case will the work be returned to the competitor, whether stamps be sent for the purpose or not.

The Editor's adjudication of the Prizes will be final, and no appeal can be received against it.

The last day for receiving the stories is March 25th (Lady-day), 1890.

A STORY WANTING WORDS.

Above: the story competition of 1889. "The competitors, or rather the majority of them, consider neither of the ladies beautiful, but are unanimous in their praise of the disposition of the older one," reported the Editor (May, 1890).

The *G.O.P.* was unusually fanciful in setting an original story competition in 1889. A picture was provided for a starting-point, similar in style to the illustrations of the regular fiction, and competitors were invited to weave a story round it. It depicted a soberly-dressed woman with a rather sad-looking schoolgirl. No fewer than 97 competitors chose to name the latter Muriel, a fact which struck the *G.O.P.* (and strikes me) as remarkable. Nearly 900 readers entered. The Editor announced:

There was no ridiculous story, no joke, no paper of which the writer should be ashamed.... On the other hand, it is a disappointment to have to state that not one story displays unusual ability, conspicuous invention, minuteness of observation, or any of the qualities that are born in a writer, and justify her in attempting to instruct and amuse the world.

In 1887 Dr Stainer, organist of St Paul's Cathedral, set a competition for the best musical setting of Longfellow's poem, *The Rainy Day*, to be judged irrespective of age. In the following year came a new competition:

Dr Stainer suggests that our musical readers shall write a short pianoforte piece in two movements, descriptive of SORROW and JOY, and the Editor has great pleasure in offering two prizes of ten and five guineas respectively for the best compositions sent to him on these subjects. There will be no certificates granted in connection with this competition, and the work will be judged irrespective of age, sex, or creed.

SIR JOHN STAINER, MUS. D.
Photo by Hill & Saunder, Oxford.

One might have supposed (at least, hoped) it superfluous to add this last, but opening the competition to the opposite sex was an innovation in 1888 and represented a change of policy; although girls competed for and won prizes in the *Boy's Own Paper*, PEGGY had been told in the G.O.P.'s first year:

Of course your brothers may not compete for our prizes. Several boys have asked the same question, and have had the same reply.

However, by 1888, in the competition for knitting *Warm Woollens for the Mission to the Deep Sea Fishermen*, there was one boy competitor— "to whom we offer our thanks and congratulations, and a first-class certificate". Both the first and second prize-winners in Dr Stainer's music competition, however, proved to be female; their ages were not stated.

In 1887 a competition was set on *My Favourite Heroine from Shakespeare*, with a ten-guinea and a five-guinea prize. The results were very gratifying; the competitors produced papers showing "an amount of excellence far exceeding anything the examiners were prepared for"; praise indeed. The youngest entrant was twelve and the oldest thirty-nine. It was noted:

There were many more papers sent in by girls between twenty and thirty than there have been in any of our previous competitions, but seventeen, eighteen, and nineteen—the ages that generally contribute quite half the MSS— were not in such force as hitherto.... The girls between the ages of twenty-one and thirty sent, perhaps, the best work we have received in any of our competitions.

HENRY RYLAND.

Above: Henry Ryland's design for the new G.O.P. masthead (see page 17) won the first prize of ten guineas and was duly adopted for the magazine.

(It is perhaps worth noticing that the G.O.P. refers to a woman of thirty as a girl; modern writers frequently imply that the Victorian woman was regarded as "an old maid" at a ridiculously early age.)

What heroines would be chosen by present-day girls? Those strong-minded characters Rosalind and Beatrice, perhaps? Or Juliet? In 1887 more than a third of the competitors chose Portia, and only half a dozen Juliet. "Who could imagine Portia being so cowardly as to commit suicide?" asked one, while another commented, "How different is Portia's love from the mad passion of Juliet!"

Although the results of this competition were clearly gratifying to those who set it, four competitors were rapped over the knuckles for introduc-

SCENES IN THE EDITORIAL OFFICES DURING THE COMPETITION.

Above: an illustration from the Editor's report on the Famous Women competition, June 7, 1884. When he recalled the immense success of this competition in his editorial for the thousandth number in 1899, the number of Post Office clerks needed to carry the sackful of entries had shrunk from five to four; but the readers' industry and enthusiasm remained impressive.

ing the question of women's rights. One young lady wrote of Portia with positively admirable cheek:

It is superfluous to describe her action and speeches in *The Merchant of Venice*. Far better will it be for me to transport her to the nineteenth century, and show how deeply she would have been interested in the great subject of women's rights.

The judges were not impressed. Those competitors fared no better who took the opposite view and deprecated "a growing tendency of women to usurp the place of men", praising Portia for her gentle and womanly nature combined with a vigorous mind. "How foolish girls are," was the editorial comment, "to become so exercised about one idea that they must fain 'drag it in', when it has nothing to do with the subject they are writing about."

The success of this competition may have prompted the Editor to institute another in which girls were required to state, with reasons: their object in life, favourite qualities in woman and man, favourite book, hymn, Bible verse, occupation, writer, painter, musical composer, character in history, character in fiction, flower, study, amusement. This ought, surely, to have proved a fascinating exercise, but the Editor wrote at the end of the time allotted, "We are not contented with the present result"; the time would therefore be extended. Only 400 entries had been received, and the Editor stated:

It is our wish that this competition should be a large one, both for the sake of our readers and also for our own sake. For our readers' sake, because so much interest, so much benefit, must accrue to those who take part in it; for our own sake, because the judgment and taste of the girls will help to give us an insight into their characters, and show us, to an extent, how we can still further benefit them and give them seasonable amusement.

At the end of the extended time nearly another 400 entries had been received, but the Editor said disconsolately that "the competition has not been so successful a one as we had anticipated". It seems that by then he had become bored with the whole thing; neither he nor posterity learns as much about the tastes of the Victorian girl as had been hoped. There are crumbs of interest; we learn that the favourite hymn was *Rock of Ages*, with *Lead, Kindly Light* a good second, nearly half the competitors choosing one or other of these hymns. The favourite writer of most girls from fifteen to thirty was Dickens, while younger girls favoured Charlotte Yonge. The Editor expressed surprise that Doré was the favourite painter, but it is not clear whether the surprise showed gratification or disapproval; Landseer came second, and the Editor said crossly that the reasons given were often "simply ridiculous—e.g. 'Because he is an animal painter'". The favourite occupation "betrays a burning anxiety on the part of girls to earn their own livelihood". Teachers, doctors, novelists and painters wrote about their choice of profession, and one girl of twenty gave her profession as a metaphysician. She said she found it "uphill work".

Above: a cartoon from the Correspondents *page, April 24, 1880. At the end of his replies (which ranged on this occasion from Queen Victoria's family name to a "preventive for bunyans" for poor* BETA) *the Editor wrote severely that he was "unable to reply to all the many unnecessary questions put to him relating to the prize competitions".*

Chapter Nine

ANSWERS TO CORRESPONDENTS

A WELL-WISHER.—1. Has it never occurred to our kind little friend that the style of our answers must be regulated by that of the letters received? Some are very silly; some give us needless trouble, as the writers had only to consult the indexes supplied [in the Annuals] to find the information required; and others, we regret to say, are of a very impertinent and unseemly character. It is our duty to reply as each case may demand, and we are only happy to say that for one ungrateful and objectionable letter needing rebuke, we receive hundreds full of gracious acknowledgements. The same hand that inscribes many of the severest rebukes inscribes very many more of the tender words of encouragement, sympathy, and praise which you admire. We are sorry that any friend of yours failed in due courtesy, and laid herself open to the strictures received. 2. Keep out of his way altogether. That is what you "can do," and that only, praying for help to banish the subject.

Answers to Correspondents
(January 28, 1882)

In 1880, the reply to a letter from AMABEL read, in its entirety:

1. Wear a white frill round your neck.
2. Consult a doctor.
3. Your writing is unformed.

If replies to letters were sometimes curt—and this was not always the case—they were, at any rate, on an enormous variety of subjects. Certain headings appeared regularly, such as *EDUCATIONAL*, *ART* and *HOUSEKEEPING*. The letters under the heading *MISCELLANEOUS* were just that.

It is hardly surprising to find the Victorian *G.O.P.* silent on the erotic problems that crowd today's teenage magazines, but queries about love appear frequently. ROSEBUD in 1886 is told:

On no account give any encouragement to a man you do not love. On the contrary, give a firm and definite refusal, and if he perseveres after that, ask your father to put an end to the matter for you.

IRRESOLUTE in the same year receives similar advice:

Far right: a page of Answers to Correspondents, *November 27, 1880.*

ANSWERS TO CORRESPONDENTS.

MISCELLANEOUS.

CANARIENSIS and OTHERS.—1. Paddle away as much as you like, it is wonderfully strengthening to the feet and ankles. 2. We are almost afraid to offer any advice as to the length of time which girls ought to pass in the water. We have frequently offered our advice at the seaside, and it has invariably been rejected. Our private opinion is that twenty minutes will make a very fair average, but much depends on the constitution of the bather. When a bather of either sex finds that the finger tips become white instead of pink, it is a sign that the bath has been too long. Giddiness on coming out of the water tells the same story.

MAIDENHAIR.—Girls of thirteen require at least eight hours' sound sleep, exclusive of the time occupied in the toilet before and after sleep; but they should manage it by going to bed early and not sitting up late.

BERYL ORSMOND.—1. Make the diet of your cockatoo as simple as possible. Perhaps you have been allowing her to nibble at bones or to eat animal food. Give her a bath by all means, but don't put her in it yourself. If she needs a bath, instinct will teach her to use it. 2. You do not mention your age, so we cannot tell how much character your writing ought to have; it certainly is not too small, and it is perfectly legible, but it has a sort of character of its own, the lines slanting downwards instead of upwards, as is the usual feminine fashion. Practise writing with black-lined paper, and you will soon find yourself falling into the right way.

ZULU HAT.—1. Of course you do not "make both ends meet of your income" if on £300 per annum you "keep three servants." One is all you ought to keep, and you should undertake all the light part of the household work yourself. 2. Wreaths of grapes and a few poppies serve best as trimming for a Zulu hat.

STUDENTA.—Go on, enquiring spirit, with your methodical reading; it is one of the secrets of progress. We understand the quotation to refer to certain inferences erroneously drawn from observations made on the brain of the frog as the seat of sensation and mental action. Theology is not likely to be so easily overthrown.

ARCHIMEDES.—1. There is no way of pressing flowers so as perfectly to preserve their natural colour. The colour always fades more or less. But there is a method of drying them with sand and exposure to heat by which they retain their brilliancy pretty well, and also their original form. By this method they will remain in good preservation for several years. 2. The way to overcome the dislike of being alone is to make excellent company of yourself. Improve your mind, then, by reading and thought. Your handwriting might be better, and it will be, Archimedes, if you practice.

ALPHONSIA.—1. Your handwriting is very good for your age. But don't be satisfied; make it still better. 2. Who is afraid? why, bring common-sense to bear upon it. You should live where we do, and go upstairs at midnight to hear the owls hooting in the wood. Whenever you feel particularly nervous repeat to yourself the 4th verse of the 23rd Psalm; it is a fine cordial for all timid folks.

JULIA.—For potato cakes take ten ounces floury potatoes, boiled and smoothly pounded. When just warm add gradually a little salt, six ounces of flour, and three ounces of butter; no liquid is required. When the ingredients are thoroughly mixed, roll the dough into thin cakes the size of a captain's biscuit. Bake in a moderate oven or on a girdle; when done, split open, butter well, and serve very hot.

A YOUNG MOTHER.—1. We are glad that the article on washing has proved so useful to you. In the second and third chapters you will probably find the further information you require. When ironing such small articles as you mention, the oval-shaped or "egg-iron" will do you good service. 2. We regret that we cannot tell you how to eradicate stains made by Condy's Fluid. An eminent chemist informs us that a long and persistent course of bleaching with chlorine might, at length, wear out the stains, but thinks the fabric itself would be worn-out or made tender during the operation. We thank you heartily for your kind and appreciative letter.

AN UNSOPHISTICATED CHILD OF NATURE.—Kindly choose a shorter *nom de plume* when next you write. Do not be uneasy about your tortoise. The little gentleman has very likely got a will of his own. Try him with cabbage or greens, but he will go off to sleep by and bye, and when summer days come, he will most assuredly make up for his long fast.

BLANCHE.—1. At your age you need not be alarmed at your hair getting thin; it is probable that your system is a little out of order. Attend to your health; eat and drink nothing that stimulates or heats the system; take a teaspoonful or two of cream of tartar now and then of a morning. Use a hard brush for five minutes every day, morn and night, and the following stimulating pomade. Go to a respectable chemist and tell him to mix you two drachms of Wilson's stimulating ointment in an ounce and a half of nicely-scented pomade. Rub a little of this well into the roots of the hair every day, and wash once a week with juniper-tar soap, or mild carbolic acid soap. 2. Take the cold bath all winter if you are *certain* you feel the benefit of it. If you have any doubts, take a *little* of the chill off.

SYBIL.—Every evening take a note-book and make a list of things to be done on each successive day, a certain time of the day being allotted to each task—some book to be read, some needlework to be continued or completed, household arrangements, or setting in order of drawers, or rooms to be done, letters too long neglected to be written, visits to be paid, or shopping, errands, and work for others if not for yourself. "Whatsoever thy hand findeth to do, do it with thy might." Life is too important and too brief for the indulgence of indolence. You write fairly well.

MARGARITA AVENAL.—The lines you quote do not appear to be from the pen of any well-known author. They are not poetry. Thank you for your nice letter.

WALLFLOWER.—The lady has the privilege of recognising a gentleman or not, at her own discretion. Your grammar and spelling should be better learnt before you attempt to write letters, and you have employed six capital letters in the wrong places within a space of eight lines.

S. W., H. H., and H. L. write a very fine free hand. That of H. H.'s is good, but less so than S. W.'s.

"ALL SOLD, MISS. WOULD YOU LIKE TO ORDER THE JANUARY PART IN GOOD TIME?"

That of H. L.'s is scarcely yet formed, but might prove very good with care.

A SCOTCHWOMAN spoils her hand by sloping it the wrong way.

JARVIS STREET.—We regret to tell you that our editorial staff is complete; and we already have close connections with Canada.

HELENA.—Much of the Litany used in the Church of England is of very ancient Christian origin, but Cranmer made some part of it. Your hand is a particularly good one.

H. S.—P. P. C. means *Pour prendre congé*; P. D. A. *Pour dire adieux*. See our articles on the subject of writing.

MADELINE and IMAGINATION.—The proper pronunciation of the name Cabul is "Caw-bull," the emphasis laid on the first syllable. Your writing is insignificantly small. "Imagination" writes very well.

MAB.—The cause of the death of your "table-plants" may probably be traced to lighting your room with gas. You appear to write with a badly-cut quill pen, so we can scarcely judge of your writing.

COURTENAY.—The pillows of a bed should be covered in the day-time with the quilt, and if the bed be an old-fashioned four-poster, the curtains at the head of the bed should be folded and laid across them, with the ends meeting in the middle. It is more usual to trim the pillows with frillings or lace than the top sheet, but of course it looks pretty to have it so finished.

MOSS ROSE.—Our answers are made to correspondents so many in number that they have to wait for them. Ivy, like most climbing plants, renders the wall on which it grows more or less damp. It also injures the masonry, although it may for some time hold a ruin together.

BETTY.—Doves eat hempseed, crumbs of bread, and indeed any grain almost. Your handwriting is good, but rather large.

MUGGINS.—If moths be already in a mattress, the latter will have to be taken to pieces, and properly baked by a man whose business it is. 2. The name Hugh should be pronounced as if written "Hu," the last two letters being mute. Handwriting not bad, but too large.

JUNETTA.—When the canary's claws have grown so long as to curl round the perch and endanger the catching of his feet in the bars of the cage they should be cut a little with very sharp strong scissors. You write a pretty hand.

RUBY.—You write with too hard a pen. Trim your dress with velveteen. See "Dress of the Month."

DIGNITAS.—You write a very good hand. We thank you for your kind and well expressed letter, and are glad that our correspondence columns interest you so much.

A. C. D.—1. You will find the tales of MM. Erckmann-Chartrain delightfully interesting. 2. The address of the Ladies' British Sanitary Association is 22, Berners-street, W. See Miss Rose Adams.

ANNA.—We could not help you in this matter, as we wholly disapprove of Planchette and all kindred amusements.

PUCK.—Chamois leather gloves are washed in a tepid lather.

LILIAN MARY GRAHAM.—Both your friends failed in good breeding. The gentleman should have taken the penny to pay for the stamp, as he had already laid the lady under an obligation by his prompt kindness in offering it to her. But allowing that the gentleman failed in good breeding, that is no excuse for the lady's declining the stamp altogether. Finding she was not allowed to pay for it, she should have accepted it with a graceful expression of thanks for the gift. Of the two, the lady's fault was the greater.

CUCKOO FLOWER.—*Vive la bagatelle* means "Success to trifling." Not a good sentiment, except interpreted that a little recreation is good for health of mind and body.

F. E. T. R.—Thank you very much indeed for your kind letter. We should strongly advise you not to work up for the examination, as it would most probably ruin what little health you have; and it is so obligatory on all of us to take care of our health. May God bless you, and strengthen you to carry out your resolutions. Your handwriting is beautiful, but the composition of your letter is marred by writing, "I think that *one* must examine *themselves* well."

A SCOTCH GIRL suggests that every girl who has a friend's welfare at heart should *give* her a copy of THE GIRL'S OWN PAPER, and she is kind enough to speak in unqualified terms of its value. She also says that she has introduced the Magazine to eight of her female friends, who are now subscribers. 1. This good little Scotch girl is informed that she can get the Index to vol. i., for one penny, or the Frontispieces to the monthly parts and Index for ninepence, and the beautiful cloth case for two shillings. This cloth case is to be had in many colours, but the editor, in strict confidence and in return for her nice letter, advises her to order the slate colour. Her bookbinder will put the book together at very little cost. 2. Stop plucking the hair from your chin. All will come right in time. Your writing is unequal, part of the letter is written well, and the other part indifferently.

FLOSSIE.—Your writing is not formed yet, but you do your best and are very careful. When you have had a little more practice, your writing will be more easily performed and will look pleasanter. We cannot possibly remember why we did not answer your previous letters.

EMMELINE MARIE LAURENCE.—Sing "Darby and Joan" at your grandparents' golden wedding. Nothing could be better for the purpose. It is simple, beautiful, and in several keys. "Always the same to your old wife Joan!" Would it not be splendid if every wife could say this of her husband.

H. M. E.—1. You should not do your lessons on Sundays. Read with earnest prayer your Bible and other good books between the hours of divine service, and maybe that the peace of God of which you speak might be imparted to you. Acknowledge your own unworthiness and sin, and implore God to receive you by virtue of His Son's merits. 2. Your writing is not good.

MILLIE E. T.—Wear a white cap and white cashmere dress. The plainer the better. Think more of your heart than your garment, and put the other questions to your parson.

CLARINDA.—1. We do not know—and do not wish to know—who wrote the morbid lines which you quote. We think you had better consult a doctor, for you are evidently in a very bad state. 2. Your writing is scandalous.

HAZELDYNE.—Why do you say that you do not care for music, and yet acknowledge that you play Bach, Beethoven, Haydn, and Mozart. Your sister says that you play well and have a very good touch. We counsel you not to be silly, for you are getting out of the dry-bones part of learning, and will be thankful, when you are older, that you are an accomplished pianist. Your writing is rather nice, and so is your sister's.

A LEFT-OUT ONE.—If it is true that you are selfish, lazy, bad tempered, plain, and unaccomplished, we do not wonder that nobody cares for you, and we trust that you will always keep at a respectful distance from us. Your portrait which you enclose, however, is that of a charming young damsel.

RUBY C.—Wash the crewel work in tepid water with soap, rinse it, and, if possible, wring through a machine, so as to make it perfectly dry.

ROMOLA.—You will find in the *Leisure Hour* for March an article on "Lamarck and Darwin," which will explain to you all about the doctrine of Evolution, showing how far it is true, with its relation to natural and revealed religion.

SPES.—Apply to the Admiralty, or if you live near a dockyard, make inquiries there.

CLAUDIA.—Use Pope's translation of the "Iliad" or the "Odyssey," if you cannot procure a more modern one. The "Conquest of Mexico," by Prescott, is an excellent book.

ONE OF ELEVEN.—There are Moravian schools at Fairfield, near Manchester, at Fulneck, near Leeds, and Pytherton, in Wiltshire. Address the Head Mistress in each case.

A SOLDIER'S FIANCÉE.—There is no other meaning than that the young lady has said "yes," and the young man is going away.

UNE GENEVOISE.—We were not at all "shock" at the style of your kind and funny little letter, and think your self-acquired knowledge of English wonderful. Order THE GIRL'S OWN PAPER from the Publisher, 56, Paternoster-row, E.C. The postage to Switzerland is 2d. each number.

SAILOR.—The belief that those who are born at sea belong to the parish of Stepney is included by Brand in his list of "Vulgar Errors."

QUERY.—There are no less than four martyrs, bishops, and saints called "Donatus," from any of whom the road may take its name.

A KENTISH GIRL.—Surnames were first used in England in the latter part of the tenth century. They were introduced by the Norman conquerors, and were chiefly derived from the names of the continental estates of the bearers of them, or from places within their seignories abroad. Camden says that "there is scarcely a single village in Normandy which has not surnamed a family in England." Families of native lineage also, after the example of the victors, adopted hereditary surnames, derived from manors and other localities. Amongst these we may reckon the De Fords, De Ashburnhams, and De Newtons.

AN INSTRUCTION SEEKER.—The names of the two thieves crucified with our Saviour are said, by tradition, to have been Dimas and Gestas, the former being he unto whom the promise was vouchsafed—"To-day shalt thou be with Me in Paradise." We believe it is supposed that the Hebrew words rendered "pieces of money," denoted a piece having on it the stamp or impression of a lamb or sheep, intimating thereby its current value. In Genesis xxxiii. 19, you will find it rendered "lambs" in the margin of your Bible. The "thirty pieces of silver" received by Judas was the "stater," a Greek silver coin, each worth about 2s. 1d., or perhaps more.

PET BIRDIE.—We have had a cat and a bird simultaneously, and watched the process of training, in reference to the former, performed daily by an old servant. She used to hold up the cat near the cage, and when it began to "chatter" at the bird she scolded and buffeted it with a handkerchief, then set it down on the floor, and drove it out of the room. The plan certainly succeeded, for whenever the cat saw the bird, after this discipline had been carried on for a certain time, it used to fly from the room as if chased by a pack of hounds. The servant was quite as fond of the cat as of the bird, and even preferred it of the two. But our bird remained in its cage; and if yours be free to fly about, its danger is far greater. We thank you for so kind a letter. Your writing is good.

CORAL.—Either the wax or the spirits of wine in which it was to be dissolved must have been of a very inferior kind, as we never knew the method to fail.

DOT and DANDY.—1. Pack the flowers in cotton-wool, very lightly, yet so as to cover them completely; and lay them in a cardboard box securely wrapped in paper. 2. A gentleman should give a lady whichever arm will permit her to take the inside of the footway or pavement. He should never place her on the outside.

JENNY JONES.—If you have no friends in town, yet have sufficient time for spending a few hours here, we advise your going direct to the British Museum or South Kensington, and make a study of one gallery after another. Then make a tour of the National and some of the other picture galleries, including Gustave Doré's, where you will find a comfortable place of rest when tired. We should advise you to go to these places provided with a

RULES

I. No charge is made for answering questions.

II. All correspondents to give initials or pseudonym.

III. The Editor reserves the right of declining to reply to any of the questions.

IV. No direct answers can be sent by the Editor through the post.

V. No more than two questions may be asked in one letter, which must be addressed to the Editor of THE GIRL'S OWN PAPER, *56, Paternoster-row, London, E.C.*

VI. No addresses of firms, tradesmen, or any other matter of the nature of an advertisement will be inserted.

notebook, and thus impress on your memory all that you have seen. A visit now and then to the Crystal Palace would compensate you for your trouble, especially as there is an excellent reading-room and library there to which ladies have access on paying one penny. On certain days in the week the South Kensington is free; on others the charge for entrance is 6d. The British Museum and National Gallery are always free when open, but you must obtain information from the newspapers. 2. Your writing is almost too large already. The large modern hand is very coarse and vulgar.

SUSIE.—Jenny Lind (Madame Goldschmidt), is living. Gentlemen in England do not usually wear betrothal rings.

AN ÆSTHETIC SPARROW.—Père la Chaise was the favourite and confessor of Louis XIV., who made him the superior of a great establishment of the Jesuits on this spot, then named Mont Louis. The house and grounds were bought for a national

cemetery, which was laid out by M. Brongniart, and first used on May 21, 1804.

A MOTHER OF A WORKING LAD.—Giddiness may arise from various causes. In your son's case we should say that it arose from weakness, and that tonics, wine, and a liberal diet would be beneficial. But we could not advise you as to what particular tonic he should take. You had better consult a medical man on the subject.

A READER OF THE GIRL'S OWN PAPER.—The different sounds of the letter "c" is one of the anomalies of the English alphabet. It is like "s" before "e," "i," and "y," as in "cell," "civil," "cymbal, except, "sceptic," "cymry;" hard like "k" before "a, o, u, r, l, t." The relative pronoun agrees with its antecedent in gender and number; in case it may be nominative, genitive, or objective, governed by a verb or a preposition. Example—"Who is that?" Answer, "The lady to whom you were introduced."

EDINBURGH.—If this young person be unable to discover a greater flaw in our magazine than an obvious oversight or misprint in reference to a single word, and that in a correspondence of such magnitude, we can only congratulate ourselves in having passed through the ordeal with rare success. We beg, at the same time, to offer her our sincere condolences on the pitiful disappointment which she must have experienced.

A CAMBRIDGE SENIOR.—1. We are not told how near the king permitted Gehazi to approach him; and without doubt he took care to keep him at a safe distance. Elisha and the servant whom he sent to speak with Naaman the leper did not catch the disease by speaking to him; nor did the "ten men that were lepers," who were healed by our Lord, communicate it by approaching Him or His disciples sufficiently near for speaking with Him. "Dwelling without the camp" was, of course, essential, as the disease was contagious; and it would not have been safe for others to enter their dwellings and touch anything which they had handled. 2. The illustration marked "a" shows a correct prism.

WALLFLOWER.—You had better try sand, glass, or emery paper, and use whichever of them answers best. Where the edges of the stone are sharp, be careful not to blunt them. "Genoa cake" is made as follows:—Ingredients required: Half a pound of flour, half a pound of butter, ditto sugar, four eggs, a small glass of brandy, and a little salt. Mix the flour, sugar, eggs, brandy and salt well together in a basin with a wooden spoon, then add the butter (merely melted by the side of the fire), and when this is thoroughly incorporated with the batter, pour it into an appropriately-sized tin baking-sheet (previously spread with butter) to the thickness of about a quarter of an inch, and bake this in an oven moderately heated. When it is done, it should be turned out upon a sheet of paper, and cut, or stamped out, either in circular, oblong, oval, leaf-like, or any other fancy shape that taste may suggest. These may then be decorated with white of egg and sugar, prepared as for "méringues," or with icing prepared as directed for wedding-cakes.

G. E. C.—We think that, with a sheet of blotting paper and a hot iron, you might succeed in taking the grease spots out of the wall paper.

ERNEST'S WIFE.—Shrove Tuesday derives its name from the ancient practice, in the Church of Rome, of confessing sins and being shrived, or shrove, that is, obtaining absolution on this day. Pancakes were originally to be eaten after dinner, to stay the stomachs of those who went to be shriven. The Shrove bell was called the "Pancake bell," and the day of shriving "Pancake Tuesday."

There never was a greater mistake made than marrying to reform a man; nor should a woman perjure herself by taking such solemn vows and making such declarations as those in marriage, if she do not really love a man. You should not marry for pity's sake either, nor as a mark of gratitude for family favours rendered by him, nor think of uniting yourself to any man, however good, so long as you feel the smallest disinclination for such a change of condition. If, as his family say, your refusal will drive him back into evil habits, he is not a really reformed character, and is acting on no high principle, and therefore, by their own showing, is no safe husband for you.

TROUBLED ONE in 1891 "thinks of shutting the stable door when the horse is stolen", which sounds ominous. The reply continues:

Why did you allow this very excellent young man to kiss you on several occasions when alone? You should have objected on the first attempt; and said that you could not allow such familiarity except from an engaged lover. Be sure he does not respect you the more for permitting him to take such a liberty so often without resistance or rebuke. You have only yourself to blame.

OLIVE ... appears to be suffering from the society of too many young men. Do not allow any man to reach the point of proposing to you if you do not mean to accept him; and do not accept any man as an intended husband whom you do not love. You ought to be ashamed of loving any man who does not love you and desire to win your love. If you need advice on such points, consult your mother. [1888]

In the reply to A COUNTRY LASSIE in 1887, class is the problem, and the gulf of a century between our day and hers is never wider:

In reference to your partiality for a working man (he being a religious man), we think you would not only act in an unseemly way, but a most reprehensible way, to set aside the natural feelings of your father and your other relatives, by marrying a man in a lower position in life, however respectable in character. We are all placed in the respective stations in life which we occupy by our Heavenly Father's appointment. You will be spared much trial and suffering as a single woman, and you had better leave your future altogether in the Lord's hands.

NOBODY'S OWN is told in 1887:

You are very unwise to set your heart so much on changing your present condition. You seem to be blessed with a comfortable home, and as you are not obliged to earn your bread, you have the more time to devote to others. Try to study what will help and please the members of your own home circle, and to organise a little society amongst your young friends for helping the sick and sorrowful by your visits or handiwork. If your Divine Master should require you to undertake new responsibilities as a married woman, He will send you a suitable husband.

The reply to BELLADONNA, who was obviously considering profiting by the fact that 1884 was a Leap Year, is more brusque:

Are you out of your mind, or were you born with any brains? A man would make a bad choice if he accepted an offer of marriage from any girl; for one who could so far set aside all natural feelings of maidenly delicacy as to ask him to marry her, would be quite unfit to be the mistress of a house and to bring up daughters of her own. Are you so utterly incapable of understanding a joke as to imagine that the recurrence of an extra day in February could justify you in throwing off all reserve, and degrading yourself thus?

TO OUR CORRESPONDENTS.

OUR readers will, doubtless, have observed that more space than usual has lately been given to that department of our paper called "Answers to Correspondents." This has, of course arisen from an increase in the number of letters received from the girls since the commencement of the magazine.

It must not be supposed, however, that these extra answers represent replies to all questions sent to us, as some of our correspondents seem to suppose. Indeed we regret to say that it is far otherwise, for every morning we receive letters answers to which would occupy more than half a weekly number.

It is, therefore, certain that many letters must remain unanswered.

Now with a view to fewer disappointments in the future, the editor wishes to say that no girl should ask more than two questions in one letter, and these should be sensible questions, clearly and briefly stated.

From this date, therefore, any letters containing more than two questions will be destroyed unanswered.

The correspondents should select initials or short and uncommon pseudonyms, avoiding "A Constant Reader," "A Lover of the G. O. P.," and other such hackneyed phrases. They should also refrain from calling themselves by such flattering names as "Fair Maid of Perth," &c., and from giving themselves the names of men.

Many letters are sent to us from various parts asking one and the same question. In this case we give one answer only, leaving the others to receive the information from that.

Of course, many questions are put to us, which, from an insufficient knowledge of various facts, we are totally unable to answer. Other letters, again, are frivolous, and prove the writers to possess an undue anxiety as to their personal appearance, as, for instance, questions on the complexion, figure, colour of the hair, &c. Such questions will, for the future, remain unanswered, as being contrary to the aims and objects of the paper.

It is therefore needless for girls to send us locks of hair and photographs for criticism.

When our girls need information that would be of real service, relating to education, domestic economy, work, recreation, and other subjects, we shall consider it a privilege to supply it, if it be in our power; and we shall also be heartily thankful to continue to give our counsel and advice to any anxious and troubled soul needing it; for, did we not say at the outset that we should "aim at being a counsellor, playmate, guardian, instructor, companion, and friend, and that we should help to prepare our readers for the responsibilities of womanhood and for a heavenly home"?

Above: an editorial comment from August 7, 1880 (the pencil marking appears on the original issue).

Far left: a page of replies, April 1, 1882.

153

The answer to A SERVANT in 1886 strikes a regrettably tongue-in-cheek note:

Not having seen, and knowing nothing of your two suitors—the cab-driver who is lame, and the flute-player who is deaf—we could not decide between them. Do they bear equally good characters as honest, industrious, and sober men? Are both good-tempered, healthy, good-looking, and equally well-to-do? Have both got a nice little home to take you to? And has either of them got a mother-in-law waiting for you, and keeping a house there already? Lastly, which cares for you the most, and have you no fancy for one more than the other?

PERPLEXED is answered in the following year:

Without being a teetotaller, we feel with you in reference to the odious practice of drinking a gin cocktail every morning before lunch. The probability is that drunkenness will, sooner or later, be the result. No wonder he is cross when you expostulate with him; the drinking of spirits has that tendency; it spoils both temper and digestion. Besides this, it is an exceedingly low, vulgar habit. Such a beginning on his part gives no promise of happiness on a wife's.

A hundred years has not altered the problem of the teenager who wants to go out with boys before her parents think she should. E.G.H. is rapped over the knuckles in 1892:

A young girl of sixteen and some months is very far too young to be in search of "lovers". Your aunt is quite right in not allowing you to "go out in the evening", especially if "very handsome", as you say you are. It is a disgrace to the mothers of "some of your girl friends, not nearly as old as you" (they must be in short frocks and bibs), if they have had lovers for some time.

Even without the full text of the letter from E.G.H. the authentic note of disgruntled adolescence can be heard at a distance of more than eighty years.

A still more mordant reply is addressed to FIFTEEN in 1892:

Your letter is a disgrace to you. The way in which you speak of your mother's care and watchfulness over you is little to your credit. It is not "chronic inquisitiveness", it is a part of her duty. She has a right to know what you do, where you go, and whom you meet. We hope that any mother who has two daughters, one of seventeen and one of fifteen who read this paper, and who take walks in the country without a maid or a chaperon, will discover the danger incurred by her daughters in meeting and walking with strange men clandestinely. Have you no self-respect, any more than no dutiful feeling? The coarse slang you employ betrays the low order of men and boys with whom you associate.

FIFTEEN can hardly have been gratified by that reply, especially if her mother happened also to be a reader of the *G.O.P.* However, bracing, tonic admonitions are the rule in these pages:

ALTA.—It is wrong to persistently refuse to sing if you have a voice. Nothing is so thoroughly wretched to a stranger as to meet a girl at a musical party who refuses to exert herself to take part in the entertainment. It is conceited to be nervous. Nobody wants to hear you. It is the music of the composer and the words of the song that they wish you to expound to them. [1880]

154

MOLLY.—Your face will often become flushed if your feet are cold, but such troubles arise also from a weak digestion, or mental work too soon after eating.

LIMY BOY.—The articles on "The Duties of Servants" will be found at pages 534, 646, vol. ii.

IMPATIENCE.—The 15th October, 1865, was a Sunday.

PANSY.—We do not know of any Institute to which old kid gloves are of value.

GING'ORING AND BLINDBAT.—A cardinal of the Roman Church is addressed as "Your Eminence;" the Pope, as "Your Holiness," and "Holy Father."

EDITH.—You must either advertise or obtain the situation by inquiring amongst your friends. Fancy-work is of little value at present, as nearly everyone does it for themselves.

E. G. B.—Wash the white feathers with curd-soap and warm water, shake dry before a fire, and then curl each filament with a blunt pen-knife, or a paper-knife.

PUSSY S. E. A.—We must refer you to page 751, vol. iii. for the meaning of the use of the letters "M." and "N." in the Catechism. The pronunciation of the name of the French town "Cannes" is like that of the English word "Can." Your writing is so illegible, we can scarcely read it. See "Tortoises," page 367, vol. iii.

QUEEN ESTHER.—The allusion to "Vanda" is from "The Betrothed," by Sir Walter Scott. She was the spirit with the red hand, who appeared in the haunted chamber to the heroine of the story. Egbert was the first king of all England. He ascended the throne A.D. 827, and was the first of the line of Saxon kings which ended with the Norman conquest.

USELESS ONE.—1. Several queries on the same subject were answered at page 496, vol. iv. (the number for May 5, 1883). It is not a text in the Bible. 2. Write to the secretary of the East London Hospital for Children, or to that in Great Ormond-street, and make inquiries direct.

LUCINI MARCELLO.—Cut the bread-and-butter very thinly, take off the crust and roll it. There are several heads under which the various styles of musical compositions are classified, amongst which are the classical, operatic, martial, dance, and sacred music, besides others.

MAYFLOWER.—Change the blotting-paper in which you press the flowers frequently. This question has been often answered.

L. E. S.—A gentleman would take off his glove, not a lady in that case.

BOOKKEEPER.—The tale of Robinson Crusoe, written by De Foe, was founded on the adventures of Alexander Selkirk, but the hero himself and his man Friday were the creations of De Foe. But we do not enjoy the story less because of its not being wholly fact, and you must accept the amusement and instruction of "Robina Crusoe" in the same way.

QUERKSY.—We do not approve of such foolish attempts to alter the appearance, and must decline to answer you.

ROSA BONHEUR.—Ladies as a rule do not fee male servants. When staying at a friend's house, therefore, you would fee the upper housemaid; in a smaller house you would fee the parlourmaid and housemaid. Where there is a butler or a man out of livery, you would fee him if he attended to your errands or letters.

THE ARTLESS THING.—Cards are not now sent out after a wedding, and cake only to relations or *very* intimate friends. When the bride receives her friends, some wedding-cake may be offered with the afternoon tea. We could not say; it would depend on the position of the bridegroom.

ELSIE CAIRD complains, like many other English girls, of having had her digestive organs completely put out of order, and to a very serious extent indeed, by a three years' residence in Germany (probably at school), where the cookery was exceedingly greasy in character. The only safe plan to adopt is to procure the advice of a good doctor, and carefully follow the course of treatment he may recommend. Medicine for the liver will be necessary, and possibly a liver tonic. A diet consisting of little if any meat for a time, and neither butter nor one atom of fat of any kind, nor of fried food. A little boiled fish or roast or boiled fowl, and light puddings, a little dressed vegetables, stewed or roast apples, but no oranges. Avoid study or any employment for an hour after dinner, and half an hour after other meals. Dine early, masticate slowly and thoroughly. If the sickness take place after eating, try a dessertspoonful of chicken broth, hot or cold, at a time, and swallow a small scrap of ice immediately after it, and remain perfectly still. This may stop the sickness and restore strength to the stomach, to enable it to do more very shortly. This is all we dare advise. See a doctor, for your case appears to be serious. One visit would at least suffice to supply you with a suitable prescription for medicine.

OLD DUKE.—"All rights reserved," means that the book or magazine and its contents cannot be translated nor used in any way for re-publication without permission of the publishers or author.

obliged to come to London, and, like anyone else, walk about your favourite localities and search for what you want.

GRISELDA.—We fear our business engagements would not permit of our undertaking any extra work.

IGNORAMUS.—If the lady be at home when you call, and not her husband, leave your husband's card for him.

MAY.—Write and congratulate the bridegroom, and express the hope of making the bride's acquaintance at some future day.

CARINA.—Mustard and cress may be grown in a sponge. Reading aloud slowly and distinctly will probably be of service to you.

NAN, NAN.—Inquire at any chemist's for the prepared charcoal, which is sold in bottles, as well as in biscuit form. Full directions are given with each bottle, and there are, we believe, several sizes and prices.

JO (Bristol).—There is no preventive for mosquitoes that we know of, save the "smudges," or little fires, used in America, and lit in the evening all round the houses in the Bush, so that the smoke may drive the mosquitoes away. Net blinds are also useful in the windows, and net or muslin curtains closely-fitting over the beds.

SUNBEAM.—There is nothing to prevent your adding the "de" before your name, if you consider you are entitled to it, and there is no one to pay for doing so.

THE SUMMER NUMBER.

Mother (restraining her tears).—"We must bear up, my darling, and must try to borrow it from a friend. Oh, why did we neglect to order it in time!"

The "Heralds' College," Queen Victoria-street, London, E.C., would be the place to which you should apply for information on the subject. They have every information relating to English families of any note. What is called an "Heraldic Stationer, we believe, would also tell you; there are many advertising in London papers.

NELLIE BURKE. — We think that the lines lack originality, so much so that we have been trying to remember the hymn from which they are taken, probably unconsciously even to yourself.

"GRANDMOTHER DEAR."—One of the great drawbacks to German schools for English girls is the diet, which seems in many cases to have affected the digestion and the health of those sent to them. Growing girls need careful treatment, and this subject should be well considered.

ALICE EVERTON.—We are gratified by your letter, which is well expressed, and fairly well written. In reference to "washing and starching a black print dress," see pages 18, 107, and 219, vol. ii., under "How to Wash and Iron."

WINIFRED.—We regret to say that your verses are not "poetry." The versification is quite incorrect, and no poetical and original ideas occur in them. Your handwriting promises well, but is not yet quite formed

one if only sloped the right way, like "Mater's," which is a good one. "Maude" writes like her mother, or at least much in the same style. "Lillian" gives good promise, but her letters are upright.

SPERANZA and PATIENZA. — The poems enclosed, "Why?" and "Infelix," we shall have pleasure in inserting in THE GIRL'S OWN PAPER (in "The Girl's Own Page"), if you send us a certificate of their being your own, a matter of rule, not personal to yourself; and at the same time state your age. We admire your poems much. Yes, we number many of your countrywomen amongst our correspondents. Your sister might use some wash for her hair unmixed with any oil or grease. It ought to shine; rough black hair would be frightful.

LILIAN C.—A person with a "white" skin and "blue eyes" could not be termed a "brunette." To be thus described, the skin should either be of a clear olive hue, like a southron, or of a nut-brown complexion, like a gipsy, and the red colour should be like that of a russet-apple. Reduce the size of your writing and slope the letters the right way, and you will write a beautiful hand.

ADA and LIZZIE.—Your quotation—

"Oh, woman! in our hours of ease,
Uncertain, coy, and hard to please,"

is from Sir Walter Scott's poem, "The Lady of the Lake." The term "blue-stocking" originated in a learned society formed at Venice in the year 1400, the members, men and women, adopting as a distinguishing mark the wearing of blue stockings. On dying out there, it appeared in Paris in 1590, the lady *savantes* taking up the idea warmly. It came to England in 1780, and was patronised by Mrs. Montague, and died out in 1840 in the person of the last member of the society, Miss Monckton, afterwards Countess of Cork.

A. A.—We consider your little poem ("Sowing and Reaping") superior to the majority which we receive for review. May you hereafter realise the full happiness of the glorious "reaping" time to which you refer.

F. C. C. and P.—A full description of Her Majesty's household is to be found at pages 21 and 154, vol. ii. The duties of the various officers are there named in detail.

FLOSS.—To make a decoction of sarsaparilla, digest two and a half ounces for half an hour of the cut Jamaica sarsaparilla in one and a half pints of boiling water; then boil for ten minutes and strain. The dose is from a wine-glassful to half a pint.

CARRIE LEACH.—In reference to the salt mines of Wieliczka, Poland, it is true that there are halls and passages, a chapel containing statues cut out of salt; the mine is perfectly dry and airy, and the miners are a fine race of men, and their labour is healthy. But it is not true that any of them live underground, for they rarely remain below the surface for more than eight hours daily. How well you write for eight years old, and you express yourself very well!

PENHURST writes to tell us that an English girl at Amalfi has suggested that, as the inscription on the monumental slab covering the grave of Queen Katharine of Aragon, in Peterborough Cathedral, is obliterated, all girls spelling their Christian name in the same way should subscribe for putting up a brass there to her memory. She has sent the first donation herself, and others have followed her example. The idea appears to be a popular one, and Mrs. Perowne will receive any further subscriptions sent to the Deanery, Peterborough. 2. "A man of Kent" signified one born east of the Medway. These men went out with green boughs to William the Conqueror, and in return had all their ancient privileges confirmed to them. They call themselves "the *invicti*." A "Kentish man" is only a resident of that county, without reference to his birthplace.

SHAMROCK.—We acknowledge your kind letter with thanks, and regret that the verses you have sent us are not suitable for insertion in our paper. They only consist of prose in rhyme.

ALICE.—We are very glad to hear that you and your friends have succeeded in saving from £9 to £12 a year through the judicious instructions on the subject of dress supplied by a "Lady Dressmaker." The names "Alice" and "Alicia" count for one and the same.

S. E. C.—If you have failed in removing the machine-oil from your carpet by means of heat and blotting-paper, by benzine, and by washing with soap, we think you had better send it to a cleaner; or else, if practicable, you had better have the nearest seam ripped, and turn the outside edges of the carpet to the middle, so placing the stain at the wall, where less noticeable, and where a chair may cover it. The table will require to be repolished.

DAISY.—We should never recommend anything of the kind. We think that plenty of soap and water, daily exercise, and wholesome food are much better.

VIXEN.—In painting on satin, you should mix a little white of egg with the colour, together with Chinese white; this will supply a good glaze, and also prepare the surface of the material. We shall give an article on the subject. Another mode of preparation is to size the satin, by brushing it over with a decoction made of a pinch of alum and another of isinglass, dissolved in a tumbler of hot water. Then leave it to dry. The Chinese white will be found to adhere longer by mixing it with a small quantity of water-colour megilp.

MAY.—We thank you for the present of your pretty specimen card. There is such a "glut" of them at present in the market, that you will have to dispose of them, if you can, at stationers' shops in your own neighbourhood, or through friends elsewhere.

Above: answers to readers' queries on art, June 26, 1880.

Far right: elegantly decorated, a page of replies from August 7, 1886.

KATE WREN.—You might as well "cry for the moon" in your position as a domestic servant. If eligible for a different calling, enabling you to have a home of your own, you might have a piano and practise if you liked. [1891]

VIOLET seems to be very young and foolish. She drinks vinegar, and writes love poems, and does not seem to have grasped the purpose of her life here, which is to serve and love God and her brother, and come short in none of her daily home duties. To take much vinegar means to destroy her digestion and deteriorate the blood, and she will cease to be a worthy object of love if she fall into ill-health through her own folly. [1889]

A DAUGHTER OF CANADA (aged 13) must be crazy, and had far better attend to her lessons than worry herself and us with such perpetually-repeated and unprofitable enquiries. [1886]

POPPY.—From the constant repetitions of questions we think our girls must, many of them, have heads like sieves. See our articles★ on "How to converse agreeably", "Good breeding in daily converse". We have done all we could to educate our girls in these matters, and cannot continue to repeat ourselves.

One wonders whether the criticism of handwriting which appears so regularly was solicited:

B.R. (Ardmore House).—Your troubles arise from a lowered state of the general health. Consult a doctor as to your home and its healthiness, diet, and exercise. Your handwriting is shocking, and the tone of your letter foolish and flippant. [1884]

AN ONLY GIRL.—We think your writing quite the most ugly we have ever seen. [1890]

Occasionally there is a dig at a reader's use of English:

MURIEL says their house "is *infected* with ants!" Had they measles, or whooping-cough, or what? Perhaps you mean that the house was *infested* with them. [1891]

One really unkind reply is addressed to SUBSCRIBER in 1892:

Oil your head and hair thickly until entirely free. We are surprised that you should ask so disgusting a question to be answered in print in a refined paper! Go to some nurse, and do not write to us again until thoroughly clean.

Probably B.R. deserved to be rebuked for her folly and flippancy, but poor SUBSCRIBER! Poor ANNIE GRAHAM, too, who is told "One of your questions respecting medical treatment is scarcely a delicate one, and we decline to answer it."

Undeterred, readers continued to write trustfully on an enormous variety of subjects. They frequently sent their poems for criticism, which was rarely enthusiastic. The reply to THEODORA is a fair example: "The enclosed poetry is harmless. We are sure it amused you to write it." So

---

★ An extract from one of the "Good breeding" articles to which the Editor refers gives something of their flavour: "It would be kind and judicious in your converse with some old gentleman to draw him out on the subject of his travels, adventures, military or naval service, and exploits of bygone years, and the interest you showed, in words ever so few, could prove quite a refreshment to him." (1883)

ANSWERS TO CORRESPONDENTS

ATHELIS must find a standard of wrong and right in reading for herself, or she will always be miserable. If on rising from the perusal of any book she feels a better girl, more wishful to act rightly, and more conscientious in judging her actions, the book has done her good. During her girlhood it is well to be strict in everything she reads, as her mind is unformed, and amusing reading means, not rest and recreation, but generally mental dissipation.

THISTLE must read the various articles by "Medicus" on the hair, and be guided by them in her treatment of it. A good cleansing and softening wash for the head is composed of camphor and borax—of each one ounce in a quart of boiling water. Keep in a bottle, and when needed apply a little with a sponge, rubbing well in.

HOMESPUN.—Your letter, so well expressed and kindly, too, was read with interest. It did you credit, and were the writing a little smaller it would be better. We regret that your former letter was not answered, and we do not now recall the question it contained. Accept our best wishes.

UGLY MUG.—As a rule, it is both polite and more considerate to repay borrowed stamps with stamps, for though you give the penny at the time, it does not repay the trouble of buying another stamp and fetching it from the post-office. With elderly people this point of view should always be considered in borrowing them.

MAUD.—We must refer you to our indexes in reference to the complexion. Probably your diet is unsuitable, or you eat too fast, or you need internal rather than external remedies.

VIRTUOUS INDIGNATION does not know what she is talking about. Where does it say that godparents are "responsible for our sins until we are confirmed"? You invent a difficulty for yourself, and then profess yourself virtuously indignant. The duties of sponsors are to see that the child be religiously instructed and shall enjoy certain religious privileges in course of time. Remember this, that, quite apart from any promise or engagement made for him, his obligations to his Maker and Redeemer are as great and binding by every law of duty and gratitude, whether such promises be made or not. As yet you only scribble, and you should write copies daily to form your hand.

PETERHOFF.—We have heard it said that "no dead donkey is ever seen anywhere," not that they never die. Many complete disappearances are always taking place. Where do all the pins go? We think the former go to the knackers. See answer to "E. Gray" respecting your second query.

H. Y. Z.—The serviette is not refolded by the guest, but left generally on the chair on which he or she sits. At home asparagus may be eaten held in the fingers, but at a more formal repast the tops are cut off on the plate and eaten with the fork, like any other vegetable.

LOTINCHA.—Carisbrooke Castle was once a British and Roman fortress. Cerdic, founder of the kingdom of the West Saxons, took it in 530. William Fitz-Osborne, Earl of Hereford (temp. William I.), gave it its Norman character. The imprisonment of Charles I. within it took place between November, 1647, and November, 1648; and the death of his daughter, the Princess Elizabeth, on September 8th, 1650, history states, of a broken heart, at the early age of fifteen. Your writing is very legible, but lacks grace.

AN AUSTRALIAN.—We could not venture to offer you an opinion as to Florida, especially as a residence for delicate people. You had better procure and study one or more books on the subject of the climate and the best locality, away from the swamps—"Down South," by Lady Duffus Hardy, and Barber's "Florida for Tourists and Settlers."

BLANCHE JANE (Canada).—This is the last notice that we shall take of your silly letters. Learn your lessons, read your Bible, and make and mend your own clothes, and waste no more time in writing such rubbish.

E. GRAY.—The sect of the Manichæans was founded by a native of Persia, who was born about the year A.D. 250. It was a fusion of Zoroastrianism and gnostic Christianity. Amongst other heretical dogmas, he maintained that the human body of Christ was a mere phantom, and His sufferings only apparent. As for Manichæus himself, he claimed to be the Blessed Paraclete promised by Christ.

FORGET-ME-NOT.—You should study our series of articles on good breeding and etiquette, under all circumstances and in every position of society. You should not bow perpetually on meeting and re-meeting an acquaintance. You can look into a shop or speak to your companion so as not to catch his eyes; but should you do so, give a smile with the slightest inclination of the head. Sometimes the Lord sees fit to permit you to be tried by temptations, and it is His will that we should look to Him for help, and grace, and strength to "fight the good fight of faith."

ENGLISH GIRL.—Pennies bearing the date 1864 have never been "called in," nor do we know where the foolish story of "the bar of gold that was dropped into the metal from which they were cast" originated; but they are of no more value than other pennies, and only one shilling can be got for twelve.

PETER CAMERON had better wear gloves, with the tips of the fingers soaked in alum-water, when she is reading, to prevent her biting her nails. A princess dress is the simplest dress to make for a doll.

I PENSIERI NON PAGANO GABELLE.—We cannot imagine how you came to think claret could be a teetotal drink, at any time. It is a wine, just as much as Burgundy or champagne.

F. A. C.—We are obliged by your letter giving the address of the Midland Reading Society—secretary, Miss Cowper, Hillesden, Buckinghamshire, which gives prizes in money and sends its rules gratis.

BEULAH TERRACE.—We can only advise you to get the "Handy Guide to Emigration," by Mr. Paton, published by Stock, 370, Oxford-street, W. In that every one of the colonies is mentioned and every information given; price 6d. only.

L. T. G. (New Zealand).—Certainly, our paper patterns are sent to the colonies, including your own. You have only to send an order for what you require and a post-office order for the money due for the patterns. Your handwriting is not yet formed. Any set of copperplate copies would suit you in small round-hand.

TROUBLED ONE.—We are told in the Scriptures that "the Gospel shall be preached to all nations," not that it will be received, nor that the conversion of all nations will be the result: far otherwise, for our Lord says, "When the Son of Man cometh shall He find faith on the earth?"—at so low an ebb will it be found; and even "the love of many shall wax cold." We cannot tell when "the end will be." We must watch.

AFFLICTED HARRIET had better leave off eating late suppers, and avoid going to sleep or lying on her back in bed. She probably breathes through her mouth by day instead of her nose—a bad habit, which she must check. It would be well for her if she did read "Luke and Belinda" under the circumstances.

HEN.—We do not think the curse in question would be a good possession, and we certainly should not give any information where to get it. Why do you want it?

KISMET.—The evil actions which you name, such as petty pilferings, and other sins, should not hinder your making a solemn and sincere preparation for presenting yourself at the Lord's table. If you have quarrelled with anyone, make it up so far as, on your own side, you can do so. If you have stolen, restore what you have taken. If you have neglected your daily prayers, resume them; and, having humbly confessed to God your utter unworthiness, and prayed for His pardon and grace, present yourself at the holy table in the spirit of that beautiful hymn—

"Just as I am, without one plea,
But that Thy blood was shed for me,
And that Thou bid'st me come to Thee,
O, Lamb of God I come!"

Certainly, you must tell your stepmother the truth about the birdcage, and clear the boy's character before you presume to partake of the Lord's Supper.

ONE IN TROUBLE.—Your question is one more for a good surgeon than for us; but we do not think that, having had one operation, you had better try another without the best possible advice.

STEPHANOTIS.—Read "Lissom Hands and Pretty Feet," page 348, vol. i. You could not have the swellings on your joints "taken out." You might as well propose that when your nose is swelled from a bad cold and becomes inflamed that it should be "taken out" likewise. Wear straight, square-toed shoes, with low broad heels and broad soles.

IVY must read the articles of "Medicus." Her question is so vague that she must only try the measures recommended by him, which are safe and reliable.

MAUDE JAMES must consult a doctor, and be guided by him as to diet and regimen.

J. WHITE.—Your quotation is taken from Campbell's "Pleasures of Hope"—

"What though my winged hours of bliss have been
Like angel visits—few and far between."

LADY CLARICE.—We should think you had better ask him not to smoke at all, if you have any influence with him under the circumstances.

EVERYTHING AND SOMEBODY.—We should think there is something wrong in your mode of living, and can only advise you to read the advice of "Medicus."

TROUBLED ONE should consult a doctor about her general health.

EDUCATIONAL.

LESLIE and ANNIE FRY.—1. We have not got our series of articles on "Good Breeding" and the "Rules of Etiquette" in separate form. In the *Girl's Own Indoor Book* and the *Outdoor Book* you will find four of the series. Others amongst them are in vol. ii., pp. 73 and 314; in vol. iii., pp. 90, 163, 278, and 419; in vol. iv., pp. 74 and 403; in vol. v., pp. 38, 98, 202, 303, and 474. We have not space to enumerate more.—2. Almost any colour would suit "Leslie" from the description given of herself—dark ruby, or a full blue, depending on the season.

POLARIS.—Ladies are trained as teachers of the Kindergarten system of instruction at the Ladies' College of Cheltenham. The sister of the Head Master at Harrow, Miss Welldon, superintends and directs it. A house is provided for students. The entire expense of board and teaching is about fifty guineas a year. In London there are six training colleges and about twenty - seven schools. Also, there are training colleges for teachers at Bedford. Address Miss Sim, The Crescent; and at Manchester, Miss Snell, 91, Acomb Street, Greenheys.

MRS. E. B. ELLMAN.—We thank you for informing us of the resignation of your daughter from the secretaryship of so many branches of education united in her Girls' Club, and also for the address of the new Secretary who has undertaken to supply her place since her marriage, viz., Miss Davies, High Street, Coleford, Gloucestershire.

MISS J. K. MORTON.—You do not name your new club, but it seems to be of a literary character, admitting girls up to twenty years of age, and requiring a subscription of 6d. a year (too little, we think, to provide a half-yearly prize). Address Secretary, at Wilson House, Wilson Road, Birchfields, Birmingham.

F. VON H. and S. R. N.—There are several Musical Practising Societies. Amongst them there is the Musical Association at Richmond House, Redland Green, Bristol; address Miss Mary Castle, the Secretary; and The Musical Society, Secretary, Miss McLandsborough, Lindan Terrace, Manningham, Bradford, Yorkshire.

MISS AMY FIRTH.—We are glad to have been the means of procuring members for your Practising Society, and give notice to our readers that your term commenced on November 1st; also, that when writing for your rules (to your address, Trinity House, Bradford), a stamp should invariably be sent. It is little creditable to the fifty girls writing for them to have omitted to enclose the amount due for postage, and of course it diminishes the amount which would otherwise have been allocated to prizes.

MISCELLANEOUS.

KITTY.—Nineteen is not too young to be engaged, but far too young to be married. And, indeed, we think that you will find occupation enough in the next three or four years in learning how to make a home happy and comfortable, and in improving your education, which seems to have been much neglected.

F. M.—"How to Study the English Bible?" A small book with this title, by the Rev. Canon Girdlestone, Principal of Wycliffe Hall, Oxford, will be very helpful to you. It is published at 5d, Paternoster Row.

A. B.—Yes; there is a small private Home of Rest for girls in business, Post Office clerks, school teachers, etc. Address, Miss H. Mason, "The Hawthorns, Framfield, near Uckfield, Sussex. Board and lodging, 12s. 6d. a week, and 5s. 3d. return ticket from London, available for a month. A stamped envelope should be enclosed to the secretary for her reply to any enquiries. We do not know whether any extension of time could be arranged for persons needing a longer rest.

A MEMBER writes to request that we will again bring the Scripture Reading and Prayer Union before our readers, so strongly recommended by the late Miss Frances Havergal. The organs of the Union are edited by the Rev. Ernest Boys, Beverley, Sidcup, Kent, one being the *Christian Progress Magazine*, and the other *Living Waters*. We have pleasure in complying with the request of our correspondent.

MARJORIE S.—One guinea a year is the tax charged for armorial bearings.

MARIE GORDON (India).—If the coloured picture should stick to the opposite page in the monthly numbers, it can very easily be set free by gently warming it before the fire.

WALTER KRUSE, of whose leaflet on "Bible Marking" to facilitate Bible study we gave a notice some time ago, writes to correct the address then given. His address is, Yew Tree Farm, Leeds, near Maidstone, Kent. It is not the Leeds in Yorkshire. We are glad his scheme has prospered.

RULES

I. No charge is made for answering questions.

II. All correspondents to give initials or pseudonym.

III. The Editor reserves the right of declining to reply to any of the questions.

IV. No direct answers can be sent by the Editor through the post.

V. No more than two questions may be asked in one letter, which must be addressed to the Editor of THE GIRL'S OWN PAPER, 56, Paternoster Row, London, E.C.

VI. No addresses of firms, tradesmen, or any other matter of the nature of an advertisement will be inserted.

DISCOURAGED.—The Married Women's Property Act would cover all your own possessions, both at the time of your marriage and afterwards. At the same time a careful inventory of furniture, etc., would be very desirable. A new Bill has been passed recently, which renders the position of a widow far better should her husband die intestate.

SOUTHSEA.—You had better arrange to go over to Boulogne by an early boat, and so leave yourself time to look for apartments before night. There is a line of steamers to Boulogne from London every day during the summer.

ROSEBUD.—It is a matter of taste and good feeling entirely as to whether you should wear your first wedding ring when you are married for the second time. The best test is, how you would like it if done to yourself were you in the other person's place. You should study your present husband's wishes.

PRINCESS had better apply to her father for protection, and tell him how she is treated. Her position is very hard, and we sympathise with her; but we feel sure all such trials of temper and patience are for our good, and will train us to be good "soldiers of Christ," "bearing hardness" for His sake, and showing love to those who persecute and treat us badly. But even so, "Princess" should ask her father's protection against personal violence.

POPPY.—Your "aunty" is right in requiring a little girl of eleven to wear pinafores. We advise you to add a "c" to the word denoting your dress. It should not be spelt "frok"; and the word "enough" is not written "inuff." But though "Poppy" should attend a little more to her spelling, her writing is good for her age.

BLACK ROOK.—1. Send to the washerwoman.—2. Poem very mediocre indeed!

KATHLEEN MAVOURNEEN should say, "My mother wishes you to do so and so," in giving orders for her mother to the servants.

LAURA.—It is the opinion of most writers on the subject that the tree that attains the greatest age, as a general rule, is the yew, that is to say, of all European trees. This distinction above its fellows of different genus may be realised as probably true when the history of the specimen at Brabourne, Kent, assigns to it, according to De Candolle, the prodigious age of 3,000 years! while one at Hedsor, Buckinghamshire, is said to be still more ancient. There is another at Fortingal, Perthshire, that is given 500 years less; and one in Derbyshire, to be seen in Darley Churchyard, 2,000. We may add to our list those of Fountains Abbey, Yorkshire, which are at the lowest computation 1,200 years old; and that at Ankerwyke House, Staines, is named as existing when Magna Charta was signed, in 1215, and as the place of rendezvous of Henry VIII. and Anne Boleyn. There is a grove of these remarkable trees at Norbury Park, Surrey, which dates back to the time of the Druids.

POOR POLLIE POLE.—There is a National Hospital for the Epileptic and Paralysed in Queen Square, Bloomsbury, W.C. Address the Secretary, Mr. B. Burford Rawlings. Also another hospital in Portland Terrace, Regent's Park (near St. John's Wood Road Station), where some patients are received free of charge, or on payment according to their means. Write to, or get some one to call on, Mr. H. Howgrave Graham, Secretary.

HYPERION.—Dew is produced by the condensation of watery vapour from the atmosphere by the cooling of the earth and vegetation bedewed. The radiation of their heat into open space produces this cooling as a natural consequence. As the sun sets and leaves them, they cool, though with unequal rapidity. Badly conducting solid matter does so rapidly, the atmosphere comparatively slowly; as do good conductors, if in contact with the earth, at a much slower rate, because the amount of warmth which they had lost they recover from the earth. The reason that the grass is so quickly covered with dew is the fact that it is the first to be deprived of the sunlight, is a bad conductor, and radiates well. Then the temperature at the level of the grass is some ten degrees colder than the air a few feet above it—say at an elevation of ten feet. Also, as stillness is essential to the formation of dew, the grass will be found quite wet when ever-moving branches and leaves of trees are comparatively dry. According to Dr. Dalton, the precipitation of dew annually in England is equal to five inches of rain.

VERA.—The hereditary successor of the sovereign (or the immediate heir) is his eldest son. The representative of H.R.H. the Prince of Wales is the Duke of Clarence and Avondale. And if the latter died without issue, his brother, Prince George of Wales, would be his successor.

M. CLARK (Austria).—Whatever may be the rank of those who may address you, you cannot err if you style them "Gnädige Frau." This applies to all German-speaking countries.

READER OF "G. O. P."—We do not recommend hair-washes excepting those home-made, such as rosemary tea, which is excellent, and may also be had from any chemist's shop. But you should refer to the articles by "Medicus" on the care of the hair.

many poems were presented to the Editor that in 1887 he remarked plaintively, "We wish our dear good girls would not send us such a quantity of verses to be criticised."

Two answers to would-be artists appearing next to each other in an 1885 issue present an interesting contrast:

MOLLY.—We cannot say much for the original sketches you enclose. We should think you had been reading a ghost book, or had been studying photographs of spirits, so spectral do they appear. One crazy girl appears about to throw herself over a precipice, and her companion, a thread paper creature, looks like the maiden all forlorn, but you omitted the cow with the crumpled horn.

NANNIE TORY.—Your drawings evince much talent. We should advise you to go to some school of art, and study thoroughly.

The answer to LADY NYASA in 1888 is still more encouraging, proving that readers were not invariably treated as, at best, harmless dilettantes:

The drawing you send is extremely well done; we should think you could make art a success, and regret to hear that you have to be taken from school. It is better for parents to practise economy in anything but in this, as in the present day it is of the utmost importance to their children. We should suggest your going to the Birkbeck Institution, Chancery Lane, E.C., or to the Polytechnic, Regent Street, W., or to some school of art near you, and making every effort to keep up your studies, and in due season to pass those examinations you have not passed. In this way you will do much better for yourself and your parents, than by trying to find a situation when too young.

Two letters follow each other under the heading MUSIC in an issue of 1891:

PIANO, ORGAN, VIOLIN. The piece you send us bears all the marks of having been composed (as you say it was) in five minutes. Not quite up to our mark yet.

A MOTHER. We strongly advise you not to waste your time, nor your child's brain power, in obliging her to continue the laborious study of any mere accomplishment such as music, for which she has evidently no natural taste. Under such circumstances she could never make her attainments available for gaining a living; and your time and hers is too valuable to be wasted. Besides, she would prove a nuisance to all who heard her.

Questions about pets occur frequently. The Victorian dog appears to have had a thin time, unless it was an eccentric opinion of the Editor's that meat was bad for dogs, and that dog biscuits provided a healthier diet; and the Victorian parrot appears, judging by a number of queries, to have been given to the distressing habit of pulling out its own feathers. It is a relief to find that EDELWEISS is told:

Cats require warmth and kindness more almost than any creatures. They should never be turned out at night nor kept out of doors by day. [1885]

The girls do not confine themselves to queries about dogs, cats, parrots and canaries:

D.H. Your pet toad must be an idiot, or at least very deficient in natural instincts, if it cannot cater for itself; it knows better than you where to find its own food. [1886]

MUSIC.

VERENA.—In reply to your question "whether the semiquaver be played with the last quaver in the treble, or not, in playing a triplet of quavers with a quaver dot, and semiquaver in the bass?" you should play two quavers of the triplet with the dotted quaver, and the last quaver in the treble with the semiquaver in the bass. Perhaps the Prize Musical Improvement Society, which has a Harmony Correspondence Class, might suit you. The other clubs for musical improvement named in the "Dictionary of Girls' Clubs" are for practising only. Address, Miss Graham, 69, Bedford Street, Abercromby Square, Liverpool. The correspondence on harmony is 15s. a quarter, which, after all, is inexpensive, though so much more than mere practising clubs' fees.

OUR BESSIE should take the trouble of paying a visit to a music publisher and look through some of the exercises and pieces for the violin. We do not know what advance she has made in playing, nor whether, as yet, any at all. The people who serve in the shop will give her a choice suitable either for beginners or those more advanced.

LOVER OF MUSIC.—To be a professor of music you must go through a course of study in one of the colleges, and obtain certificates on passing certain examinations. There are several colleges in London; amongst them is the Guildhall School of Music. There are three terms of twelve weeks each, and the fees vary from £4 10s. to £33 1s. 6d. a term, according to the subjects taught, and the number of lessons given. There is also an entrance fee of 5s.

BASHFUL FIFTEEN.—There is no harm in your singing any more than the young birds attempting to do so, or the young cocks to crow, however hoarsely. What would be injurious is a regular course of training of the voice by a master, which should only begin, and very carefully, too, when infancy is giving place to maturity. 2. You should hold the eye that is so blood-shot in an eye-glass full of very hot water when you go to bed, and avoid reading or doing fine work by candle or gaslight, and of exposing your eyes to a cold wind until quite recovered.

NINETEEN.—We cannot assist you in the matter of slowness in reading music. The acquirement of it rests with yourself. The strengthening of the fingers by rubbing with oil is recommended. Vaseline might still be better.

Above: answers to queries about music, January 25, 1890.

Far left: an interesting collection of replies, May 2, 1891.

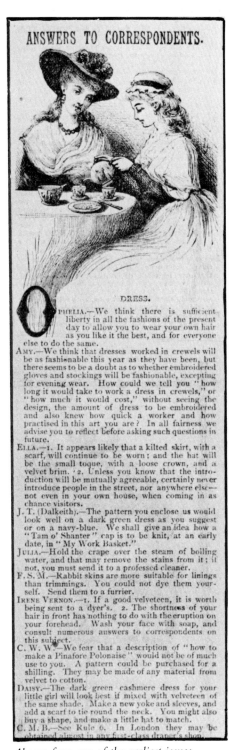

ANSWERS TO CORRESPONDENTS.

DRESS.

OPHELIA.—We think there is sufficient liberty in all the fashions of the present day to allow you to wear your own hair as you like it the best, and for everyone else to do the same.

AMY.—We think that dresses worked in crewels will be as fashionable this year as they have been, but there seems to be a doubt as to whether embroidered gloves and stockings will be fashionable, excepting for evening wear. How could we tell you "how long it would take to work a dress in crewels," or "how much it would cost," without seeing the design, the amount of dress to be embroidered and also knew how quick a worker and how practised in this art you are? In all fairness we advise you to reflect before asking such questions in future.

ELLA.—1. It appears likely that a kilted skirt, with a scarf, will continue to be worn; and the hat will be the small toque, with a loose crown, and a velvet brim. 2. Unless you know that the introduction will be mutually agreeable, certainly never introduce people in the street, nor anywhere else—not even in your own house, when coming in as chance visitors.

J. T. (Dalkeith).—The pattern you enclose us would look well on a dark green dress as you suggest or on a navy-blue. We shall give an idea how a "Tam o' Shanter" cap is to be knit, at an early date, in "My Work Basket."

JULIA.—Hold the crape over the steam of boiling water, and that may remove the stains from it; if not, you must send it to a professed cleaner.

F. S. M.—Rabbit skins are more suitable for linings than trimmings. You could not dye them yourself. Send them to a furrier.

IRENE VERNON.—1. If a good velveteen, it is worth being sent to a dyer's. 2. The shortness of your hair in front has nothing to do with the eruption on your forehead. Wash your face with soap, and consult numerous answers to correspondents on this subject.

C. W. W.—We fear that a description of "how to make a Pinafore Polonaise" would not be of much use to you. A pattern could be purchased for a shilling. They may be made of any material from velvet to cotton.

DAISY.—The dark green cashmere dress for your little girl will look best if mixed with velveteen of the same shade. Make a new yoke and sleeves, and add a scarf to tie round the neck. You might also buy a shape, and make a little hat to match.

C. M. B.—See Rule 6. In London they may be obtained almost in any first-class draper's shop.

Above: from one of the earliest issues, answers to queries on dress and fashion, March 20, 1880.

WENONA. Place your spider's nest under a small glass shade. [1885]

One wonders at the Editor's sangfroid in the latter case, unless the assumption was that the object was no longer inhabited.

A query which recurs frequently concerns a use for old postage stamps. The reply to AN ELDER SISTER in 1880 is:

No. Old postage stamps are of no use, except for the manufacture of "stamp snakes", which are very nice playthings for children. They require about 4,000 penny stamps for the body alone, while half-penny ones are needed for the tail. The head is made of black velvet, having bead eyes, but we think that you would require to see one, before you could manufacture one properly yourself.★

Etiquette is the subject of frequent enquiries:

CODLING.—The exclamation "Hang it!", although not swearing, is a vulgar slang expression. [1892]

IMPULSIVE.—If no one else were by to find his coat-sleeve for him, you were not guilty of any serious breach of etiquette in helping him to it. But such acts of friendship might lead to undesirable acquaintanceships, and you had better keep out of the way. You cannot safely perform such little attentions to strange men as a general rule. Were he a very old and infirm person it would be another matter. [1892]

TIBBIE.—If accompanied by your sisters (or one at least) you need feel no scruple in accepting the rector's Sunday hospitality, as you are helping his services by playing the organ. [1898]

A.B.C.—You were quite right in not returning the bow of any man with whom you were not acquainted. Girls who travel by train to school should be most particular in their conduct, and keep up an appearance of gravity and reserve. [1887]

HUGH, MAUD, AND GUS.—Never look at any strange man as you approach him in passing by, for sometimes a look may be taken advantage of by forward and impertinent men. Look straight onwards, and do not speak loud nor laugh in the street. It is generally a girl's own fault if she be spoken to, and, as such, is a disgrace to her, of which she should be ashamed to speak. But we must hope and believe that the liberties thus taken were owing to no light manner, nor indiscreet conduct in your case. [1881]

EUSTACIE wishes to know "up to what age a girl may climb a tree?" If a pack of wolves were after you, we should advise you to climb a tree up to ninety or a hundred! Otherwise, why make yourself look so like one of Dr Darwin's monkey-progenitors? [1880]

DUBBS.—It is not unladylike to ride a tricycle. It is enough to say that Her Majesty the Queen has patronised it for her granddaughters. But your dress may be unsuitable for it, and you may hold yourself ungracefully, and work the pedals in an ungainly way. If your elbows be spread out, your head much bent forward, and your dress be so ill-arranged as to show your stockings to a considerable extent, the general appearance behind will be decidedly inelegant and froglike. [1885]

★ A "stamp snake" appears in the illustration on page 36.

SACK.—How comes it that you sometimes walk with a gentleman, if not engaged to him? If your intended husband, you may, of course, walk under one umbrella; but otherwise you had better keep your own to yourself. If needing one, he can buy one as well as you can. [1885]

BLACK AND WHITE.—It would be utterly unseemly, and as much as your reputation is worth, to walk out at night with any man but your father or brother. There are certain rules of society, in the lower and middle classes as well as in the higher, which were made by common consent, for the protection of young women, and this is one—that they should not be out in the streets or roads at night, unless under the care of a member of the family or middle-aged woman. You should get home before dark, if possible; and always be accompanied by a friend, if walking (even by daylight), with a man to whom you are not engaged. [1892]

PANSY.—Why uncertain in a question of thanking for any little attention paid you? Be sure of one thing, that you can never err on the side of graciousness, and no trifling act on the part of another is too insignificant to be accepted with a kindly acknowledgment. Always say "I am obliged to you for your escort", or words to that effect. [1901]

Perhaps my favourite reply on the subject of etiquette is the following, addressed to PERPLEXITY in 1891:

We can see no cause for perplexity in such a case as yours. The man who sent you a mouse in a match-box could scarcely be called a "gentleman", and such vulgar practical jokes are unknown in "polite society".

The *G.O.P.* could not invariably provide what was asked for. EMILY FRANCES must have been disappointed to be told in 1886, "We cannot undertake to give a recipe for making woollen parrots." Perhaps understandably, the query put by HURLY-BURLY in 1880 received in reply only another question: "Are you serious in asking 'whether eating eggs, and wearing high-heeled shoes, make you deaf'?"

Some of the replies are mysterious, such as this to ELLEN in 1886: "They are, and always will be so, although not universally worn, nor ever will be." (Beards? Hats? Corsets?) The following at first glance seems even more baffling:

E.E.E. (Cape Colony).—We know all about the appliance to which you refer, and strongly advise you never to use it again. It is, as it were, a stepping-stone to what is highly dangerous and evil; and many who have made a toy of it have discovered its real character, and destroyed it. [1889]

A flash of inspiration—could the nasty thing have been an ouija board? Present-day magazine correspondents tend to be uninspired in their choice of pseudonym, all too frequently settling for WORRIED. Those of the Victorian *Girl's Own Paper* are of a far richer variety, verging, indeed, on the rococo. Among them are TEAPOT, COREOPSIS TINCTORIA, THE TOAD, A PRINCESS OF THULE, THE DAUGHTER OF AN IRISH LANDLORD, MAD CRICKETER, MARQUIS POFFWHISKER, A BASHFUL YOUNG POTATO, QUEEN OF THE WUNKS and DISTRESSED CRUMPET. After these, a mere PERPLEXED tends to pale.

Serious family problems are dealt with from time to time. Questions about marital difficulties are not frequent, but V.I.S. is advised in 1887,

WORK.

JANIE.—Finding that you and one or two other readers have not been able to work the "Fly pattern tricot stripe," described on page 332 of our March number, we gladly re-write it, making some slight alterations, by which means we hope all difficulty will be removed. Commence by making a chain of twelve stitches. 1st Row.—Miss two, tricot one to end of row, you will then have five loops on the needle; make four chain into the last loop in chain. 2nd Row.—Take off first loop on needle, make one chain, take off *two* together, continue making one and taking off two to end of row. 3rd Row.—Make three chain, * draw a loop through the first open space, a second through the perpendicular stitch, and a third through the second opening, take off *three* together, make one chain, and repeat from *, commencing in the same space as last worked into. Make four chain in the third chain stitch at the end of row. These *two* last rows are to be worked until the stripe is the length required. The number and colour of the stripes must depend upon the size and purpose for which the couvrette is intended.

Above: queries about work (in the sense of handicrafts) were often sent in (June 18, 1881).

"Your sister could certainly get a separation, and could protect herself and property from her worthless husband, and she could punish him if he were caught." And MAUD in 1886:

Go to the police office and inform the inspector of your trouble and the cruel treatment to which you are subjected, and he will take you to the proper quarters, where you may obtain a separation and an allowance. Do nothing rashly and nothing wrong, be your trials and provocations what they may. What you suggested to us would be very wrong indeed, and we think and hope you must have done so under great excitement. If by word or act you thoughtlessly gave cause for jealousy, you might not obtain the separation and allowance, to which otherwise you could lay just claim. Pray God to guide you and preserve you from evil.

LIZZIE HASLAM is told in 1883:

Your little nephew and niece—who are dependent on your support, as well as motherly care (being orphans), and who at so tender an age refuse to obey you or to call you "auntie", as in their mother's lifetime—should be punished until you can again bring them under control. Try mild measures, such as standing them in a corner, or take away their toys for a time; this failing, give a good slap or two with your own hand on theirs, and if the rebellion be too determined for this to put it down, nothing remains then to be done but to give the unruly little people a good sound whipping. Instant obedience must be obtained, or later on your authority will be irretrievably gone, and they will grow up without due moral training.

What story can have lain behind A.C.'s letter to elicit this reply in 1889:

Could you not arrange with your clergyman or minister to come and have an interview with the wild, unmanageable girl—unexpectedly to her—and let him tell her of the injury to her character and her future prospects in life this conduct of hers must be. You could not send her to a reformatory, unless she were guilty of some criminal offence. If the clergyman's representations have no effect in shaming her, you had better consult him as to any school at which she could be placed, or she might perhaps be sent to some quiet distant place—put to service in a farmhouse, where there would be a strict hand over her.

The sense of family duty was strong throughout the epoch. The great majority of marriages were made for life, but the risk of early death meant that a widowed parent might be left with a number of small children to care for, or faced with years of loneliness. In an early issue (November, 1880), a reply from the Editor deals firmly with the question of a parent's remarriage:

PERPLEXITY.—You are very cruel and quite in the wrong to annoy your father about his second marriage. As there seems to be nothing against the new wife, you have no right to resent the union and to talk about leaving home. We know a case of a dying wife making her husband promise never to re-marry, and the man's life was a wretched and lonely one ever afterwards. We also know of girls who love, and justly so, their stepmothers very dearly and do not consider it an injustice to the memory of their own mother. Your writing is rather nice.

Far right: a page of answers to correspondents in the style of the later issues (March 9, 1901).

Proper family feeling is set out still more plainly when the Editor answers a later enquiry from bereaved daughters, and one from a restless teenager:

ANSWERS TO CORRESPONDENTS.

STUDY AND STUDIO.

MISS BIRRELL, 31, Lansdowne Crescent, Glasgow, sends us a prospectus of the Queen Margaret Correspondence Classes, for S. I. We regret that our rules forbid us to forward matter by post in connection with this column, but we cordially recommend the classes to our readers. They prepare for examinations of various grades, and also assist students in private studies. The Hon Sec., Miss Birrell, will be glad to give all information.

WANDA DE GORKIEWICZ.—Many thanks for your delightful letter, which interested us very greatly. We are glad you have received so many cards, and are informing our correspondents that you are no longer at the High School, Constantinople.

MISS HENRIETTA M. CROSFIELD, noticing our answer to PANSY, suggests *Easy Lessons in Egyptian Hieroglyphics*, by E. A. Wallis Budge, published by Kegan Paul at 3s. 6d. *First Steps in Egyptian*, by the same author, costs 12s. We thank MISS CROSFIELD for her kind letter.

MISS F. O. ANDERSON, Lea Hall, Gainsboro', Lincolnshire, asks us to mention her Literary Club for amateurs, in which prose compositions are criticised and circulated bi-monthly. All particulars as to rules, etc., will be forwarded on application.

ONE OF PEGGY'S FRIENDS.—We should paraphrase the lines by Burns something as follows :—When life is bright and all goes merrily, it is comparatively easy to stifle the conscience and to disregard religion in pleasure; but let dark days come, and the mind be troubled and tempest-tossed, then will be felt the need of "the anchor for the soul" which is given by Christianity.

*** We have pleasure in directing our readers' attention to competitions at the Royal Academy of Music for the Goring Thomas and the Dove Scholarships. The Goring Thomas Scholarship offers free tuition for three years at the Royal Academy. It will be awarded to that British-born candidate of either sex who may show the greatest promise of ability as composer of lyrical dramatic works. The Dove Scholarship is of the value of about £32 yearly for three years. It will be awarded to that candidate of either sex who may show such talent in violin-playing as to give promise of future distinction. The literary examination for each competition will be held on Monday, April 29th, 1901, and the Musical Competition on Wednesday, May 1st, 1901. Full particulars may be obtained from the Secretary, Royal Academy of Music, Tenterden Street, Hanover Square, London, W.

INTERNATIONAL CORRESPONDENCE.

Exchange of view post-cards is requested by (MISS) NELLIE H. RAE, Raeburn, Hamilton, Scotland ; SOPHIE GARBEA, Horezani, Gara Bibesci, Jud Gorjiu, Roumania ; ELSIE BIGGS, Station Road, Victoria, Australia (Australasian stamps or a card for foreign stamps or a card) ; MAY GRAHAM, Station Road, Otahuhu, Auckland, New Zealand ; MILICENT McCLATCHIE, 62, Edith Road, West Kensington, London, W. ; S. TACHDJIAN, 115, Grande Rue de Pera, Constantinople (views of Constantinople offered for all others, except those of England and France) ; MARGARET SPEEDIE, Surrey Road, South Yarra, Melbourne, Victoria, Australia ; LILY TROLLIP, Spring Valley, Bushman's Kop, Orange River Colony, S. Africa (cards for postage stamps, especially Mexican, not less than eight).

MISS E. M. DALE, Port Chalmers, New Zealand, writes to inform MISS L. HARDENBROEK that she has sent post-cards and New Zealand stamps to the address first given.

ELSIE G. JONES, 27, Southfield Road, Middlesboro', Yorkshire, would like a girl about 14, in England or abroad, to write to her.

MISCELLANEOUS.

MERCIER.—We have given articles on the subject—illustrated ones—in this magazine within the last two or three months. Look back yourself and you will find them. These may suffice without purchasing a book on calisthenics.

J. W. G.—Are you acquainted with the "Governesses' Benevolent Institution"? It gives temporary assistance to those in distress, has an annuity fund, a provident fund, an asylum for the aged, etc. Secretary, C. W. Klugh, Esq., 32, Sackville Street, W. There is a "Governesses' Guild," 139, Fulham Road, S.W. The former would, we think, meet your requirements.

CHERRY and MOTHER'S HELP.—With reference to making the eyelashes grow see our answer to "Lord Roberts." As to making your nose "thinner by pinching the end of it," we do not think it would, but it might inflame and make it red. We do not approve of any attempt to thin yourself unless a doctor pronounced you to have "fatty degeneration of the heart," in which case he would prescribe for you and watch your case. Taking much butter, cream, and fatty foods might be limited to a certain degree, however, without injury to the system in general.

A QUAVER.—The Royal College of Organists, Hart Street, Bloomsbury, W.C., admits women, by examination on equal terms with men, to fellowship and associateship ; and should you be desirous of making way as an organist, you should pass their examinations, which are held half-yearly, and consist of solo-playing tests and paper work. There are not many openings for women, however, except in small country churches, we are told.

BLACK EYES, ETC.—Hardy ferns do well in a north aspect, and so do the following plants : myosotis, mimulus, violas, pansies, vincas or periwinkles, and hardy primulas, the lily of the valley, hydrangeas, ivies, and clematis, and some climbing roses, such as the Dundee Rambler.

CLAUDIA.—We have answered your question many times. Those who fail to understand our Lord's words recorded by St. Matthew (xii. 31, 32) and St. Mark (iii. 28, 29) have overlooked the explanation given in the 30th verse of the last-named chapter, *i.e.*, "Because they said, He hath an unclean spirit" ; and in verse 22, "He hath Beelzebub, and by the prince of the devils casteth He out devils." Now, reflect a moment. If our Blessed Lord was possessed by Satan and his evil spirits, He could not be the incarnate, only-begotten Son of God, and in this case there could not have been any atonement for man, and His sacrifice on the Cross was of no avail for our salvation. So those who reject Him as their divine Redeemer cannot be saved through Him ; and in regarding Him as doing all things through the power of the devil, they necessarily reject Him as their saviour. They place themselves outside the pale of salvation, and so long as they reject him as the pure and holy One, the God-Man, One with the Father and the Holy Ghost, and deny that His miracles were performed by the indwelling omnipotent power of the Holy Ghost, they simply cut themselves off from participation in the redemption wrought by Him. They are living in a reprobate state ; they blaspheme the divinity that dwelt and acted in Him. How could one possessed by devils and unclean spirits be a Saviour to them ?

LORD ROBERTS.—We are not sure that your eyelashes would grow again if you cut them. Were they in the habit of growing, they would be hanging down over your cheeks by this time.

M. A. S.—Photographers will tell you that to take the shiny sort of glaze off a photograph before painting it they pass the tongue over the surface. This is one of the little secrets of the art.

A. T. S.—*Fier, sans tache*, "Proud, without stain."

MATTY RAY.—We do not know that there are any more particulars to be given of the mobbing of the lady students than those you have read. Your writing is very legible.

MUSE.—The letters mark the series of the stamps, the others the time when posted, we believe.

RAINY JUNE.—The dust accumulated on the top of the leaves of a book must be brushed off with rather a hard brush. If they be uncut, and a subsequent rubbing with crumbs of bread be not sufficient, we advise you to put it into a bookbinder's hands to be cut and "marbled."

MARIE ARNOLD.—The German tradition respecting a fabulous hunter,—called *Der Wilde Jäger* (or, the Wild Hunter), one who appears by night surrounded by dogs, and with a train of attendants joining in the chase,—has its counterpart in England under the figure and name of "Hearne the Hunter." See Shakespeare's "Merry Wives of Windsor," act IV. scene IV., where the legend is related by Anne Page, in connection with the "Hearne Oak." It was supposed to have been the trysting place or *rendezvous* of the spectral hunter; and is counted,—for its antiquity, and legend connected with it,—as one of the sights to be exhibited to visitors.

A MAGPIE.—The author of the verses called "Home, Sweet Home," commencing with "'Mid pleasures and palaces, though we may roam," was J. Howard Payne, who flourished 1792–1852. The song occurs in the opera of "Clari the Maid of Milan." 2. The name "Jane" is the feminine of John; which latter means "the gracious gift of God." "Lillie" is merely the name of a flower, which need not be described.

SNOWDROP.—1. Not having mangoes, we use other ingredients in the making of chutney. See our "Useful Hints." 2. See a former reply on the subject of cleaning marble. 3. Verdigris is the blue-green rust which is formed on copper and brass, not on gold. You may clean gold by first washing with soap and water, using a soft toothbrush, and then applying ammonia, sal volatile, or spirits of wine to it, then wipe, or hold near the fire, and shake and rub it well in a bag of box-wood sawdust.

Above: miscellaneous replies of August 21, 1880. This particular issue included predictable advice to STEPHANOTIS, *grieving over a disappointment—"Try to do something useful for others"—and referred* VIOLET *to her doctor with the austere comment, "It is not seemly to describe your ailments on a postcard."*

BIRTHDAY.—It seems very strange for loving daughters to inquire, "What month would it be etiquette for us to go to a dance, our dear mother having died very early in February?" Seven months only had elapsed (when writing in September) since that "dear mother" was laid in her grave; and you are eager to go to a dance in the first month that mere "etiquette" would permit. What has "etiquette" to do with the love and respect you should feel for your mother, and the sense of an irreparable loss? You ought to wear the deepest mourning for a year; and how soon, after that, you would like to go to that kind of entertainment, it is for you to decide. How would your father like it? Would he consider it both loving and respectful? [1894]

F.C.J.—Every girl should be so educated as to be able to support herself if necessary. So long, however, as the necessity for your leaving home does not exist, it is your duty to endeavour to remain there, to be a comfort, as a daughter might be in a thousand little ways, to her parents. They have had the expense of your education, and of all else you have enjoyed, and to arrange to leave them the moment your schooling is over, and to make no return in those watchful loving attentions that mere gratitude demands of you, not to speak of filial affection, would be a most discreditable and undutiful act. How could you be "dull at home?" You might be engaged in perfecting your education in so many ways—in housekeeping, cookery, nursing, reading, and plain needlework. The proper place for a little girl in her "teens" is at home, when not at school. We feel sure that it was only want of due reflection—not want of natural affection, or, at least, good feeling—that made you contemplate a removal from home when your schooling shall be over. We request the attention of all our girl readers to this answer. [1884]

AN ORPHAN GIRL (1882) writes in some anxiety about the brother for whom, it seems, she keeps house, and is told:

Merely talking to your brother will not suffice to keep him at home at night if he be a pleasure-seeker. Perhaps if you could invite some pleasant and suitable companions to the house to tea, from time to time; had music, and practised glee or chorus singing; or introduced some small games, and made home bright and cheerful, he might find it more agreeable than his haunts outside. Do not grumble and look doleful, but let him see that you try to make home more attractive.

Many of the correspondents ask if the Editor can suggest ways of earning money at home. Sadly, there is little he can advise:

DOG ROSE.—Perhaps in your position as an only daughter, with an invalid mother, you may do more by saving than by earning. Make yourself a good housekeeper, dressmaker and general needlewoman, and you will soon make a great many shillings by your helpful ways. [1880]

However, readers regularly ask for and receive information and guidance on careers. Here the answers are almost invariably careful and informed:

A. R. LEWIS.—Naturally, the constant use of the telephone is injurious, creating what M. Gellé calls "aural over-pressure". The working of the telegraphic apparatus, and constant attendance amidst the jar and noise of machinery, likewise tend to overstrain the ear and to induce nervous excitability, giddiness, and neuralgic pains. But how long the delicate nerves may be exposed to this over-pressure without inducing any of these evil results we are unable to tell you. Only it is well, when choosing a vocation in life, to look beyond the present into such possible eventualities; and if of a nervous temperament, and at all subject to headache and neuralgic pains, it would be well to choose some other calling. [1896]

TRIXY.—The salaries earned by librarians of either sex are so low that we are not inclined to recommend you to think of such work. At the same time, if you are really drawn to it by fondness for books, there would be no harm in writing to the head librarians of the public libraries in the towns you mention, and asking them whether they could receive a woman assistant. In the Manchester Free Libraries women are considerably employed as assistants at very small salaries. At the People's Palace, London, women enjoy better positions, but there are few of them. [1897]

JESSIE A. PINKER.—At the London National Training School for Cookery, Buckingham Palace Road, S.W., the training for the post of Cookery Instructor in all branches of plain cooking costs 13 guineas for the full course of twenty-four weeks. You will find further particulars as to cookery instruction in London in our articles *What is the London County Council doing for Girls?* (March). But we have made further enquiries and it seems highly probable that you will be able to obtain what you want at the new Municipal Technical School, Brighton.... As the building is not yet completed ... perhaps your daughter could stay a little longer at school till the classes ... are fully established. We are gratified to learn that, having taken the *Girl's Own Paper* as a girl, you now take it for your own girls, and consider its influence "like that of a sweet and gentle lady". [1897]

Sometimes a warning note is sounded:

LILLIE MORE.—We feel very much the enormous responsibility that you have placed upon us in asking us to advise you on entering the profession to which you refer. But we dare not do other than counsel you to abandon all ideas of thus engaging yourself. Believe us you are not alone in your particular aspirations. Most girls above the ordinary abilities have the same unhealthy craving at some particular period of their life, but when they grow older and see how incongruous is that position to a good honest girl's they are filled with a life-long thankfulness that they did not join the profession. In addition to great abilities, unusual physical strength, and personal attractions, a Christian girl or woman would need the steadfastness of a more than Job or St Paul to come out unscathed from the fiery ordeal. We happen to know many things of the life and character of the lady you mention which would lead you to either despise or pity her very much. [1880]

Did LILLIE hope to follow Mrs Langtry as an artist's model—or to go on the stage?

Questions about religion are not uncommon in these pages, and the answers are generally long and serious:

KITTY SCOTT and LAURA.—Judging from the questions perpetually asked, our young converts seem to regard conversion as consisting in denying themselves certain amusements (music, etc.), various articles of women's usual dress, and restriction in reading religious books. Religion is not of a negative, but positive and active, character. [1884]

OLIVE.—You say you are "greatly troubled" about the thoughts with which you are beset. Now, so long as you are "troubled", you have the evidence in yourself that God has *not* "given you up to hardness of heart." Do you not remember what St Paul says in his Epistle to the Romans vii., 20, "now, if I do that I would not, it is no more I that do it, but sin that dwelleth in me." Sin confessed, repudiated, prayed against, and fought against, is sin forgiven, and atoned for by the bloodshedding of Christ....

Your letter is very well expressed. [1883]

appreciation on "Marion's" part. It is so nicely written too! Kind hearted-Heppie.

FLORENCE.—Choose the handwriting you most admire, and copy it carefully. We once knew a girl who quite changed hers in six weeks by so doing.

HAPPY DOT.—James Montgomery is the author of a poem called "A Mother's Love."

ZARA.—A turkey carpet looks best when frequently shaken.

A. G. B.—We could not recommend you to take a situation on the Continent, unless you know exactly to whom you are going. The English chaplain in Paris, in a recent number of the *Times*, begs English girls to stay at home, and details the miseries of many who have gone there to be swindled, and left penniless and friendless.

CLARA and ANON.—Brush the leather which has been inked with a solution of oxalic acid in water. Your second query is not one we should answer. Read "How to Look My Best."

IVY and MAY.—There is no way of pressing leaves or flowers except between leaves of blotting-paper, or else by ironing with a warm iron.

TAMMY.—Are you quite serious when you ask us to "explain the working" of a "scent fountain" which we have never seen? Write to the manufacturer.

LILY OF THE VALLEY.—The words are those of a very ordinary ballad song, apparently. You might inquire of a music seller.

TWO RING DOVES.—Doves are grain eaters. Give them peas, barley, wheat, and tares, a little hempseed, small beans, a little rock-salt to peck at, crumbs of bread, and plenty of gravel and water.

FLOSSY.—1. See answer to "Ivy and May." The voice is trained by practice. 2. Very hard brushes are not good for the hair. You have spelt envelope rightly.

JESSIE.—1. We know of no other method for curing a habit of stooping than wearing a face-board stuck into a belt in front for a certain time daily while reading or working, and a fixed resolution to remember and check the habit all the rest of the day. 2. It is impossible to lay down a rule that will apply to all alike in reference to suppers. Much depends on the hour of the previous meal, and that of retiring to bed, on the nature of the supper, and on the state of health, and on the individual peculiarities of the person who hesitates about eating just before bed-time. A heavy meal at a late hour could not be wholesome for any one, for the body is fatigued, and the digestive powers are thereby enfeebled. Some sleep the better for partaking of a slight refreshment, others do not. Those who sleep little, and have some hours of fasting before them, would probably be benefited by taking a biscuit and a small cup of broth; or of milk with a teaspoonful of lime-water in it.

Above: some other miscellaneous replies to readers' letters, June, 1880.

THREE ENGLISH GIRLS, GERMANY, sent in a query on extra-terrestrial life in 1884. They are told:

We consider it to be utterly absurd to imagine that our little world should be the only speck in the vast universe of worlds—either within or beyond our view—that is inhabited by intelligent beings, and acquainted with their Almighty Creator. But how many may be fallen like ourselves and needing a Saviour, has not of course been revealed to us. The side of our own little satellite the moon, which is turned towards us, presents the appearance of a world destroyed by volcanic action. Many may be so. But even this would not necessarily preclude its being inhabited by disembodied spirits, or bodies having different attributes and constitutions to ours. All is veiled in mystery for the present.

The usual practice of the *G.O.P.* was to print answers only, but on occasion readers' letters did appear. In June, 1883, an issue includes *A Dip into the Editor's Correspondence*. Nine letters are printed, among them one from A HAPPY YOUNG WIFE:

DEAR MR EDITOR.—Pray forgive me for troubling you, but as I have taken your most charming paper from the first, and have only written to you once, I think you will not be very cross at my writing to thank you for a good husband and a comfortable home. I wish you could come and stay with us, we would try to make you enjoy your visit.

No doubt you wonder how you can possibly have aided such a happy state of affairs: it just happened like this. When *The Girl's Own Paper* first appeared three years ago I was twenty-five, and never had received an offer of marriage. As I had always been taught to consider that woman's first duty was to marry, you may suppose I was in rather a melancholy, discontented state of mind, but thanks to my dear *Girl's Own Paper*, both from tales and articles, and most of all from the "Answers to Correspondents", I learnt differently, and tried by God's blessing to fill my life with work for Him. I took up French, music, etc., which I had sadly neglected, asked for and got a district, and determined by God's help if I were to be an old maid I would at least be a contented one and make others happy....

I had quite left off thinking of the possibility of marriage for myself, when I was electrified by receiving a proposal from a gentleman much my superior. He tells me how that he was first attracted to me by the bright, contented expression of my face and total lack of self-consciousness. So you see, dear Mr Editor, I have indeed great cause to be truly grateful to *The Girl's Own Paper*....

In this batch of nine letters are three of praise and gratitude from Australia, one from Hungary, and one from Italy.

The volume of overseas readers swelled increasingly as the years went by, until in January, 1901, the Editor started a new column, *International Correspondence*, in which readers sought correspondents in foreign countries:

E. N. DRUMMOND ... Dublin, asks for a French girl correspondent aged 16 or 17, each to write in her own language, and inquires whether Miss Natalie Gorianoff of St Petersburg would care for an Irish correspondent.

Very often an exchange of more than mere letters is proposed:

MISS DAISY and MISS EDITH LE FONTAINE ... Smyrna, Asia Minor, would like to correspond and exchange stamps with girls in Italy, Spain, Norway, Hungary and America. The former will send Turkish, Levant, and Persian stamps to anybody who will send her a few humming-birds' eggs.

Below: a page of answers adorned with two line decorations which admirably sum up the G.O.P.'s unfailing advice to readers (March, 1881).

I.—BEFORE SUBSCRIBING TO "THE GIRL'S OWN PAPER."

WORK.

MARCH.—Read "Seasonable Dress," and have your dresses made very wide in the chest, and endeavour to correct your round shoulders by constant care and thought. Black silk should be chosen with a moderate sized rib, a very large one generally denotes the presence of cotton. Purchase at a good shop where they care for their reputation. Your writing is very neat and clean.

IRISH BIDDIE.—We should send the black silk velvet to a cleaner's. A recipe for reviving black cloth is given at page 316, vol i.

MITTEN THUMB.—To knit the thumb on a mitten see page 144, vol. i.

FLO.—We regret we cannot assist you to dispose of your mother's work. Try a draper's or a fancy wool shop.

AGNES.—Make a narrow hem for the top of your frilling, not a roll. The whipping is very well performed.

MADCAP.—Trim the pale violet dress with deep red satin or silk broché. Select the right shade carefully.

ART.

MARGUERITE.—The outline of flowers for painting should be carefully drawn in pencil, not too hard nor black, as as to prevent their subsequent erasure. Your writing is very legible and neat, and your note well expressed and ladylike.

LITTLE BUTTERCUP.—Varnish the whole plate if you do not admire the white look of it. It will keep much cleaner also.

BARBARA.—Spirits of wine and turpentine are used to clean pictures and to dissolve the hard old varnish ; but they will attack the paint as well if not washed off at the proper time with cold water. Your varnish must have been poor or badly mixed.

COOKERY.

EDITH CHURCH.—We are quite at a loss to understand your difficulty, as nothing can be more explicit than the directions given on page 28. "Rinsed out of boiling water, squeezed dry, and floured well," is surely simple enough? Your writing might be improved by writing copies.

A YOUNG COOK.—1. We cannot give addresses nor recommend "kitcheners." 2. Inquire at a music-seller's.

THE DAISY CHAIN.—For toffee recipes, see pages 15 and 176, vol. i. You should be guided by your schoolmistress.

MISCELLANEOUS.

LOCH LEVEN.—The name of the Navigators' Islands was given to them by their discoverer, from his observing the natives to be in possession of superior canoes, which they managed with the most dexterous skill. Your writing should be more flowing and free.

MURIEL.—There is no occasion for bowing to a gentleman whom you do not know. Your writing is not pretty though so legible.

J. O. U. W.—1. "Primrose way" appears another way of saying "flowery way," or "gay spring-like paths." Shakespeare used the same expression in Hamlet, act i., scene 3. And a recent author, Motley, also makes use of it in the same poetical way. 2. It is better to take your parents' advice as to your reading.

C. P. C.—"Ling's Exercises," which have been translated by Dr. Roth, would perhaps suit you.

ENILEC.—We should advise you to have your hand well rubbed with fresh lard, which will probably give strength and lessen the stiffness. Thank you for your kind letter.

SWEETBRIAR.—The 4th March, 1863, was Wednesday. Your writing is anything but good for your age, and you would do well to take to copies again.

DISRAELINA.—We think you have mistaken the initials. Your writing is very good.

AN ONLY CHILD.—See page 624, vol. i., on the falling of hair, also 80 and 111 ; also the articles at pages 259, 400, and 416. We thank you for your kind letter.

MADELINE MURPHY. — Ammonia might affect the colour of some things perhaps, you had better make a trial before using it.

VIC.—Perhaps your garden soil is not suitable for fern culture, or you do not give them moisture enough.

MARY CARPENTER.—1. Thank you for your suggestion. We think our paper is sufficiently general to be useful to every class of life. 2. We hear that there is a very clever new seat for using behind the counter just patented, and now that a practical step forward has been taken like this, we hope the "standing evil" may be overcome. Thank you very much for your kind expressions of satisfaction with our efforts.

FIDUS ACHATES.—The gentleman's mother would pay the first visit. Fish is eaten with a fish knife and fork. If these are absent, with a fork.

MIDSHIPMAN EASY.—It would be impossible to say, we think, who first invented rudders. The first people who tried navigation probably.

POPPY.—Read "Sketching from Nature," page 23, vol. ii.

POLLIE FLINDERS.—Your writing is not good for your age.

COLLEEN BAWN.—Thank you for your kind letter.

SNOWDROP.—See article on "Puddings," at page 27, vol. ii. Your writing is clear and legible.

AN INQUIRER.—Gently and kindly tell your friend that it is a duty to refrain from "playing with edged tools"; and that no greater evidences of a pure and straightforward friendship in private than can be honestly manifested in public. A religious person will not only abstain from evil known and undisputed, but from all that is even doubtfully permissible. The more your friend trusts you the more scrupulous you should be.

CARROTS.—You do not say of what substance the white tracings on the black marble are composed. Perhaps the groove might be filled in with white paint. Should you see a similar style of decoration in any clock shop, inquire of the manufacturers.

A CONSTANT SUBSCRIBER.—Table-cloths are used at afternoon tea, and at a late tea substituting a late dinner A long napkin or cloth should be laid over the sideboard, but not to hang down at the front. You write fairly well.

TEASE OF STRETFORD.—A little girl of sixteen writes to inquire whether, at that time of life, she should be "cold and proud," and whether she should "ponder and screw." We fail to understand what she does when she performs the operation called "screwing." We have heard of "screwing-in a waist," and hope she does not contemplate any practice so baneful and silly. Let her be gentle, modest, and natural, putting on no "airs" of any kind. When well in health and kindly cared for, and trying to do her little duties well, she could not be other than "lively and gay," instead of, as "T. S." expresses it, "cold and proud." 2. "Navy blue" would suit our little correspondent very well.

CISSY writes, "Will you kindly take pity on me, for I am a very poor girl?" We would willingly express our sympathy, for we love all our readers, and especially those who are in trouble. But surely, Cissy should tell us the cause of her unhappiness. Cissy is asked to furnish us with particulars that we might know how to help her.

J. H.—Your verses have the merit of earnestness, but are not up to the standard required for publication.

CORA ORMAN.—1. Read "Health and Beauty for the Hair," which appeared in vol. i. 2. A verse of some good Easter hymn would be suitable for the memorial card. Such a verse, for instance, as :—

. "Lord, by the stripes which wounded Thee
  From death's dread sting Thy servants free,
  That we may live and sing to Thee
                              Alleluia !"

Your writing needs improvement ; there is no character in it.

DAMASK ROSE.—We have received a long illegible letter from you, which we think is sent to inform us that we have not answered previous letters sent by you. We suppose that they were equally badly written, and so received the fate of being instantly destroyed, or that we had others worthier of the space.

II.—AFTERWARDS.

1819

1901

[PRICE ONE PENNY.

Above: the memorial notice published in the issue of February 16, following Queen Victoria's death on January 22, 1901.

Whether he liked it or not, the Editor seems by 1901 to be acting as a Post Office:

We have a letter for KOMURASKI SAN, with a silver leaf from Table Mountain and some African stamps.

ART STUDENTS AT BREAKFAST IN PARIS.

Trustfully, readers continued to write from all over the world, seeking the Editor's advice which, blunt or not, was always straightforward. One reply, to a letter from CUSHILDA D.C. in 1888, may be said to embody the philosophy of *The Girl's Own Paper* in its first twenty-one years, although that philosophy was often expressed less sternly:

Your chief desire in leaving school early is to go the sooner to balls and parties every night. Alas! What a frivolous idea! Is this the object of existence? Have you no work in life to accomplish? Have you, to say the least, no idea of the duties of home life in "requiting your parents", devoting your mind, strength, and all you have learnt at school (paid for by them) to do them loving service and add to the comfort and cheerfulness of home? What are you going to do with the talents committed to you by your Divine Master—health, time, education, competent means, and knowledge of the way of holiness and salvation? A little schoolgirl of fifteen has three more years of school discipline, and then, at the very least, three more of home-work and education, literary and practical. "Knowing a lot of German and drawing well", you might only be a poor little empty-headed nonentity.

Above: the last illustration from the last issue of 1901, the year which marked the opening of the Edwardian era and the magazine's "coming of age" at twenty-one. Very different from the girls in the line illustrations of twenty years earlier, these students, photographed in Paris, are enjoying a picnic breakfast in public, and three of them are even bare-headed.

169

"THREE LITTLE MAIDS FROM SCHOOL."

Conclusion.

A HAPPY ENDING.

The Editor, Charles Peters, and his staff were professional journalists. They had to sell their magazine, and to do that they had to give the readers what they wanted in exchange for their pennies. Yet, looking through these old Annuals, one feels the desire of the writers not only to entertain, nor even only to inform and instruct, but to guide, influence and mould. The readers were "our girls"; the writers wrote, in general, as adults to girls, or sometimes as adults to slightly younger adults, not as teenagers to teenagers. Obviously they aimed at satisfying their readers, and if they had not succeeded in doing so, the magazine would never have seen the new century; but perhaps they did much more than that.

However that may be, the *Girl's Own Paper* must have played its part in making the Victorian girl and the Edwardian woman what she was. The magazines of the late twentieth century are, in their turn, playing their part towards shaping the women of the twenty-first. Journalists do well to remember it.

Above: the closing instalment of The Studio Mariano *by Eglanton Thorne (April 2, 1892).*

Far left: three schoolgirls dressed for the autumn term, from How a Girl Should Dress, *by "Norma": August 31, 1901.*

INDEX

Page references to illustrations are given in italic type. Captions (*cap.*) are indexed only if they do not appear on the same page as the illustrations to which they refer.

Chapter headings are given in small caps.

Titles are indexed in *italic* type. The genre "fiction" includes short stories, serials, and story features. The genre "article" includes series of articles as well as one-off items and features.

British royalties are indexed by their Christian name, members of the peerage by their title.

Pseudonyms are given in inverted commas.

If a reference runs over two or more pages (*e.g.* 112–118), those pages may include illustration material which does not bear directly on the item being indexed.

" DON'T LOOK SO SAD, MY DEAR, ANOTHER VOLUME IS ABOUT TO
COMMENCE."